Carolina Evangelical Divinity School Library

REDISCOVERING THE POWER OF THE GOSPELS

Jesus' Theology Of The Kingdom

D1526173

by

J. ARTHUR BAIRD

North Carolina Wesleyan College Library

Scurry - Drum Collection
Given by:
*Dr. Frank Scurry and
Carolina Evangelical
Divinity School*

THE IONA PRESS / *Wooster, Ohio*

COPYRIGHT © MCMLXXXII   THE IONA PRESS

All rights reserved — no part of this book may be reproduced in any form without permission in writing from the publisher, except by a reviewer who wishes to quote brief passages in connection with a review in magazine or newspaper.

Scripture quotations from the Revised Standard Version of the Bible are copyright, 1946 and 1952 by the Division of Christian Education of the National Council of Churches, and are used by permission.

ISBN 0-910789-00-2

Library of Congress Catalog Card No. 82-083623

Printed in the United States of America

226
BAI   Baird, J. Arthur   2031
      Rediscovering The Power Of
      The Gospel

REDISCOVERING
THE POWER
OF THE GOSPELS

NC WESLEYAN COLLEGE LIBRARY
ROCKY MOUNT, NC 27804

*With The
Compliments
of The Author*

J. Arthur Baird

To

Andrew and Paul

Beloved Sons and Sailors

Contents

Abbreviations

JGTJ	Baird, J. Arthur, *The Justice of God in the Teaching of Jesus*, Westminster Press, 1963
ACHJ	Baird, J. Arthur, *Audience Criticism and the Historical Jesus*, Westminster Press, 1967
CAC	Baird, J. Arthur, "Content Analysis, Computers and the Scientific Method of Biblical Studies," *The Journal of Biblical Literature*, June, 1976
UG	Baird, J. Arthur, *The Uniqueness of the Gospels: A Comparative Study of the Gospel Genre*, unpublished manuscript
HW	Baird, J. Arthur, *The Holy Word: A Study of the Genesis and Historical Authenticity of the Synoptic Gospels*, unfinished manuscript

Preface

Of all the problems that plague the modern world and threaten to send it reeling back into the nineteenth century, the most crucial would seem to be that of power. Humanity is rapidly outrunning its resources, and in our own country we are beginning to come awake to that fact by engaging in a series of crash programs to discover new sources of oil and coal, to harness the power of the sun and wind, the tide and the atom. Some are saying that we are facing the greatest depression in our history because of the problems of power. Whatever be the answer to that economic question, one thing is certain: the world in general, and America in particular, has been going through a period of great depression of spirit, a time of the recession of values, an era of the pollution of mind and heart, that is far more damaging to the nation than any depression in our economy, or any pollution of our ecology.

But there is a tragic blindness within this secularized age which prevents us from seeing deeply enough into what ails our time; and this blindness threatens our existence. The power we are looking for is the power to raise the value of the dollar, and this is obviously essential; but what is even more seriously needed is the power to raise the level of people's values. The power we have been looking for is the power to clean up the land and sea and air, and this is obviously important; but the most serious pollution problem is the pollution of mind and heart. The power we have been seeking is the power to alleviate poverty, and the land weeps with the agony of those caught in the grip of hunger; but even here, the more deadly problem is the power to alleviate our poverty of spirit. Whether it is the power to raise our economy, or to raise the moral level of society, there seems to be little question that power is our most serious problem.

This book is addressed to those who are interested in knowing what kinds of power the Christian church has to offer in these days when many are confidently predicting the demise of civilization. My thesis is two-fold. First of all, the overriding concern is to demonstrate that in Jesus' Gospel of the Kingdom of God we have the greatest undiscovered, undeveloped, unexplored source of power available to mankind. The corollary to this is that before the disciples of Jesus and the Christian church can be effective in the extension of the Gospel, whether it be to problems of personal morality, social justice or world peace, we must first intensify the Gospel within our own lives and that of the church. We must discover a God who *commands* our attention, a Christ who *compels* our allegiance, a Gospel that presents mankind with alternatives it *cannot ignore.* That is, we must rediscover the Gospel in some semblance of its original explosive power.

The second thesis is more subtle and more scholarly. We live in an age which has been having great trouble in believing this Gospel, in affirming with its mind what it has been accepting with its heart. We are going through an agonizing re-appraisal of the relevance and authority of the Bible, and our understanding of the person of Jesus Christ that is as radical and open-ended as those thunderous discussions on the nature of Christ in the first six centuries of our era, out of which came the creeds that united Christendom for many hundreds of years, but which are now dissolving. How much can we know about him, and how certain can we be that the Gospels and those who commented on their story in the rest of the New Testament have given us a record that is believable in this modern age? My second thesis which weaves in and out of every page is that in the light of the problems of critical scholarship, and within certain reasonable limits, it is more possible than ever before to recover a sufficiently accurate picture of the life and teachings of Jesus to be relied upon, using the same techniques of higher criticism which have brought this matter into question.

Today the church is properly searching for relevance; for civil rights programs that are effective, for meaningful expression in worship and its on-going life. This book attempts to remind the church that its supreme relevance is its Gospel. Its supreme attraction is its Christ. Its supreme imperative is the God it proclaims. Here is an attempt to rediscover the power of the Christian Gospel for those who sense that both head and heart are needed in apprehending that

Gospel, that both social and charismatic renewal are essential to the Christian message, that critical scholarship and evangelical proclamation are both indispensable ingredients in a modern resurgence of the power of the church.

These pages are written for a "middle audience," which is neither scholarly nor popular, but somewhere in between. I am concerned to make the results of professional biblical scholarship available to a wide spectrum of Bible students in ways that are meaningful to the practical concerns of faith and the life of the church. Behind this book lie several others listed above which are more technical and scholarly. In these are contained the critical documentation for what is said in the present volume. At times, where it is helpful to the argument, detailed support will be reproduced from these other studies; but mostly I shall assume that if one is that concerned, he or she can consult at least the three published works.

I am especially indebted to the Wooster Laymen's Academy of Religion for the invitation to give the series of lectures which forced me to try to bring thirty years of scholarship into clear homiletic and practical focus. I want further to acknowledge my debt to my brothers, Dr. James W. Baird and Dr. Paul J. Baird, for sharing their insight into the church, which they have long served with distinction; to the members of the Lay Academy board for their continued support; to the board of The Iona Press for their enthusiasm in launching this new venture of faith; to the seminar in the Fifth Avenue Presbyterian Church of New York, who carefully and critically reviewed these pages, and to their leader, my former student, Mrs. Victoria Galbraith for her theological insight far beyond anything she learned from me; to my editor and friend of many years, Dr. Roland Tapp, for his steady belief in what I am doing; to the administration of The College of Wooster for its continuing support of my writing through a leave policy in the best tradition of the liberal arts; to the staff and residents of the Ecumenical Institute for Advanced Theological Study in Jerusalem, for the excellent accommodations in which to do my work and the stimulation of ecumenical discussion that has contributed so much to my thinking; and finally, as always, to Mary, whose loving support and keen editorial instincts are acknowledged on every page.

J. Arthur Baird
Jerusalem

PART ONE

THE HOLY WORD,
THE PROCLAMATION OF THE KINGDOM

Chapter I

There is Power in Believing the Gospel

The Christian Gospel dares us to believe that time has been invaded by eternity. It dares us to believe that God has become uniquely available in Jesus Christ. It dares us to believe that this is not a beautiful myth, not just a plausible philosophy, not just a workable ethic, but an event in space and time that really happened. This that we are describing in the Christian Gospel is either the greatest folly in intellectual history, or the most exciting news ever to invade the human mind.

From the beginning, one of the greatest sources of power in the Christian Gospel has been its historical realism. John summarized his Gospel in just such terms: "These are written that you may believe that Jesus is the Christ" (John 20:31). John was concerned that people be able to make a rational acceptance of this Gospel; for this was apparently a very real problem in that sophisticated hardheaded, skeptical age, as it is today. The author of II Timothy put it this way: "I know whom I have believed, and I am sure that he is able to guard until that Day what has been entrusted to me" (II Tim. 1:12). Paul and his disciples were concerned that what they affirmed with their lives be rationally defensible. There was a desperate need, then as now, to be able to believe that something really did happen in space and time; something that was compatible with what John and Paul and the church knew about life, and what we today know about history and the scientific world.

And yet throughout the years, one of the real problems of Christian power has been the intellectual resistance to the Gospel. As Paul put it, "The word of the cross is folly" to the wise and to the debators of his day (I Cor. 1:18-25). What Paul said is true today, and there are many facets to the intellectual charge of "folly" in the twentieth

1

century. One of the most sinister challenges comes from my own discipline of biblical scholarship. It emerges in the form of a deep and abiding historical skepticism where at least two generations of biblical scholars in America and Europe have lost their hold on the historical realism of the Gospels. This, I think, is one of the most serious threats to the power of the Christian church today. It is clear, for example, that one of the major sources of that strange "Death of God" movement in the 1960s that found its most extreme expression in some of the more radical students of Paul Tillich, was the loss of the restraining influence of the historical Jesus. Typical is Thomas Altizer, who began by assuming that we really can't rely on the Synoptic Gospels for a valid account of the life and teachings of Jesus. This then permitted him to go almost anywhere he wanted for the sources of his theology. He went to Tillich, Buddha, Nietzsche and William Blake, among others. The result was a kind of psychedelic unitarianism that seemed more like a revival of the old Sabellian heresy of the fourth century than an adequate statement of the Christian Gospel.

From time to time, I am called upon to speak to groups of ministers who have come up through the New Testament classes of the last twenty-five years. Regularly the question they want to discuss is, "Do we have any real basis for believing that what the Gospels say about Jesus really happened?" This historical skepticism, is a very important part of our age, and is a product of a revolution in biblical scholarship which we all need to understand.

The Biblical Revolution

In the last seventy-five years a profound change has taken place in biblical research, manifested in three types of challenge to biblical realism. First of all, there has come a literary challenge to the authorship and dating of the materials. Traditionally it was assumed that Moses wrote the first five books of the Old Testament. Today very few Old Testament scholars would make such a statement. Historically, Christians have taken for granted that the four Gospels were written by Matthew, Mark, Luke and John. Today most scholars would probably accept only Mark and Luke as authors, and would say that at best, Matthew and John supplied some of the basic material for those Gospels, which were probably written by their students. Whether or not one agrees with these and other similar conclusions, it can hardly be denied that this kind of scholarship has had a significant effect on the church's assessment of the authority of the Bible.

The second challenge has to do with historical analysis. What was the influence of social and religious history on the formation of the biblical material? Hermann Gunkel, an early twentieth century Old Testament scholar, convinced many of this generation that the Genesis stories are what he called, "mature, artistic creations reflecting more about the history of the environment that nourished them than the originals that they described." In the New Testament field, Rudolf Bultmann is probably the chief figure in this challenge to historical authenticity. He described the Synoptic Gospels as a "sociological product" of the early church. It was the church that produced them; and what they report is so overladen with first century concerns that we really can't get back to the historical Jesus. This has proven to be one of the most disturbing ideas ever to confront the church in its study of the Bible.

The third challenge has to do with the influence of the editors upon the materials. It is generally insisted that the Synoptic Gospels are so heavily edited that all we can really know is the theology of the editor: of Matthew, Mark, Luke or the author of John. This approach to the Gospels is called "Redaction Criticism," and is one of the most popular methods for Gospel study today. The focus for such an approach then is not the historical Jesus standing behind the text, but rather the editorial level of the text itself; and great amounts of scholarly energy are going into discovering the vocabulary, the literary peculiarities and the theological motivations of the Gospel "redactors." Those who examine the texts primarily in this way are understandably reticent to talk about the theology of Jesus, since from that point of view all we can know with any degree of certainty is the theology of the redactors.

The Challenge of Form Criticism

These three challenges coming out of the biblical revolution have had an enormous influence on Christian theology in the last fifty years. One of the most important results has been a severe criticism of the historical realism and authenticity of the Synoptic Gospels; and before we dare to talk about the theology of Jesus, we must examine this matter carefully. The heart of this challenge is concentrated in what is called "Form Criticism," a school of New Testament thought which arose in Germany at the beginning of the twentieth century, revolving around the work of Rudolf Bultmann. I will always remember my first introduction to the form critics. I had

3

been reading Bultmann at the University of Edinburgh, and one day Professor William Manson, my graduate thesis advisor, overtook me as he was hurrying down the hall — black robe flying behind him. I called out, "Professor Manson, what do you think of the form critics?" He whirled about as if he had been shot, and replied, "Sawdust, Mr. Baird. Sawdust!" and rushed on to class. This, of course, did not give an adequate statement of his sophisticated assessment of form criticism, but it aroused my curiosity and led to thirty years of research and a term at the University of Marburg, studying in the shadow of Bultmann, who still lived in retirement in his home overlooking the seminary. Out of this I learned to appreciate much of the creative spirit of this movement which intended to approach the study of the Bible in a more scientific way.

Certain results are, I think, well founded. The work of the form critics has given us a greater insight into the influence of the early Christian community on the formation of the Gospels through its worship, preaching, teaching and debate. Certainly there was interpretation going on as the original words of Jesus were heard, understood, remembered and recounted. The form critics have created a genuine breakthrough by demonstrating the manner in which the Synoptic Gospels are composed of independent units of tradition, which probably circulated in detached fashion in the earliest period of Gospel formation. It would also seem clear from their work that certain elements of the historical and literary arrangement of the Gospels are of dubious authenticity. Beyond this, however, the scholarship of the last fifty years has called into question many of the conclusions of the form critics, and also the critical bases upon which they are founded. Basically, there are three foundations to Bultmann's conclusions, which have become so deeply imbedded in popular scholarship that they are seldom discussed and commonly taken for granted. My scholarly pilgrimage, however, since Professor Manson aroused my curiosity thirty years ago, has led me to the conclusion that each one of these is open to serious question.

1) The most fundamental insight of form criticism is that the Gospels are composed of a series of independent units held together by a few words and phrases, much like beads on a string. If one pulls out the string and separates these units according to their form, they fall into five consistent groups: parables, sayings, miracle stories, legends, and what are called pardigms (apophthegms), brief sayings surrounded by a short narrative necessary to the understanding of

the saying. The phenomenon of form is easy to observe, and I would agree with the general consensus that this has been a most helpful insight. The problem lies in the interpretation of this phenomenon. The form critics have insisted that the form of these units was the product not of the original historical events, but of the *use* to which the *early church* put them in its preaching, worship and debate. The accounts of Jesus' life and teaching were so overladen with the concerns of the church that one can't get back to original bed-rock history. There is some truth to this, especially in the legends and miracle stories, where the words of Jesus are imbedded within considerable narrative. But when this phenomenon of form is subjected to critical scrutiny, it appears that, generally speaking, the form of the material was a product not so much of the *use* to which the early Christian community put it, as of the *intrinsic nature* of the material itself. That is, certain types of data had to be presented in certain ways because of the built-in demands of the material itself within the historical situation (cf. JGTJ-23; ACHJ-163). Form, therefore, is not a barrier, but a window into the necessities of reporting or the characteristic practice of someone who taught and acted in these consistent ways — most likely Jesus of Nazareth!

2) The form critics further argued that there was a period of about thirty years following the death of Jesus before anything of what he said or did was written down. During this "strictly oral" period, the Jesus recollections were handed on by word of mouth alone; and in the process of forgetting or elaborating, the material was changed, so that like a snowball rolling downhill, the final product was greatly enlarged from its original historical form. This assumption still plays a large role in the work of modern New Testament scholars.

There are really two questions here. The first has to do with the fate of the Jesus story during the oral period. There seems little question that for a time, whether years, or only a few minutes, the things Jesus said and did were carried in people's memories, and transmitted orally. The question is, was the material altered drastically during this time? Bultmann assumed that it was, and based this on what he called the "laws" of folk transmission, which he derived from some early folk lore research going on in Germany at the turn of the century. Actually, folk lore scholars have never agreed about any such "laws" of folk tradition. As a Norwegian scholar, Thorlief Boman, has shown again recently, more sophisticated research has revealed that when folk material like the Gospel story is circulated orally, it tends to be passed on by individual story tellers, whose capacity for memory *preserved*, rather than distorted, the original (*Die Jesus Uberlieferung im Lichte der Neueren Volkskunde*, 1967). The work of Birger Gerhardssen (*Memory and Manuscript*) has further demonstrated the probability that the Jesus recollections would have been handled with the same scrupulous care given to preserving the words of the Jewish rabbis of that day. The Gospels reflect many of the same devices for aiding memory which were common to first century rabbinic schools. My own research into the teachings of Jesus has also demonstrated the probability that the sanctity with which the Jesus words were regarded by the early church would have further disciplined the process of oral transmission (cf. HW).

There do indeed seem to have been various versions of sayings and narrative incidents within the four Gospels, reflecting changes within the oral period (ACHJ-137-149); but more recent research has, I think, shown that Bultmann vastly overstated this matter. There are just too many patterns of agreement between independent sources on Jesus' words and ideas for there to have been the wholesale development to which Bultmann referred (cf. pp. 20 f).

The second question has to do with the time when this material began to be written down. Was there indeed a moratorium on writing for thirty years, giving opportunity for extravagant oral manipulation of the Jesus story? Or did this material begin to be written down much earlier, providing the kind of discipline that written records would give to oral recollection? Bultmann offered three defenses for this insistence that written material did not begin to appear until about thirty years after Jesus' death. a) The first is that since Jesus and his followers expected the end of the world within that generation, there was no motive for recording his words and deeds for a generation that would never come. Besides what seems to be the fact that Jesus did not predict an immediate end (cf. Ch. XIV), there is a fallacy in the logic of this argument. As many have shown, even those like Paul, who believed the end of the world was imminent, were not hindered from writing voluminously about Jesus, so why should the editors of the Gospels?

b) A second support has been the assumption that since the first disciples were uneducated people, one must not attribute much literary activity to them. After all, Peter and most of the others were poor fishermen who could not write, or probably even have access to expensive writing materials. On the contrary, more recent research has shown not only that Matthew was probably a literary person, but that the larger group of disciples contained many who would

6

have had an interest in writing, including priests, scribes, and pharisees, as well as wealthy supporters who could certainly have afforded the luxury of writing materials (ACHJ-37-43).

c) A third support for Bultmann's rejection of early Christian writing is the assumption that the devout Jews had such high regard for the written Torah, that it was generally considered improper for them to record the words of their rabbinic teachers. Again, I think, more recent biblical research has shown the fallacy of this argument. For one thing, it has become more apparent that although there was this popular prohibition against writing in the first century, *in fact* the Jews were a people long accustomed to writing down the words and deeds of their great figures, and even in Jesus' day there is good evidence that the students of the great rabbis recorded the words and acts of their teachers to aid their memories (JGTJ-24). There is no reason why the disciples of Jesus would not have done the same.

Even more to the point is a growing body of evidence that many of the earliest sources of the Gospels were in writing long before they were gathered together into the large collections which we have, and that writing was a common activity among the early Christians (JGTJ-25; HW-II; cf. below, pp. 23 f). This is what Luke was referring to about 80 A.D. when he said, "Inasmuch as many have undertaken to compile a narrative of the things which have been accomplished among us..." (Luke 1:1-4). If, as would seem probable, the writing down of Jesus' words and actions began at a very early period, and I see no reason whatsoever for denying that this could have begun during his lifetime, then we are not dealing with a strictly oral transmission of thirty years subject to the vagaries of spoken repetition, but rather with a more complicated, disciplined oral process combined with much literary activity, all of which would have given considerably more stability to the recollection than the form critics have allowed.

3) One of the most deeply imbedded axioms of form criticism comes from the work of Adolf Julicher in his book, *Die Gleichnisreden Jesu* (1899). In his understandable concern to keep people from unduly straining the interpretation of Jesus' parables, Julicher insisted that anyone like Jesus who expressed himself without great deliberation, would probably not have used a form as highly artificial and rhetorical as allegory, where every symbol has some meaning. Jesus rather used the parable in its classical Greek manner, where it is a simple analogy that has only a single point.

7

Many of Jesus' parables have several points, and even some allegorical explanations like that appended to the parable of the sower (Mark 4:13-20). The reason for this is the "development" that took place within the early Christian community. All one had to do then was to decide which was the main point, and the rest could be dismissed as the creation of the early church. Such logic is still probably the main reason why many scholars are nervous about deriving too much theology from an interpretation of Jesus' parables. This is tragic, for the parable is Jesus' most characteristic form, and contains the largest amount of teaching about the Kingdom of God.
contains the largest amount of teaching about the Kingdom of God.

In this book I shall make abundant and constant use of the parables as sources of the theology of the historical Jesus; and I shall do so on what I consider to be justifiable critical grounds. For this reason, it is only proper that I give a slightly more detailed critique of Julicher as he has been used by the school of form criticism. There are three main problems with this axiom. a) To begin with, Jesus was not a Greek, but a Hebrew, and it would seem more appropriate to derive one's understanding of his use of parable, not from the classical Greek concept of a simple one point analogy (*parabole*), but from the Hebrew use of parable contained in the word *mashal*, which not only permitted many points, but also detailed allegory. It is commonly recognized that the rabbis of Jesus' day used allegory, and it is very difficult for me to see why one must deny Jesus this privilege. My best explanation of this curiously arbitrary restriction is that Julicher did his work at the end of the nineteenth century when most New Testament scholars were primarily students of classical Greek literature, and it was fashionable to interpret the New Testament from that perspective. Since then, students of the New Testament have become increasingly familiar with the Old Testament and rabbinic literature; and that, along with many new discoveries like the Dead Sea Scrolls, has shown us that the most basic environment for interpreting Jesus and the early Palestinian church is not a classical Greek, but a Hebrew one.

b) A second problem with this axiom is that it doesn't work. It involves the interpreter in such an arbitrary process of deciding which of the several points in a parable is the authentic one that his critical interpretation becomes completely trapped in subjectivity. A better plan would seem to be to make our definition of parable fit the use to which Jesus put it (JGTJ-27), which permitted as many points within a parable as he wished to make, in good Hebrew fashion.

8

THERE IS POWER IN BELIEVING THE GOSPEL

c) A third problem with this restriction of Jesus' parables to one point is that it necessitates doing violence to the Gospel text, and in the process misses a very important pattern contained therein. In the Synoptics there are eleven parables with what I would call "semi-allegorical" features. They are not pure allegories, because every symbol within them is not interpreted in the explanations that follow. They are distinctive in that they all contain explanations of the various symbols within the parables, usually as separate units at the end. Now if Mark is to be believed, Jesus regularly explained his parables to his disciples privately (Mark 4:11, 33-34). Julicher, however, insisted that this is an impossible example of allegory, and Mark must have been mistaken.

Some years ago I did an exhaustive analysis of this phenomenon, and the results were most interesting. The new factor in my study was the audience situation, to which neither Julicher nor the form critics had paid much attention. I discovered that there were not just these semi-allegorical explanations to Jesus' parables, but other types as well: thematic, contextual and internal (ACHJ-104-109). If all four types of explanation are correlated with the audience to which they are given, what emerges is the fact that among the 71 different Synoptic parables, 42 are explained in one of these four ways, and 21 are left unexplained. Here is a pattern suggesting that the predominant motive of Jesus was to explain his parables. Furthermore, to the disciples there were 30 explained and seven unexplained — to those groups or individuals who opposed him, twelve were explained, but fourteen left without explanation. Here is a further pattern corroborating the generalization in Mark that it was Jesus' custom to explain the parables to the disciples, but leave them without explanation to those "outside." The patterns are not perfectly consistent, and that is what one would expect in a living situation; but they are too wide-spread throughout all the sources, too recurrent, to have been the work of editor or early church. They most probably originated with an historical figure who operated in that way, and whose consistent practice, generalized by Mark, emerges unconsciously from an exhaustive study of all the parables in their audience contexts. Jesus seems clearly to have used allegorical parables.

There were two conclusions consistently drawn by the form critics from the above and other similar arguments. The first was that one can know little or nothing for certain about the historical Jesus. The only thing Bultmann would admit with real certainly was what he

9

called "*das dass,*" the *fact that,* Jesus did live. The second conclusion was an accommodation to the first; it doesn't really matter whether we can get back to the historical Jesus or not. The result of this logic has been that for two generations of biblical scholars, the faith of the early church has been erected as a "barrier" between us and the historical Jesus. All we can really know is what the church thought about him, and if one takes Bultmann's logic seriously, this cannot be relied upon. The result has been a deep historical skepticism that has settled over the field of critical Gospel studies, and had an enormous effect on biblical scholarship and the theology of the church.

I have tried to show that each one of the three bases for this skepticism has in recent scholarship been successfully challenged. It has been long in coming, but I think the signs are clear that the world of New Testament study is gradually releasing itself from this strange "Bultmannian Captivity". But the legacy remains in the two questions which still haunt Gospel scholarship: can we know anything for certain about Jesus, and does it matter? Before we can go any farther in our examination of the theology of the historical Jesus, we must find some positive answers to these questions which have stifled such research in recent years.

It Is Important: The Pathology of Historical Skepticism

Let's reverse the order and ask the second question first: does it really matter whether or not we can recover the historical Jesus with any degree of accuracy? I am going to suggest that it matters so much that this problem is one of the major sources of the loss of power within the mainline Protestant churches.

(1) In the first place, it is important for a mature faith. Bultmann reminded us that historical research is so uncertain and filled with so many new and surprising discoveries, that it would be impossible for our faith to be based upon it. I agree; but this is too shallow an analysis, for faith has many levels. Ultimately, Bultmann is right; faith must rest on one's personal encounter with God and not on the answers to historical questions. But the problem is that faith also involves rational belief, which is the intellectual level of faith, even as spiritual encounter is its more emotional, "existential" level. For faith to be mature it must be total. It must involve not only the bottom of our hearts, but also the top of our minds; and historical considerations are important for the intellectual support that augments faith. If we feel the necessity of hanging our rational minds in the narthex with our hats and coats as we enter the church, we are prob-

10

ably suffering from "theological schizophrenia," which is the name for the divided personality who cannot believe rationally what he or she embraces emotionally. There are many intelligent Christians today suffering from this disease, and it is a great source of weakness in the church.

(2) In the second place historical belief is important for the authority of Jesus' teachings. He is recorded saying many things about every kind of theological question. That is what our book is about. Much that he said was quite different from Moses, or his own contemporaries, or from what people have generally believed about religion, then or now. What he said often involved him in some preposterous claims concerning his own part in the drama of salvation; and men challenged him, asking, "By what authority do you do these things?" (Matt. 21:23) This is still the most relevant question; for if he is the Son of God, and if our record of what he said about these important matters of God and salvation is sufficiently accurate, then we have a source of knowledge about such questions that shines like a beacon of light in a great darkness. We have some authoritative knowledge about theology direct from the Son of God. But if what we have is only the faith of the early church, based on an irrecoverable kernel of authentic Jesus material, or created out of whole cloth by the church to serve its own purposes, then unless we canonize the entire Palestinian church, we must reduce the authority of the Gospels to that of any other document coming out of the entire history of Christianity. The effect of this logical schizophrenia has gotten through to scholars, and now to laymen (See Irving Wallace's recent book, *The Word*); and the authority of Jesus as a source for the theology of the church has been widely abandoned because we can't be sure of anything he is recorded saying or doing. So the sharp point of the Gospel is blunted, and much power has gone out of the proclamation of the Holy Word.

(3) This, then, is important because Christianity is an historical faith. It is not a philosophy, nor a cleverly devised mythology, nor a set of useful rules for personal conduct; but on its own terms it is the incursion into history of the living God at a point of space and time and in the person of Jesus Christ. This is what electrified the early community; this is what gave authority and power to its message. Bultmann's early research convinced him that it was impossible to recover the historical Jesus. As a result he turned to existential theology which concentrates on one's inner, personal involvement with God. As he said to me one day in Marburg: "If you can't believe

11

in the historical Jesus, where else is there to go except the Christ of faith." What I am saying is that this misrepresents the nature of Christianity, and substitutes certain philosophical concerns (Bultmann turned to Heidegger and Kirkegaard) for Jesus as the source of Christian theology. It was perfectly consistent then that Bultmann in his later writing denied not only the importance of the historical resurrection, but its fact. The resurrection became for him merely a mythological symbol for what really happened, which was that Jesus was crucified, and then rose in people's hearts as they came to believe that God was somehow working through the cross for their redemption. The point is that this historical skepticism has made some radical changes in the basic nature of the Christian faith, for Bultmann, as for great numbers who have followed his lead.

(4) This means, then, that one's answer to this question of historical authenticity is very important for accurate interpretation of the Gospels. Those who wrote the material obviously appear to have believed that these things really happened. Unless it is all an extremely clever subterfuge, this historical orientation clearly had an influence on what the authors meant, and on what Jesus would have meant, for example in his insistence that in him the Kingdom of God had come near in space and time. Furthermore, unless one is to ignore certain inconsistencies in the New Testament, and insist that every word is equally authoritative, a position which I believe to be incompatible with modern critical scholarship, we need to be able to distinguish between what is authentic and what is not. If one compares the sayings of Jesus with the surrounding narrative, it soon becomes clear that there is a sharp discontinuity between them. This is seen for example in the use of the phrase Kingdom of God. In the sayings, Jesus presents a Kingdom that is intensely spiritual, personal and embraces both the present and the end time. Those in the narrative who speak of the Kingdom, however, like John the Baptist (Matt. 3:2), or the disciples (Luke 19:11; Mark 11:10) picture it in highly Jewish terms as political (Mark 11:10), or a final event about to happen (Mark 15:43; Luke 23:42). As Luke comments: "They supposed that the Kingdom of God was to appear immediately" (Luke 19:11). The vocabulary, theology and general world view of the editors is often at variance with that of the recorded Jesus, and this helps to document a running theme within the Gospels that Jesus was misunderstood as often as he was understood. We dare not assume uncritically that the faith of the Gospel writers was inevitably true to the teachings of Jesus (ACHJ-74-89).

(5) The historical question is also important in terms of the consequences of historical skepticism. Protestant scholarship has now had about fifty years in which to work out the logic of the extreme skepticism which came out of the work of the form critics. The results have been most illuminating. Years ago, Donald Baillie in his book *God Was in Christ* noted the strange contradiction between the conservative theology of Karl Barth and his radical biblical criticism. The Jesus material was used by Barth and other Neo-orthodox theologians "as if" it were authentic, when the basic premises of their critical scholarship logically denied its authority. The logic of this incongruity has gradually permeated the theology of the church, especially in America, where German biblical criticism is taken much more seriously than it is in Britain, or even sometimes in Germany.

As far as I can see, and there isn't space here to do more than state the situation, these fifty years have revealed the increasing sickness of Protestant theology, and the progressive weakness of the church. The theological giants like Barth and Tillich, Brunner and Baillie, Niebuhr and Ferre, whose grandeur was based upon their biblical rootage, have died off, and been replaced by a generation of theologians some of whom have led us in a bewildering chase after theological relevance from one extreme to another. There has been some justification for this, for theology must constantly adapt its approach to these rapidly changing times. But unfortunately theology has become a "faddist" game, where a bewildering variety of trends have appeared in books on the Honest to God debate, or the Situation Ethics debate, or the Death of God debate, or the Theology of Hope debate, or the Process Theology debate, or most recently the Liberation Theology debate. And here is the point: there is one thing that most of these interesting, creative, often helpful, yet idiosyncratic theologies have in common. They begin by accepting in one degree or another, whether consciously or unconsciously, Bultmann's extreme historical skepticism. As a result, they usually go elsewhere than the Gospels, or even the Bible in general, for the primary substance of their theology: to modern philosophy or other contemporary theologians, to psychology or sociology, to nonwestern religions or secular literature and poetry. In most of these theologies, if the Bible is used at all, it is at best an illustrative device for theological conclusions derived elsewhere.

The result has been a series of brave and even noble attempts at making theology relevant, but causing the Christian community to be as Paul described the church at Ephesus, "tossed to and fro with every wind of doctrine" (Eph. 4:14). This is what happened to the early Christian church in North Africa and elsewhere when it lost its hold on the historical realism of the Gospels and turned to Greek philosophy and oriental religions as the source for its theology. Jesus was turned into a vague mythical figure, or a baby monster who killed his playmates because they displeased him. In *The Infancy Story of Thomas*, a book produced within those circles in the third century, Mary and Joseph are approached by their neighbors in Nazareth who complain about the baby Jesus: "Since you have such a child, you cannot dwell with us in the villiage... for he is slaying our children." The church had lost its hold on the historical Jesus, and this is what resulted. The same spirit of Gnosticism has plagued the Protestant church for the last fifty years, and we are sick; and the heart of our sickness, as far as I can determine, is this theological schizophrenia, resulting no doubt from many things, but chiefly I would say from the extreme historical skepticism I have been describing.

(6) The effect of this has been a very practical one. When a Christian minister stands up in the pulpit and reads from the Gospels, "And Jesus said...", and a small voice within replies, "Oh yes? Isn't this the word of the early church that cannot be relied upon?" then the power of the proclamation of the Holy Word goes out of his or her message. Not only are they in agony because of this intellectual-spiritual tension, but their parishioners also recognize that something is lacking. What happens is that ministers turn to Psychology, or as Bultmann did, to an extreme existential theology, or they turn to various faddist group techniques to buttress their emasculated Gospel. Or they compensate by an extreme radical activism or avant-grade life style that often splits churches and drives away its members. Or they drop out; and the professions of our country are filled with former clergymen who are victims of this disease. Some simply agonize in silence, wishing nostalgically that they could believe with their minds what they feel to be true in their hearts. It is no secret that all of the mainline Protestant churches have been losing members, while those who have maintained a strong hold on the Bible can't build mammoth churches fast enough to house their adherents. I cannot endorse the uncritical biblical scholarship of some of these churches; but I recognize the vital importance of having a word to proclaim that is credible, not only in some complicated theological way, but in the simpler, more

14

understandable terms of its historical authenticity.

To what extent this illness has infected the Roman Catholic church, I am not competent to hazard more than a guess. But now that this ancient communion since Vatican II has emerged into the modern world of critical biblical scholarship, an event much to be applauded, I would presume to give a warning. There are many ways of doing critical scholarship that do not result in losing the church's hold on the historical Jesus. I would pray that this great church exercise its new biblical freedom with wisdom and considerable caution. Let me put it bluntly. The extremes of form critical historical skepticism have been a Trojan horse for the Protestant churches, and we have been ravished by its influence. Roman Catholic theology is still strong, producing theological giants such as the Protestants produced two generations ago before the influence of this skepticism began to take effect. There is some indication, contained in a basic contradiction within the Pontifical Biblical Commission's statement of 1964, that the Roman church has accepted a modified, but still doctrinaire form criticism as its guide into the new world of biblical scholarship. *Caveat emptor!*

If we must accept this extreme historical skepticism, then let us face up to that fact and accommodate ourselves to a malingering illness that may have no cure. We must make the best of it, and perhaps follow Bultmann into an internalized existential theology where faith is not concerned with the facts of history. But if this is not necessary, if the evidence does not demand it, then it is too bad to accept what I see as the adverse practical results of this extreme skepticism simply because this is the prevailing mood in critical scholarship.

It Is Possible: The Therapy of Historical Optimism

My main reason for believing it is important to recover the historical Jesus is that within certain limits it is possible to do so. We live in a new day which is going beyond the skepticism of the past. It was a noble, and for many a very painful, effort to be honest and scientific in their biblical study. It was a necessary part of the emergence of biblical research out of the middle ages into the modern world. But now we must move on; and new insights are emerging that present a more hopeful and positive picture. I want to initiate this reconstruction of Synoptic theology by presenting three methodological "clues," which represent my own intellectual pilgrimage along this difficult critical path.

15

We must begin by narrowing the parameters of this discussion. In the first place, in talking about the historical authenticity of the Synoptic Gospels, one must distinguish between the teachings of Jesus and the narrative material that surrounds them. The historical problems and possibilities, and the methods of historiography for each, are necessarily different. The teaching material stands in a unique position in the emergence of the Gospel story. By its very nature it is easier to document, and we can be more certain therefore of its exact details. We shall therefore concentrate on the teachings of Jesus. What I shall say will also point toward the authenticity of the narratives, for teaching and narrative are intimately bound together; but strictly speaking in terms of this methodology, the historicity of the former is more securely founded.

A second limitation of this discussion has to do with the fact that we are dealing with what one might call "qualified historicity." The fact is that the phrase "historical authenticity" must be viewed in at least two different ways. Bultmann defined the problem by distinguishing between two German words for history: *Historie*, which he used to identify the objective facts of history, and *Geschichte* which represented for him interpreted history, which was the faith understanding of the historian. Since he could not believe in the validity of *Historie*, what he did was concentrate on the *Geschichte* of the Gospels, which was the faith of the early church.

It would seem quite clear that what we have in the Gospels involves the interpretation and faith of the early Christian community. There were no tape recorders or movie cameras at work among the disciples, and any responsible examination of these records must recognize evidence of the activity of the editors. At times the Gospels disagree with each other on the wording of a saying, or its literary or geographical location. Certain words and phrases are peculiar to one and another of the Evangelists, and one can detect clear editorial activity (ACHJ-138). Furthermore, the ways in which the words of Jesus and the events of his life are arranged at times show clearly some consistent plan, for example in the editorial arrangement of sayings in Mark 13 (cf. p. 203). I have pointed to the discontinuity between the vocabulary, theology and world view of the editors and that of the teachings of Jesus. So sharp is this that at times one must recognize what I call "anti-patterns," which are places where some pattern emerges that goes against the general tenor of the Jesus material (ACHJ-172). For example, the editor of the material peculiar to Matthew was especially interested in Jewish concerns, and at one point seems to have wanted to limit Jesus' ministry to "the lost sheep of the house of Israel" (Matt. 10:6), which goes against the universality of Jesus' message elsewhere, and would seem to represent the bias of the editor more than that of Jesus (ACHJ-114-117). Certainly there was interpretation going on. My discovery has been, however, that when it occurs, it is at a minimum, and can usually be detected, so we are not at the mercy of the editors.

Actually, it is inevitable that history must be interpreted, lest it be merely a series of unrelated and incoherent clusters of data. I would go further and say that, up to a point, the best history is an interpreted one. I sometimes throw a book at a student in class to illustrate this point, hoping not only that he will catch it (I usually choose an athletic looking student), but that in reporting the history of that event he will correctly interpret it, lest the word get out that the instructor has lost his mind. There is no problem in accepting the inevitability of interpretation in the writing of the biography of Jesus. The Gospels are partly *Geschichte*. The problem comes when the validity of the element of *Historie*, the objective fact of the matter, is so downgraded that we can no longer believe that the interpretation is an authentic representation of the actual occurrence. This is what Bultmann and a whole generation of form critics have done; and so my concern is to recover the *full* authenticity of Gospel history, not only *Geschichte* but *Historie* as well. The latter is a product of hard-headed historiography, and it is in historiographic methodology that I find three clues to a greater appreciation of the element of *Historie* within the Synoptic Gospels.

The First Clue: Content Analysis, The Computer and the Scientific Method

The more I have worked on this question, the more apparent it has become that the most basic problem of the form critics is one of method. The very intellectual, critical technique they used in doing their research was pre-scientific, and their radically skeptical conclusions were built into the method itself as presuppositions. There is a whole series of assumptions, like the insistence that Jesus' parables must have only one point, which operated to prejudice the conclusions of these scholars. The method Bultmann used was so highly subjective, so impressionistic, so filled with phrases like, "it seems to me," or "there can be no doubt," when there actually was much doubt, that the method had no way of checking its own presuppositions. What is needed is a more scientific method, one that examines the evidence first and then out of that builds its conclusions; a method that provides careful checks on one's own pre-judgments by demanding evidence for everything; a method that deals in probabilities that are empirically and even mathematically induced, and not absolute certainties intuitively arrived at. What I am describing is the need for a revolution in biblical method. This, I think, is coming, and I am encouraged by the developments of recent years. Although the historical skepticism I have described is still normative for Protestant scholarship, especially for America, there is nevertheless emerging a climate within biblical studies that is more open to new methods than during the hey-day of the "Bultmannian captivity." What I want to do here in a very brief form is just to mention some work which is described at length elsewhere (ACHJ-15-31), and shows various ways — some of them quite new — in which modern historiographic methods can be applied to the study of the authenticity of the Gospel material. The first is what is called "Content Analysis" (cf. CAC). This is a method widely used in other disciplines, but almost nonexistent in biblical studies. It represents the application of the scientific method to literary study, whether it be Homer, Shakespeare or the Bible. The key to it is the search for "patterns" in the material being studied. Any such phenomenon that occurs more often than chance would allow is the indicator of something "real" in the world, and is the substance of the conclusions of chemists, sociologists, psychologists, historians and all who would approach their data in a scientific way.

Now when applied to the study of the Synoptic Gospels, this means that we must search for patterns of regular recurrence in every conceivable way, correlating each word of the text with every phenomenon of form, source, audience, history, grammar, syntax and the like. This of course is monumentally difficult, and is one of the chief reasons why Content Analysis has not been applied to biblical studies. After spending an entire summer on such an analysis of one word in the Synoptics, I was ready to abandon the effort, when a friend alerted me to the possibilities of the computer in literary research, and the results have been most exciting. For here is a tool that enables one quickly and accurately to do the kind of massive analysis of every bit of data that is essential to scientific research. When the Gospels were subjected to a computer-assisted Content Analysis, there emerged a whole new world of information;

entire new dimensions of data, hundreds of patterns never seen before. I learned later that this was the first time this had ever been done. One result has been the production of a series of computer generated concordances of various "levels" of biblical material called, *The Computer Bible*, which is making the scientific method more available to the student of biblical literature.

The Second Clue: Audience Criticism and the "Hard Core" of the Holy Word

My first use of computer-assisted Content Analysis was to examine the audiences to which Jesus is recorded giving his teachings in the Synoptic Gospels. This story is contained in detail in my book, *Audience Criticism and the Historical Jesus*. I discovered these Gospels agreeing with each other on the audience to which Jesus' words were addressed, more than on any other matter. There is hardly a word of Jesus not directed to one of the four audiences: the twelve, the larger group of disciples, the large opponent crowd, and the small core of opponents (priests, scribes, pharisees, sadducees). The Gospel editors go out of their way to make this clear. It became apparent that here was a solid pattern that could possibly serve as a basis for other patterns. With the use of the computer, I correlated the audience situation with everything else I knew about these Gospels, wording, theology, form, source, teaching method, historical context, to discover whatever patterns there might be. The results were unbelievable. When they first began to emerge, I took some of my observation down the hall of the graduate library where I was working to show to a visiting German scholar. His remarks were brief and unequivocal: "Very interesting, but I don't believe it!" I didn't either to begin with, but gradually I have come to believe that something entirely new and thoroughly credible was coming out of this new methodology. The first discovery was that the direct words of Jesus showed up quite differently from the editorial narrative surrounding them. The vocabulary was different, the style was different, the reference to the audience was different, the theology was different, the use of certain key words was different. It did not seem possible that these editors could have created the sayings of Jesus, as many scholars in this generation have assumed, because they were so unique in every way. It took a computer to reveal this in an exhaustive fashion.

Furthermore, as I looked carefully into these quoted sayings of Jesus, it became apparent that they revealed many patterns of "con-

19

tinuity" that cut "horizontally" across the three Synoptic Gospels, and all of their earlier sources. They showed Jesus using certain words, metaphors, teaching techniques and theological emphases to certain audiences so consistently that when the audience changed, one could observe the theology, wording, form and teaching technique also changing. As the editors themselves said, he spoke to them "as they were able to hear" (Mark 4:33-34); he modified his language, theology and practice to suit the audience. These patterns are principally of four types. 1) The first is the verbal pattern. T. W. Manson in his book, *The Teachings of Jesus*, discovered years ago by a laborious longhand method that there were 191 words in the Synoptics that were used consistently to certain audiences. The computer turned up at least 309 such pattern words in a matter of minutes. The word *amen* (verily), for example, seems to have been a signature word for Jesus, occurring fifty times as part of his teaching and almost always (45 times) to a disciple audience. Certain types of words tend to cluster about a particular audience, like the nineteen Jewish terms directed almost exclusively to the opponents (ACHJ-91). An over-all summary reveals that 17.5 % of all important words in the Synoptics (omitting articles, prepositions etc.) are used in some such consistent "pattern" fashion (ACHJ-171).

2) There are also many metaphors showing the same consistency. Those dealing with salt, light, business, servant-master relations and parts of the body seem to be reserved for the disciple audiences, while the metaphors of houses, dinners, fathers, sons and weddings are given characteristically to the opponents. Again, an exhaustive survey reveals that 88% of all the teaching units have at least one pattern word; twenty have 50% or more pattern words, three have 80%, and in two, every word is a pattern word (Matt. 9:22; Luke 5:9).

3) Even theological emphases vary according to the audience, with the teaching about the end time, for example, being given almost exclusively to the disciples and that about the wrath of God stressed to the opponents. Ninety-two per cent of all the sayings of Jesus have at least one such theological pattern.

4) Finally, the Gospels reveal a Jesus who acted in "pattern" ways to his various audiences. To the opponents, he is pictured deferring to their Jewishness by making many references to Jewish history and institutions, while in his sayings to the disciples, this kind of language is notably absent. It was to the disciples that he seems to have most completely spoken his mind, stressing both the love and

the wrath of God, both the present and the future aspects of the Kingdom, and it was to them that he deliberately explained his parables. In 97% of all the units of Jesus' teaching there is at least one pattern of some kind.

Now some of these patterns can be attributed to the editors, and others to the obvious necessities of the material itself (ACHJ-136-152); but to attribute them generally to the early church or editor would mean that the broad spectrum of audience-saying correlation would have to be the result of the creative activity of the church, universally known and widely understood. It would mean that it was generally agreed that Jesus used the metaphors of body, salt, light, business and harvest only to the disciples, and those about weddings and dinners primarily to non-disciples — or that all these verbal, metaphor, theological and praxis patterns are the merest chance — all of which is highly improbable. For these patterns to have been created by the church would demand an editorial body capable of somehow controlling the editors of all sources and Gospels so strictly that departures from these patterns would be minimal. According to any defensible theory of Synoptic origins, this is highly unlikely. Such a theory would demand a lack of concern for the facts of evangelical history that would allow a community to compose or drastically alter the original teachings of Jesus without opposition; but this is out of keeping with the evidence. The agreement between the editors on the sayings of Jesus, coupled with the discontinuity between their narration and the teaching material, suggests a conservatism on the part of these editors in handling Jesus' sayings that cautions strongly against attributing such license to the early community of which they were a part (ACHJ 136f, 145, 150-157).

These patterns are rather too subtle, too widespread, too deeply imbedded in the material, too generally agreed upon to have been the product of either the editors or the early church. What they seem to reflect is the activity of a single mind, operating at the deepest historical level, who thought and taught in certain consistent ways (ACHJ-136-152). This kind of verbal-theological practice continuity which I shall be demonstrating throughout this book, represents a growing body of data pointing to the stability of the Jesus material coming through the process of Gospel formation surprisingly intact (ACHJ-98-102).

It is also important to note that the abundance and quality of these patterns within the sayings of Jesus stand in sharp contrast to

21

the patterns of wording, theology or praxis evident in the narrative material. This suggests as a general principle that there are more "horizontal" patterns cutting across the teaching of Jesus in all the Gospels and sources, than "vertical" patterns persisting only within one Gospel or source. As a consequence, it would seem more possible to talk of the characteristic teaching of Jesus, than the characteristic style, vocabulary or thought of any particular evangelist (ACHJ-136-152). It is this hard core of teaching material which the early church called "the Holy Words" of Jesus. The new principle emerging from this kind of research is that at these points, where there are demonstrable patterns, it would seem we have broken through the "historical barrier." What we possess in the Synoptic Gospels is a hard core of Jesus data concentrated in his teaching which antedates the work of the editors, surrounded by some rather obvious narration, and organized in certain editorial ways; but handled with a carefulness that enabled these subtle patterns to survive to this day.

The Third Clue: Historical Analysis and the Stability of the Holy Word

Now let us back up and take another run at this question of the historical Jesus, this time with a more traditional approach (cf. HW). If one examines all the literature of antiquity, from the first to the fourth century when the New Testament was canonized, one sees four major factors contributing to the stability and authenticity of the church's reproduction of the life and teachings of Jesus. 1) The first is the "sanctity" of the holy apostles. By Paul's day, it was well established that the twelve apostles were the authorities in matters of church discipline and doctrine, and this authority acted as a standard of conduct and a check on the doctrine being preached in the early church (see Acts 5). Even Paul felt that he had to clear his message with those "pillars" in Jerusalem (Gal. 2:2). Now it was these holy apostles which the various records describe as the chief line of transmission for the Gospel material. That is why their names are attached to so many New Testament documents, whether they wrote them or not. It is their teaching that was the major source of early Christian instruction (Acts 2:42). This apostolic authority seems to have acted as a control on the life and thought of the early church, and we must not assume that anyone could simply write anything he wanted about the teaching and activity of Jesus. The constant battle against "heresy" that began in the first century and lasted for hundreds of years, prompting the several ecumenical conferences and the writing of the various creeds, is eloquent testimony to the fact not only that there were those who were changing the original Gospel, but that there were even more who were determined to keep it accurate. One of the natural products of the sanctity of the apostles was to produce sources and standards for doctrine which were the prime ammunition in the church's battle against heresy.

2) A second factor contributing to historical stability lies in the "school" environment out of which the Gospels emerged. From the time of the "school of Jesus" where the teaching mode was predominant, the disciples, and then the disciples of disciples of disciples, were students whose masters were concerned to catechize them (Mark 8:27-30), to repeat their material to them, and to explain the Christian Gospel as Jesus explained his parables to his disciples in private (Mark 4:10-12). The pattern established there was continued through the years. Later it was the school of the apostles in Jerusalem that acted to stabilize the early church; and then, as they scattered after Jerusalem's destruction in 70 A.D., this took place in the schools of each of the apostles. This pattern then continued in the great schools of sacred learning in Alexandria and Caesarea, where the careful recording of the words of one's teacher was obligatory and widespread. Such seems to have been the environment out of which these Gospels and most of the rest of the New Testament material emerged. As Luke had followed all things "closely for some time past" (1:1-4), so also had a great many others in the early church; and it was this, not some kind of loose, freewheeling tradition of extravagant creativity, that lay behind our New Testament, and especially the Synoptic Gospels (cf. HW).

3) A third stabilizing factor coming from such historical study is that of the early literary activity of those who were a part of the original disciple fellowship. The form critics insisted that it was twenty to thirty years before anything was written down. It would appear that this insistence on a long oral period was an arbitrary model which Bultmann and others borrowed from the Old Testament form critics and which does not really apply to the process of Gospel formation. Some of the members of the larger group of disciples were rulers of the synagogue (Mark 5:36), and others were pharisees (Luke 7:36-50), elders of the Jews (Luke 7:3) and scribes (Luke 20:39-Mark 12:34-Matt. 8:19-20 etc.); certainly a literate company. Others were called "ministers of the word" (Luke 1:1-4),

and their specific job was to deal with the written records of Jesus' life and teachings. Furthermore, there are passages in the New Testament referring to the "sacred writings" in which Christians like Timothy were instructed "for salvation through faith in Jesus Christ" (2 Tim. 3:14-15); and these would seem to be references to early *Christian* scripture (cf. 2 Peter 3:15-16; I Tim. 5:18; 4:13; Ro. 16:25-26; cf. HW, Chapt. IV). Luke called himself a "minister of the word," and gave every indication that he and others like him had compiled careful narratives "for some time past" that they might know the "truth" of what had transpired (Luke 1:1-4). The evidence points to the first century Christian community from the time of Jesus himself as a highly literate group of disciples oriented to a disciplined "school" experience. They were concerned and trained to reproduce the Jesus "memoirs" with a carefulness that is consistent with the hard core of pattern data turned up by computer analysis. These three lines of evidence would all seem to point to the historical probability that the Gospels were carefully preserved and produced.

4) A final stabilizing factor coming from historical analysis lies in the "sanctity" of the words of Jesus. The question that has haunted me throughout this research is how the Gospel material could have been preserved with such fidelity as to reproduce the patterns I have observed. The answer I think is deceptively simple: beyond all else that one could say, ultimately it resides in the sanctity which they attributed to Jesus. They called his teaching "holy words," and they treated them with a carefulness that has never to my knowledge been duplicated in the history of human literature, because *they really believed he was the Son of God.* Bultmann was right that the authenticity of the written Gospels ultimately depends on their accuracy as *oral* words, however quickly they may have become fixed in writing. But the impressive fact with which any assessment of Gospel historicity must reckon is the stabilizing influence of the sanctity of this word. All the Evangelists want us to know that it was the "words of Jesus," the "word of Jesus," the "word" (cf. pp. 35). that caused the disciples to leave their nets, and impressed the woman at the well in Samaria. The sanctity of the holy apostles, and the authority of the holy writings is ultimately based on the sanctity of Jesus' Holy Word. It is this which functioned from the beginning as the basis for Christian Gospel and tradition, and was the primary check on heresy: a solid, stable body of data, preserved with a uniquely slavish attention to the original because of the unparalleled

sanctity of that figure and his word in the eyes of the beholders. Writing quickly aided in stabilization; but it was the oral Holy Word that authenticated the writings in the first century, and continued to authenticate and eventually canonize them out of the living memory of the church.

It is therefore not only important but increasingly possible to talk with cautious certainty about the historical facts (*Historie*) of the Jesus story, and especially about his Holy Word; and it is to a detailed examination of this Word that we now turn.

NC WESLEYAN COLLEGE LIBRARY
ROCKY MOUNT, NC 27804

Chapter II

No One Ever So Spake

It is a surprising thing that Christian theology has not taken Jesus seriously as a theologian. Emil Brunner traced the ranking of the Gospels below the teaching of the apostles as a relic of the first centuries of the Christian era. Certainly it is apparent in the present age that Paul, not Jesus, is the dominant source for Christian theology. But surely, this is inadequate. If, as the church has insisted from the beginning, Jesus is the Son of God, if he is the head of the church, and if Paul represents a valid restatement of his life and thought, then it would seem that even the sainted apostle is a secondary source. There is a real probability that Paul himself would be unhappy with this situation; for in one way and another he constantly referred his readers to the "mind of Christ" (I Cor. 2:2, 16). As far as I can see, it is Jesus himself who stands in judgment on the church; it is he who stands in judgment on Paul; it is he who stands in judgment on Christian theology; and it is his mind and person, his teachings and life that should be the chief cornerstone of Christian doctrine. It is strange that this simple thesis should have such a bizarre and radical ring, even to the author. The truth is that before one can elaborate such a thesis in this day, he must first examine carefully the place and validity of the written Gospels as sources for the theology and life of the church.

The Centrality and Uniqueness of the Gospels

From the end of the first century, the four Gospels functioned as the center of Christian belief. Such is evident in the fact that there are more ancient manuscripts of this material than of any other portion of the New Testament. This is particularly interesting for the literary historian in view of another fact. Although the term Gospel

(*Euaggelion*) does occur in Greek literature as far back as Homer to refer to the "good news" about the birth, coming of age or succession to the throne of the Emperor, nevertheless, as a self-conscious literary type, that is, as a Gospel, this appears for the first time in Christian literature. As a literary device it seems to have originated in the early church as a composite of several standard forms. Created for a particular purpose, it lasted within the Christian community as an active literary genre, for approximately 300 years, and then disappeared. After about 325 A.D. there were no more Gospels written. So here is a peculiar literary vehicle created by the Christian church to proclaim the life and teachings of Jesus; and when that particular need was satisfied, the Gospel genre disappeared, and so far as I know, has not been used again in the history of human literature (UG, Chapt. VI).

Actually, there were many Gospels produced by the early Christian community in the first three or four hundred years of its existence, besides those that found their way into the New Testament. There was the Gospel of the Hebrews and the Gospel of the Egyptians, the Gospel of Thomas and the Gospel of Philip, as well as a great number of others which are available for study in complete or fragmentary form, in what is called "The Apocryphal New Testament." It does not take much examination to see why most of these never made the Bible, picturing as they did the baby Jesus stretching boards, or killing his playmates with a wave of his hand! But some, like the Gospel of Thomas, contain much material also found in the New Testament Gospels, along with other new sayings of Jesus which might well be authentic. It is the four that are in the Bible, however, that emerged quickly and survived 300 years of testing as the most highly regarded of the many possible Gospels.

Of these four, John has proven to be the most widely used for devotional purposes. It was written later than the others and directed specifically to the questions of faith and spiritual need that occupied the practical life of the early church. It is my thesis, however, that the other three, the so-called "Synoptic" or "viewed-together" Gospels, represent the hard core of Christian belief from the very beginning, and so contain in its most pristine and primitive form the nucleus of the atomic power of the Christian proclamation. These contain the most information about the life and teaching of Jesus. In comparison with John, they seem to be less highly interpreted; and that observation, in company with the fact that they regularly give us two or three accounts of the same event or

27

teaching, makes them the best avenue for getting back to the historical mind of Jesus Christ. As far as I can see, Matthew, Mark and Luke functioned as the earliest prototype of what a Gospel was supposed to be; and it is on these Synoptic Gospels that we shall concentrate in identifying the center of power of the Christian message.

The Centrality of The Word

In the Synoptics we have a constant interplay between two types of material; between a lively and credible narrative about his life, death and resurrection on the one hand, and a solid body of the teachings of Jesus, what they later called the "holy word," on the other. The two are inseparably related; for what Jesus was and did are crucial to what he said. Nevertheless, there is a second observation that has taken me quite by surprise, and has commended itself as a significant new insight. In the tension between the narrative and the "Word," the emphasis is clearly on the "Word." This is surprising because we usually assume that the center of focus in these Gospels is the life, death and resurrection of Jesus. This was the emphasis of Paul, and became the focus of the life and theology of the developing church. But the fact is that *for the editors of these three Gospels*, it was not so much what he did as what he said — about the Kingdom of God — that was considered most important. This can be seen in several ways, some of which involve a subtle and highly complex analysis of the Gospels as a literary type or genre (cf. UG-Chapt. I). Perhaps most simply it is revealed in two ways. 1) If one thumbs through the Synoptics, it becomes quickly apparent that Matthew and Luke begin and end with two and then three chapters each, which are mostly narrative (Matt. 1-2, 26-28; Luke 1-2, 22-24); but between these narrative sections the vast bulk of material is teaching of Jesus. In Mark this is less clear because of the abundance of miracle stories, but even here, Jesus' healing ministry is secondary to his teaching, as Jesus insists to his disciples who remind him that people are searching for him in order to be healed: "Let us go on to the next towns, that I may *preach* there also; for *that is why I came out*" (Mark 1:38). 2) If one compares the number of separate narrative and teaching units, this fact is even more dramatically revealed. There are in all three Gospels 56 different narrative units (miracle stories, legends) compared with 306 separate teaching units (parables, sayings, paradigms). The narrative material, although it has immense value in its own right, is ultimately most significant as a setting for what the early church called "the Word of Jesus," which is the Gospel of the Kingdom of God. This suggests that if we are to take these Gospels seriously as sources for our preaching and teaching, we must put more emphasis on the theology of Jesus than is usually done in the life of the church.

It is in keeping with this that those who were most active in producing the Gospel were called *huperetes* in Greek, which is translated, "ministers of the word." As Luke says in his prologue (1:1-4), "Inasmuch as many have undertaken to compile a narrative of the things which have been accomplished among us, just as they were delivered to us by those who from the beginning were eyewitnesses and ministers of the word, it seemed good to me also..." Luke sees himself as a "minister of the word," and it is the *word* that is the heart of what he produces in his Gospel: not only what Jesus did, not only his life and death and resurrection, but the supreme importance of what he *said* about God and his Kingdom. For me, this insight has served to bring Jesus' teaching about the Kingdom of God into blazing focus as the center of the "fire" which he came to cast upon the earth (Luke 12:49). This does not reduce the importance of his person, as some might fear, but does just the opposite. For he pictured himself in his teaching; and if we look at Jesus through his own word, we see there a figure whose conscious stature rightly caused John to identify him as the word made flesh.

The Inner Nature of the Holy Word

If this is so, then we need to look more closely at this word to discover how it has functioned as a source of power for the church. One thing seems clear: the word of Jesus by its very nature is filled with power.

A Familiar Word Renewed

In one sense it was a familiar word, and this gave it power. Much of what Jesus taught was well known in Hebrew law. For example, in the Talmud, the large compendium of Jewish civil and canonical law, one finds this statement: "And Rabbi Gamaliel said, 'So long as you are merciful, God will have mercy upon you, and if you are not merciful, He will not be merciful unto you.'" That is exactly what Jesus said in Matthew 5:7. In another place the Talmud says, "Him who humbles himself, God exalts, him who exalts himself, God humbles." That is very much like Luke 14:11. In many ways Jesus talked like the Jewish rabbis of his day.

He also regularly quoted the Old Testament, and is recorded using the phrase "It is written" (in the Old Testament) on at least nineteen occasions. The law, the prophets and the writings of the Old Testament are referred to with equal authority, but he allied himself principally with the prophets, quoting them thirty-one times. Isaiah seems to have been his favorite. Luke describes him beginning his ministry in his home synagogue at Nazareth, reading a messianic passage from Isaiah 61, and then preaching a sermon which Luke summarizes in one sentence: "Today this scripture has been fulfilled in your hearing" (Luke 4:21). The judgment oracles of Jesus also sound very much like those of the Old Testament prophets: "Woe unto you Pharisees, you whited sepulchres, you hypocrites, you sons of Satan." This has the distinct flavor of Amos: "Woe to those who are at ease in Zion...I hate, I despise your feasts, and take no delight in your solemn assemblies" (Amos 6:1; 5:21).

The parables of Jesus are also similar to the Old Testament. For examples, in II Samuel 12:1-14, the prophet Nathan comes to David and tells the story of the rich man who stole the one ewe lamb from his poor neighbor. The king asks, "Who is this man?" and Nathan answers, "Thou art the man," applying the parable to the king. This is exactly the kind of thing Jesus did, directing his parables to his audiences, and protraying them in the parable. Besides the Old Testament, many of Jesus' parables were derived from common Jewish folklore. For example, the parable of the faithful and unfaithful servant was an adaptation of an old Jewish parable found in the book of Ahikar, contained in the Pseudepigrapha, a collection of Jewish writings coming out of the inter-testamental period, between about 300 B.C. and 100 A.D. Jesus, in other words, got some momentum for his teachings by beginning where people were, with methods and material that were familiar and respected.

A Distinctive Word

But Jesus was more than just a borrower. His was a radically new, dramatically different word, and this also was a source of its power. He called his message "new wine," a "new garment" (Mark 2:21-22), and rarely did he borrow material without putting his stamp upon it. One of the best ways of getting at the essence of what Jesus said is to find a place where he quoted or alluded to something from his environment, a popular Jewish folktale, a quotation from the Old Testament or something the rabbis were teaching, and then see where he differed. He always did three things to the material he borrowed which brought these religious ideas to a new dimension of meaning. As he said, "I am not come to destroy the law, but to fulfill it" (Mark 5:17). In the first place, he always strengthened the spiritual content of these ideas. Secondly, he broadened their context, lifting them out of their more parochial Jewish environment into a universal one. Thirdly, he added himself; and this was what always offended the Jews and excited his disciples. A fascinating illustration is his use of Isaiah's parable of the vineyard. "My beloved had a vineyard on a very fertile hill...When I looked for it to yield grapes, why did it yield wild grapes?...What will I do to my vineyard? I will remove its hedge, and it shall be devoured" (Is. 5:1-6). In Jesus' adaptation of this parable, with one stroke of his parabolic brush he spiritualized and universalized the story by making the vineyard stand for the Kingdom of God instead of the Jewish nation. Then he added himself in the figure of the "beloved son" sent to remind the unfaithful servants of their obligation to God, the owner of the vineyard (Mark 12:1-12). This kind of dramatic novelty electrified his audiences or severely antagonized them, and served to remind them that his Gospel was not just a refined Judaism, but something radically and dramatically new.

Jesus as Preacher

More exactly, they said, "No man ever so spake," and in this typical response one can see the reflection of his creative novelty as a preacher. This is particularly true in his use of the parable, the preaching form that was his trademark; and one can detect several ways in which his parables reveal the distinctiveness of his word. In the first place, they mirrored his own life and times. The figures of speech he used were drawn from farming, business, husbandry, homemaking. People heard him gladly, because he spoke to them out of their own experience in words they could understand.

Secondly, his parables reflected the moral and spiritual condition of those he addressed. The fascinating thing about them is that they became a two-way mirror, reflecting the audience to which the material was given, and also Jesus himself. He saw the audience in the parable. He saw himself in them, and often one finds a picture of God in them. There is a brilliance in the way he held this form up to his audience that enabled them to see themselves as rebellious servants, or as prodigal sons and daughters. As Mark says about his parable of the unfaithful servant, "They perceived that he told the parable against them" (Mark 12:12).

In the third place, the distinctive power of the parables lay in the crisis use to which he put them, challenging persons with the judgment of God. That of the sower, for example, is a parable about the telling of parables (Mark 4:1-9). "The sower went forth to sow," and here Jesus saw himself as the sower and those in the audience as various kinds of soil — rocky, weedy, hard trodden, or as good soil, plowed and prepared for the coming of the seed, which was the word of the Kingdom he was giving them in the parable itself. He was sowing the word as he was speaking. The word was in the parable, and this was a vehicle for the judgment of God as various soils (persons) accepted or rejected the seed. Only he who had eyes to see and ears to hear would understand, because there needed to be spiritual preparation; the soil needed to be plowed in order for the seed to be received and the mystery of new life to begin. These parables performed a very important selective, judging, crisis function, and that, too, is part of their distinctive power.

Jesus as Teacher

The power of Jesus' word lay not only in his brilliance as a preacher, but also as a teacher. The "saying" or teaching form is the most abundant among the various forms that he used. There are 185 sayings in the Synoptics, compared to 71 parables, and this is important for understanding the material. The most typical form in which he couched his message was that of the classroom, the way a teacher would speak. This "school" environment is clearly seen in the incident at Caesarea Philippi, when he asked, "Whom do people say that I am?...Whom do you say that I am?" He was testing them, and the teaching situation seems to have been the normative environment out of which the Jesus material emerged. So it was that later, as Jesus' disciples preserved his word, the "school" situation continued to function as the "pipeline" of the Gospels. Each of these disciples had his own school of disciples. Peter, John, Andrew, Thomas, and even Matthias, Judas' substitute, all seem to have founded schools of Gospel teaching (HW, Chapt. II).

Jesus as Theologian

Preacher, teacher, the distinctive character of Jesus' word is also a function of his ability as a theologian, and I suspect that this falls strangely on our ears. We are used to talking about the life, death and resurrection of Jesus, about his divinity and atoning sacrifice, about his abiding presence with us, all crucial parts of the Gospel.

But when it comes to talking about the mind of a man named Jesus in Palestine in the first century, who thought and taught in certain ways, and whose intellect operated according to identifiable patterns, we are not prepared for this. To call him a theologian may seem to reduce his grandeur to the level of some of the bickering pedants who argue in professional societies over obscure points that nobody cares about and who write scholarly books which only a small inner circle understands. Certainly not! Jesus was not such a person. But if one understands "theologian" to mean someone who thinks deliberately, consistently and coherently about God, whether professional or layman, whether highly educated or not, and who tries to convey these ideas to others, then it is very natural to call Jesus a theologian.

In this broader sense, Jesus' teachings reveal the talent of a consummate theologian, at once creative and poetic, but also brilliant with the integration of a disciplined mind. The apostle Paul, for all his ability and education, leaves many theological loose ends dangling...for example the way he tries to explain the concept of predestination, and God's election of the Jews in Romans 9-11, and then finally throws in the towel with the remark, "Great indeed is the mystery of our religion!" Jesus also presents the Gospel as a "mystery" (Mark 4:10-12), but gives us to understand that this is one which he is able to explain to those who have eyes to see. The Synoptic Gospels are not systematically organized, except in small blocks such as Mark thirteen which is all about the end, or the ethical sermon on the mount (Mark 5-7), both probably the product of editorial arrangement; but there is an internal theological system to the Synoptic material which is breathtaking. Surely here was the master theologian, whose parables and even short sayings were so comprehensive, and whose theology was so clear, that again and again he would encompass the entire essence of his thought in short, brilliant utterances. This whole book will be a discussion of the beautiful integrity and coherence of Jesus' theology as it revolves around his central concept, the Kingdom of God.

At this point, it is important to make my reference to Jesus as a theologian very clear, for this will operate throughout the rest of the book. Actually, the theology of Jesus emerges from the Gospels at three levels, not just one. The first level is that which is reported as direct quotation of Jesus. This is what the early church called "the holy word;" and for reasons I shall be explaining is that which can be taken most seriously as a source for Jesus' theology.

But there is a danger of limiting his theology to specific proof texts, lest we restrict their meaning and miss the deeper levels of his intention. For Jesus' theology emerges not only from particular passages, but also out of the deeper substructure of his thought, out of a whole set of basic assumptions which control and inform everything he said and did. This is evident in the patterns which cut across all that he taught, and demand that the study of any one passage be done in the light of everything else he is recorded saying. One has to interpret all of Jesus' thought to understand him in depth at any one point. This is time consuming, and is where most interpreters fall down. In the pages to come, I shall be illustrating this comprehensive method at many points. For example, Jesus is recorded very seldom using the phrase, "justice of God." But actually it is this concept which ties together all his thinking in the use of many different words and ideas; and this appears only when one brings together all that he said into a coherent picture. At this level, the justice of God runs throughout his teaching, bursting out regularly in direct utterance like the surging up of an underground stream.

Then there is a third source for our knowledge of Jesus's own theology; and that is not so much what he said as what he did. He acted in the light of what he believed and taught. In a unique way which we shall explore more fully later, it is in this "word made flesh" that we find some of the profoundest insights into his theology. Here is the mystery of Jesus the man, acting deliberately in a theological way, where his self understanding of identity and mission expresses his own relation to this God about whom he is speaking. In that eliptical tension between the word and the life of Jesus, we come perhaps the closest to the heart of his theology.

It is common among New Testament scholars to avoid systematizing the teaching of Jesus. Norman Perrin calls this an act of "violence against that teaching, which is a constantly interrelating and interlocking whole" (*Rediscovering the Teaching of Jesus*, p. 109). I would agree that Jesus did not treat subjects in neatly systematized fashion; but this is obvious, and not really the point. Jesus' thought was indeed interrelated and interlocking; but it is just this fact which leads me to disregard Perrin's warning. There is a deep, underlying system of ordered and coherent thinking within Jesus' teaching which we must understand if we would interpret him in depth. Failure to do this condemns much Gospel interpretation to shallowness and inadequacy. For this reason, I am deliberately presenting Jesus' thought in a systematic way, in an attempt to place his thinking at any one point in its proper context as part of this total coherent stream.

A Holy Word

When Mark characterizes Jesus as one who spoke "with authority and not as the scribes" (1:22), he is describing one of the most uniquely important facts about him. There was a majestic, oracular quality to his teachings that mystified, offended or excited people, and immediately commanded their attention. This is centered in the phrase, "verily, I say unto you," which occurs fifty times in the Synoptics on the lips of Jesus, but never again in the words of any other ancient writer or teacher, as far as I can determine. The manner in which he spoke, what he said, and the way his teachings were received testify to a quality of authority beyond anything they were familiar with. It can only be described as *sanctity*. They were "holy words," and one can clearly see the recognition of this within the early community in the escalating sanctity attributed to them.

Jesus ascribed heavy significance to his own words: "Whoever is ashamed of me and of my words...of him will the Son of man be ashamed" (Mark 8:38). Matthew says that "the crowds were astonished" at his words, because he "taught as one who had authority" (Matt. 7:28). In Luke, the plural "words" of Jesus have become singular in the growing recognition of their sanctity: "The Jews were astonished at his teaching, for his word was with authority" (Luke 4:32). By far the most abundant use of this term in the New Testament is where the "words of Jesus" or the "word of Jesus" has become simply "the word." "With many such parables he spoke the word to them, as they were able to hear it" (Mark 4:33; 16:12; Acts 10:44). This is "the word" of the Kingdom, preached by Jesus or by others who "went about preaching the word...the good news about the Kingdom of God" (Matt. 13:19; Acts 8:4, 12; 19:10). There are eighteen different clusters of expression within the New Testament referring to the words of Jesus in this oracular, authoritative sense, like "the commandments of Jesus," "the mysteries of God," "the things received from the Lord," "the law," "the truth," and that which was "taught with authority." Later, Clement of Rome (about 120 A.D.) reflects the continuation of this sense of sanctity, which reverberates throughout the writings of the early church: "Let us...walk in obedience to his hallowed words" (Epistle 13:3). It is this recognition of the authority unto sanctity of the words of Jesus, which I shall refer to in this book as "The Holy

Word."

Not like a rabbi, not like a prophet, he spoke like no one they had ever heard before. The closest I have come in the examination of ancient literature to the oracular quality of the teachings of Jesus is in the sayings in Ezekiel where *God himself* is speaking. They said no one ever talked like this; and such an editorial generalization can be documented in terms of modern comparative literary research (UG-Chapt. VI). No other charismatic phrase-making teacher of antiquity, no rabbi, no prophet, no one, as far as I can see, ever spoke this way. And it is this distinctive authority, as a product of his brilliance as a preacher, teacher and theologian, the startling independence of his mind, the coherence of his thought, and the oracular quality of his word, that is the key to the power residing in the intrinsic nature of this Holy Word.

PART TWO

GOD, THE SOVEREIGN OF THE KINGDOM

Chapter III

We Know God as He Is

The real power of the Gospel resides not in the vehicle, no matter how brilliant or authentic, but in its content. It was what Jesus said about God and his revelation, about man and his needs, and about himself and his part in the judgment drama, that electrified his hearers, and either drove them to distraction, or to their knees. So we are concerned about the content of what we have identified as "the Holy Word," the solid center of the theology and life of the early church, and the core of the Gospel's power.

The heart of this is what Jesus called the Kingdom of God. It is here that the substance of the Gospel's power resides; and like the theme of a great opera, its melody runs hauntingly throughout his entire message. It is this which gives unity and direction to his teaching; and most of his ideas are merely variations upon this theme. So it is that Mark introduces Jesus coming into Galilee proclaiming, "The Kingdom of God is at hand, repent and believe the Gospel." This is a fine summary statement, and is accurately documented by the constant repetition throughout his teaching of the phrase, "The Kingdom of God is like..." Jesus was not a systematic theologian in the modern sense, but as I have suggested, his mind was beautifully systematized, with a coherence and clarity testifying to long and mature reflection on the questions of God and faith; and it is in his concept of the Kingdom of God that this fact becomes most clearly apparent. It is therefore upon the Kingdom that we shall concentrate our attention in the pages to come, as we attempt to rediscover something of the power of the Christian Gospel.

But this is a tremendously large and complex concept, and one of great importance to the church. So we must examine it from many different angles in order to get some sense of its magnitude and proportions. Each chapter will be a look at the Kingdom of God from a slightly different perspective, viewing it in terms of each of the major areas of Jesus' theology, and attempting to show their interrelation as we do.

A Clear and Compelling View of God

The present chapter is about the Kingdom as it reveals the person and nature of God himself. Here is where any theology must begin, for every concept of theology depends ultimately for its character upon its view of the nature of God. This was particularly true for Jesus. His mind was literally consumed by his awareness of the person of God, and it was this which was the exact center of that nucleus of power bursting forth as the Christian Gospel. There has been no one in human history who ever presumed to say as much about the person and nature of God, and to say it as clearly and intimately. This was why the Jews hated him, and the early disciples adored him...and some areas of modern theology have had so much trouble with him. No one ever talked about God quite like this before.

Not only was Jesus very clear about God, but the images he gives us reveal a God of immense power who cannot and must not be ignored. Today this is the measure of our theological illness. We worship a God who can easily be ignored, and the God of Jesus intrudes on that comfortable image. In our modern sophistication, without realizing it many of us have disposed of the shocking clarity that is the distinctive mark of the Hebrew Christian God. We have "civilized" the awesome biblical Deity into an innocuous twentieth century nonentity, and it is no wonder there is a power failure in the Christian church. Without a clear and forceful revelation of God, Christian theology flounders hopelessly through the mists of theological confusion, at the mercy of philosophical annihilation, with the Bible gradually being substituted by an arbitrary collection of contemporary theological fads, and the word of God replaced by the word of man.

At the outset, we must get one thing clear. The God of the Bible and of Jesus is not a vague oblong blur about whom we may speak in awkwardly solicitous subjunctives. He is rather a particular kind of God, about whom the biblical revelation speaks with a blunt clarity that has always shocked the sensitivities of the pharisaic mind. The name of this God is "Power" (El), and my proposal is that in our search for power, we attempt to discover anew the magnificent proportions of this biblical God who called the church into being and is revealed in a uniquely vivid way in Jesus' teaching about the Kingdom.

The Existence of God

For the Hebrew mind, the existence of God was not a subject of debate. The Old Testament simply begins with the assumption, "In the beginning, God..." The most primitive name for Deity, *Yahweh*, seems to have arisen from some form of the Hebrew verb, "to be" (*hyh*); and so when Moses asks God for his name (Ex. 3:14), which for the Hebrew would be the same as asking "Who are you?" the answer he receives is, "I am that I am." God is the one who "is."

Jesus took the existence of God for granted, and never in the recorded tradition did he seem to feel the need for defending this assertion. Instead, he referred to God constantly, specifically and with vivid clarity. There are approximately sixty-seven separate sayings in the Synoptics where the term God appears, a striking thing in view of the rabbinic practice of avoiding direct mention of the divine name.

But today, God has become a problem, and my bookshelves are filled with popular as well as scholarly books discussing the difficulty of belief in God. This is a consequence of our Western background in Greek philosophy, for which God has always been a subject of intellectual discussion. What this does is create the impression that somehow the believer has to be able to prove the existence of God, and much useless energy is wasted attempting to defend it. One thing has become evident to theologians from hundreds of years of philosophical discussion: that although a reasonable defense of God is helpful, ultimately the existence or nonexistence of God cannot be proven in any absolute way according to the normal lines of rational demonstration. The reality of God is by very definition an ultimate concept, and there is nothing prior which can be used for proof. The existence or nonexistence of God is one of those assertions that are what Soren Kirkegaard, a nineteenth century Danish theologian, called "knots" in the end of the thread of your logic. You must simply assume it. Because of the limitations of the rational process, there is no other way. So the believer must take the "leap" of faith, just as the nonbeliever must take the "leap" of nonfaith, and both are equally vulnerable to the charge of begging the question.

The Hebrew theologian, and in this case Jesus, instinctively knew this philosophical fact, and so he began by assuming God's reality, knowing that there is nothing so unusual about that. As the apostle Paul reminded his readers, all men know there is a God (Rom. 1:19-20). The problem is not the intellectual assertion that there is a God, but rather the deeper assertion that we will honor him as our God (Rom. 1:21). There is the rub, and there is where Christian theism goes far beyond this superficial philosophical discussion of God's existence. It is our existence, not God's, that is at stake. It is *we* who need to be defended, not God. And as we shall be seeing throughout this chapter, if we allow God to be discovered on his own terms, there is evidence that commends itself to us on an intellectual level, as well as on this deeper more immediate level of experience.

The Being of God

What is God made of? This is a question a child would ask — or a philosopher, especially a Greek one from the centuries preceding the Christian era. The Stoics, for example, were very much concerned over the "stuff" (*phusis*) of the universe, and identified what they called God (*theos*) with law, reason and fire: all physical (*phusikos*). The Hebrew, on the other hand, was little interested in such questions of physics, preferring to talk of God not as "stuff," but as personal being. In a way this is unfortunate, for we today are more Greek in our thinking than Hebrew. Many of the scientific questions we might ask were simply not important to the Hebrews, and so have been difficult to reconcile with Hebrew-Christian theology. For example, how exactly is God related to the physical universe? There are, however, three Old Testament terms regularly used in connection with the names for God which do give us a clue to what these authors thought of the "essential being," that is, the "stuff," of God. These terms are "spirit," "glory," and "power;" and each, in its own way, is a graphic metaphor that tries to say something essential about God.

Spirit (*ruach*) literally means "wind," and describes the being of God in ways that relate to and also transcend our three-dimensional world of "stuff." God is *like* the wind. He is invisible, yet we feel his presence. He is everywhere, and yet we can exclude him from our inner lives. Like the wind, he is necessary for life, a caressing breeze or a raging hurricane. If we abide by the laws of the wind, we can "mount up with wings as eagles" (Is. 40:31), but if we break those laws, we destroy ourselves against them. The wind is a wonderful metaphor for God.

But more exactly, in biblical terms, spirit is the active agent in creation (Gen. 1:2), the author of life (Job 33:4), the source of wisdom and ability in certain persons at certain times (Ex. 28:3). Spirit is the command of God directing a Moses (Num. 11:17) and an Ezekiel (Ezek. 11:5). It is the presence of God impinging upon his creation; and it is this unique awareness of God as inbreaking spirit that characterizes the prophetic figure, and shines unmistakably from those portions of the Old Testament to which Jesus most often referred. "Whither shall I go from thy spirit? Or whither shall I flee from thy presence?" (Ps. 139:7).

The word "glory" is an even more graphic metaphor, identifying God in terms of light. His glory is a "devouring fire" (Ex. 24:17) that consumes the sacrifice in the temple (II Chron. 5:14), a voice that "flashes forth flames of fire...and strips the forests bare; and in his temple all cry, 'Glory!'" (Ps. 29). God's glory is his unapproachable holiness that drives Isaiah to his knees with the cry: "Holy, holy, holy is the Lord of hosts; the whole earth is full of his glory" (Is. 6:3). Glory is the radiant presence of God.

But perhaps the most essential in terms of physical phenomena is the metaphor of power. This is the basic semitic meaning of *Elohim*, another Hebrew name for God. Power describes the very essence of creation (Jer. 10:12), and the mighty deeds of God (Ps. 78:26). It is identical with his spirit (Micah 3:8) and glory (Ps. 29:1) and represents the majesty of his sovereign rule over men and nature (I Chron. 29:11). Wind, light and power: the Hebrew is trying to describe the essential "stuff" of the God who transcends the physical universe, but who can nevertheless be compared to certain elements within it. And how interesting that these are the very elements that describe our modern energy shortage!

Jesus seems to have begun his thinking with these basic Hebrew insights. For example, he is recorded using the word "spirit" to refer to God on twelve occasions in fairly consistent Old Testament fashion. In the synagogue at Nazareth the "spirit of God" is that which anoints him to preach the good news of God's salvation (Luke 4:18); it is the gift of love which God gives to his children (Luke 11:13); it is the "finger" of God with which he drives out demons (Luke 11:20); it is the very being of God himself whose rejection is the definition of sin (Mark 3:29). He also uses the term "power" in Old Testament fashion to describe the being of God in terms of his ability to act and perform mighty works. Power is that which enables him to heal the woman with the flow of blood (Luke 8:46); it is the ability of God to raise men from the dead (Mark 12:24); it is that which accompanies the returning Son of Man (Luke 22:69) and attends the coming of the Kingdom (Mark 9:1). Ultimately power identifies God himself as he acts upon and within his creation (Mark 14:62; Luke 22:69). In all of this, Jesus shows his basic Hebrew orientation.

But Jesus had a curious way of adding his own distinctive ideas, and we must be prepared for him to go beyond the Old Testament in some rather decisive ways. He does so in his use of the phrase "Kingdom of God" where he might be expected to use the words spirit and power. It is sometimes said that Jesus had little to say about the Holy Spirit; and it is certainly true that the word *pneuma* (spirit) does not occur often in the Synoptic Gospels. It would seem, however, that there is a simple answer to this: Jesus preferred to use his own terminology, and the phrase he chose was the Kingdom of God (*malkuth shamayim*). In its simplest and most essential meaning, this phrase describes the sovereign presence of God as spirit and power. This one fact, fully grasped is more important for an understanding of Jesus' theology than any other single item. At times the Old Testament comes close to this use of *malkuth shamayim* in passages which refer to the Kingdom as God's sovereignty in the heavens (Ps. 103:19; 22:28; Dan. 4:3, etc.). Mostly, however, in the Old Testament this phrase identifies the Kingdom of Israel, a real theocracy within the present age (I Chron. 28:5), or the future reign of God at the final judgment, but still localized in Jerusalem (Is. 9:7; 65-66; Dan. 2:44; 7:14, etc.). It was Jesus who took the high points of the Old Testament use of this expression and spiritualized them into a full-blown doctrine of the spirit.

It is difficult to find him defining Kingdom quite as clearly as this. He was not accustomed to definitions, but rather taught by implication, by parable, simile and metaphor. There are, however, several places where Kingdom of God is used in parallel construction with some phrase clearly referring to God himself as spirit and power, and therefore validating this definition. For example, in his debate with the pharisees, after healing the man said to be possessed with the dumb demon (Luke 11:20), Jesus is recorded saying, "If I by the *finger of God* cast out demons, then the *Kingdom of God* is come upon you." The phrase "finger of God" is a common Hebrew idiom to describe the spirit of God in a particular manifestation of his power (cf. Ex. 8:19; 31:18; Deut. 9:10), and its parallel in this passage with "Kingdom of God" rather clearly identifies the Kingdom as the spirit of God at work in their midst (cf. Mark 9:1).

This aspect of the Kingdom in Jesus' mind is perhaps best seen in more subtle ways, not dependent upon particular words: when we see the Kingdom as something outside the mind of man or woman that comes into their lives as a gift and a treasure; when the Kingdom appears as an inner reality within our psyche as a power and a presence; when we find the parables of the Kingdom describing the very person and nature of God. In other words, Jesus attributes to the Kingdom the same characteristics which he ascribes to God as spirit and power, and we are justified in seeing the Kingdom as his most characteristic way of talking about the Holy Spirit.

This has many implications for our ability to come to know God. For one thing, it tells us that like any other reality, God must be known on his own terms. He is not an intellectual concept to be proven, but he is like wind and light and power. If we would know this spiritual God, then we must know him spiritually, as spirit is known. But if we begin by denying the existence of spiritual reality, then we cut ourselves off from such knowledge before we even start. This is the tragic blindness of so much that styles itself as atheism. Beginning with the assumption that there is no such thing as spiritual reality, it demands that God's existence be proven in ways that are congenial to the atheist, but totally untrue to the reality of God. So atheism operates in a logic-tight circle, denying the only kind of evidence that would prove the contrary. The theist, of course, does the same, but theists usually seem more aware of this than are those whose superficial claim to "complete objectivity" makes them victims of their own logical circularity.

Within the religious tradition, there is a whole realm of activity that deals with coming to know God on his own terms. It is called prayer, worship, dedication, meditation, and involves all the various techniques of spiritual discipline invented by men and women through the ages for "tuning in" on the deeper levels of experience. These are ways of coming to know God as spirit, and on their own terms are just as valid evidence for his existence as are logical proofs or substantial demonstrations. For any reality must be known on its own terms.

But the distressing thing about the Christian church is that periodically it loses sight of this fact. We inadvertently accept the logic of atheism, and then wonder why those groups who stress the spiritual dimension of the church's life are growing so rapidly, or why there are charismatic groups springing up within those denominations where "many are cold and a few are frozen," to paraphrase a word of Jesus (Matt. 22:14). God must be known on his own terms; and if those are the terms of spirit and power, then without a rebirth of the spirit, there can be no rebirth of power within the church.

The Person of God

It is necessary to go beyond the concept of spirit to understand the Hebrew prophetic mind, and especially that of Jesus; for God is not the impersonal, incomprehensible force suggested by the metaphors of wind, light and power. He is rather *personal being*, whose revelation is always one of intelligence that speaks to persons. From the crude pictures of God as a man walking with Adam in the cool of the day (Gen. 3:8) — imagine the eternal Lord of the universe hunting for Adam behind a bush! — to the more sophisticated concept of God as creative word (Gen. 1:3), the Hebrew rarely, if ever, spoke of God except in terms of personal intelligence. Hence it is not in the ideas of eternal being, power, spirit or glory, as divine essence in some philosophical sense, but rather in the description of God's nature as personal being, that we come to the heart of the prophetic Hebrew concept of God.

Jesus, especially, reflects an intensely personal concept of God. He refers to him as "father" on approximately forty-six occasions in the Synoptic Gospels in some of his most graphic references! "How much more will the heavenly father give the Holy Spirit to those who ask him?" (Luke 11:13); "Love your enemies...so that you may be sons of your father who is in heaven" (Matt. 5:44-45). "Fear not little flock for it is your father's good pleasure to give you the Kingdom." His own relationship with God comes to most initimate focus in the Aramaic phrase preserved in the Greek by Mark (14:36), "Abba," which is what a small boy would call his father.

It is, however, in the parables that this dramatically personal concept of God takes its most vital form. There are fifteen parables in the Synoptics where the subject and principle actor can be identified as God. Within this body of teaching there are three general types of figures which portray God. 1) He is a man of authority, a householder who makes a reckoning with his servants (Matt. 18:23-25), and expects them to serve him dutifully (Luke 17:7-10).

44

He is a husbandman who owns a field of wheat and weeds (Matt. 13:24-30), a judge who avenges his elect (Luke 18:1-8), the owner of a vineyard (Mark 12:1-12) and a fig tree (Luke 13:6-9), a king who gave a great feast (Luke 14:15-24) and required that his guests be properly dressed (Matt. 22:11-14). In all these there is a stress on the sovereign authority of God in dramatically human terms.

2) A second picture that repeats itself within Jesus' parables is that of God as one who searches for what is lost: God is like a woman probing in the dirt for the coin she has lost (Luke 15:8-10), a shepherd searching in the darkness for the wayward sheep (Luke 15:1-7).

3) Perhaps most characteristically, Jesus pictured God as a father with various kinds of sons, rebellious, prodigal, dutiful (Matt. 21:28-32; Luke 15:11-32), a father for whom there is one special son sent to remind his servants of their obligations (Mark 12:1-12), a bridegroom for whom he prepares a wedding feast and invites all who would respond and prepare (Matt. 22:1-10; 25:1-13). It is in these intensely vivid similes and metaphors that we come to what is perhaps the heart of Jesus' description of God.

Now let us draw some implications from the above. These parabolic pictures of God are highly significant for Christian theology. Note the logic: *If* Jesus is the Son of God (and I shall not argue Christology at this point, but just raise the question), and if, as is commonly assumed, the parables are his most characteristic form of teaching, and if I have correctly identified the figure of God in these fifteen parables, then it would seem that here we have a series of word pictures of God painted not only with rare skill, but with striking clarity and unique authority. Ponder this for a moment. No one has ever seen God; but if in the teachings of Jesus we have word pictures of God painted by his only son, then here is a new glimpse of God that makes every other attempt to describe him pale into insignificance.

Secondly, if we would be true to the Bible and especially the teaching of Jesus, we cannot deny the Christian the right to speak of God with clarity and a certain degree of confidence, and to use symbolic, mythological, metaphorical, parabolic language to describe him. There are many today so sensitized by the warnings of Bultmann against myth, and the analytical philosophers against meaningless unverifiable language, that they feel the only thing a Christian can do is speak of God tentatively, vaguely, or not at all. This defensive, apologetic posture is, I believe, irreconcilable with the biblical tradition. The Bible speaks clearly, and at times very graphically about God, and this is absolutely characteristic of its proclamation in both Old and New Testaments.

Another German theologian, Julius Schniewind, is a shrewder mind at this point when he reminds Bultmann, in the book entitled *Kerygma and Myth*, that mythological language about God is inevitable; for without mythological language, which describes God in terms of three dimensional reality, one can only speak of him in negatives, by saying what he is not. This is valid in religious philosophy; but runs completely counter to the revelation of God as found in the Hebrew-Christian Bible. If we must do away with the Bible, then that is another matter; but let us be very clear at this point: such reticence in speaking about God can never be called a biblical position. Nor is speaking clearly about God the crudely naive thing it is sometimes said to be. One must simply keep in mind that whenever he says anything three dimensional about God, he is not speaking crudely about a man in the sky somewhere "out there." He must immediately apply the Bible's own de-mythologizing sign, "God is spirit," and know that these metaphors are thereby transformed into symbols for that which transcends the three dimensional world "out there" (cf. pp. 69 f)..

There is one further implication. If God is Person, not "a" person, but PERSON, then whatever else it means, it says to us that we must come to know him as persons know other persons. This old biblical insight has been popularized in a highly philosophical way in recent years by Martin Buber, a Jewish philosopher, in his book, *I and Thou*. For the Hebrew-Christian Bible the point is this: a person is not an object, but a subject. We talk *about* objects, treat them "objectively," and come to know them by describing them. But we talk *to* persons and inevitably come to know and relate to them more subjectively. Personal communion is the proper means of knowing another person. So it is with what the Bible describes as man's knowledge of God. The Hebrew "know" (*yadah*) has more of this personal, existential sense than does the more rational, objective Greek concept of knowledge. To know God is not only to know *about* him, as we have been trying to do and will continue to do throughout this chapter. But to really "know" him in the deepest sense, *on his own terms*, is to know him personally, immediately, subjectively; to talk to him in prayer, to commune with him in worship and the secret meditation of the heart, to do his will in living a life of service for others. Because God is person, and to know him

46

personally is to know him as he is.

This is what it means in Hebrew-Christian theology to say that man is made in the image of God. Our most human capacity, our highest ability as human beings, is the ability to talk to God person to person. There is a correspondence between us as persons and God as person. This is what prayer is all about. This is what worship is all about: coming to know God by talking to him. The problem with so much discussion about the reality and existence of God is that it is all third person. It is all talking *about* God, and you can never know God by talking about him. Ultimately, somehow, you have to get down on your knees and talk *to* him, because God is person.

The Mystery of God

At this point I must add a typically Hebraic caution. God is not to be taken for granted. He is not to be reduced to the level of the human mind. Ultimately for the Hebrew, and I think for Jesus, God is mystery. The Hebrew prophetic mind was always overwhelmed by the sense of the vastness, the eternity, the mystery of God. Job cried out in the perplexity of his trouble, "Who can understand the thunder of his power?" Jesus said to his disciples, "Unto you is given to understand the mystery of the Kingdom of God" (Mark 4:10-12). Paul, after he had written everything he knew about God was forced to conclude that God's will was a mystery (Eph. 1), God's word was a mystery (I Cor. 2), Christ was a mystery (Col. 2). The greatest mystery of all, he said, was "Christ within you, the hope of glory." "How unsearchable are his judgements and how inscrutable his ways!" (Rom. 11:33).

This also has many implications. Ultimately our knowledge of God is limited by our humanity. We are three dimensional creatures, and God transcends our limitations. The author of Isaiah put it clearly: "As the heavens are higher than the earth, so are my ways higher than your ways and my thoughts than your thoughts" (Is. 55:9). The problem is that the very words and ideas I am using here are all trapped in three dimensional frames of reference. And so, when I try to reach out of my human entrapment into dimensions that go beyond my ken, all I can do is speak in analogies, and this is exactly what Jesus did. When he said, "the Kingdom of God is like," he spoke in similes, and this is all a person can do when talking about God. If we say that God is "father" or "king," what we are really saying is that God is "like" a father or a king. These tell us not what God *is* in some absolute sense, but what he is *like*. We are using what the philosopher calls "the Analogy of Proportion." The word father is to a human father, who has two legs, two arms and a nose, as the word father is to God, who is spirit, glory, power and mystery. The same word has different proportions when applied to man than it has when applied to God. The analogy is valid only if you recognize this difference in proportion. And so as we try to take a puny three dimensional word like "father" and use it to reach beyond the spiritual sound barrier between man and God, we are helped by these analogies, but ultimately our words are shattered. So again we are driven to our knees, and instead of talking about God and trying to use all of these elaborate symbols, we had better start talking *to* him, person to person, for God is spirit and God is person and God is mystery.

Chapter IV

He Is A God of Justice

It is sometimes said that a theologian has only one great idea in his lifetime. Whether or not this is true, my own theological pilgrimage has been dominated by one powerful insight. It was in the cold and musty basement of the Edinburgh graduate theological library that I first began to see how the nature of God tied Jesus' theology together into a coherent system of such clarity and grandeur that I have spent my life trying to understand and express it. This came as an intellectual conversion and a heart-warming sense of God's power which has never left me, and which the years of teaching, preaching and research have only served to confirm. The key is the justice of God, and how this summarizes the theology of the prophetic Old Testament and provided the framework for the theology of Jesus.

There are many terms whereby the Bible describes God as personal being. He is sovereign, creator, covenanter, teacher and father. He is righteous, loving, majestic, correcting, commanding. But behind all these stands this supreme concept that dominates them all, gives them primary meaning and absolutely captivates the prophetic mind: God is a God of Justice. As the author of Job put it: "He is great in power and justice" (37:23). This is the key to biblical theology; this is the throbbing heart of its vitality. And this is the catalytic agent that clarifies more Hebrew-Christian theology than does any other single idea.

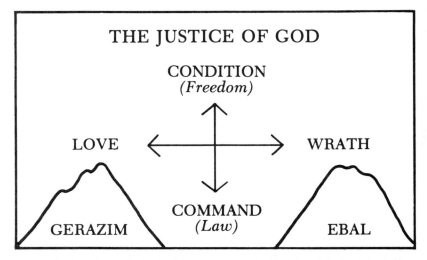

On the heights of Moab, Moses is recorded giving his final instructions that when the children of Israel should come to the Land of Promise they should ratify the code of Deuteronomy at a solemn assembly in the plain of Shechem. Whatever exactly may have been in Moses' mind at such a time one can only conjecture; but certain it is that in this great acted parable which I have diagrammed above, we have an almost perfect picture of the prophetic concept of justice (Deut. 27:11 ff.). Six of the tribes were to gather on Mount Gerizim, the Mount of the Blessing, and as the blessings of the Law were read, they were to shout "Amen." God is a God of blessing, a God of love. The other six tribes were to gather on Mount Ebal, the Mount of the Curse, and when the curses of the Law were read, they were to shout "Amen." God is a God of punishment, a God of wrath. In the narrow valley between were to stand the priests with the Law, for God is a God who commands. And implicit in the tension between God's love and his wrath and the inevitable assumption behind the commands of the Law lies the "condition" that men and women are free to make their choice for Ebal or for Gerizim. In this thundering dialogue the author of Deuteronomy has pictured for us in most vivid form the four basic elements that comprise the prophetic concept of the justice of God: love, wrath, command, condition (cf. JGTJ). All of them together constitute the *Mishpat Elohim*, the justice of God. It is upon the frame of this fourfold concept that the Hebrew prophets, Jesus, and indeed Paul and the rest of the New Testament writers, weave the fabric of their theology.

50

God's Justice Is His Love

One of the popular fictions regarding the Bible is that the Old Testament talks about the wrath of God, while the New Testament talks about his love. Nothing could be farther from the truth. Actually, the Old Testament has a great deal to say about God's justice as a revelation of his love. One of the most beautiful expressions of this comes out of the agony of Hosea's experience with an unfaithful wife. He loved Gomer dearly, but she was constantly untrue to him; and through his recurring need to forgive, Hosea learned something about the love of God, which he described as a mother loving her child: "When Ephraim was a child, I loved him, I bent down to him, I took him up in my arms, I fed him" (Hos. 11).

There are really three ways in which the love of God is presented in the Old Testament, and all within a context of his justice. In the first place, the essential nature of God is described as love. This is seen where love describes the "name" of God, for in Hebrew thought, the name identifies the person himself: "It is good to give thanks to the Lord, to sing praises to thy name...; to declare thy steadfast love..., and thy faithfulness" (Ps. 92:1-2; cf. Ps 138:2). In the second place, love refers to an *act of God* that expresses his nature: "I have loved you with an everlasting love; therefore I have continued my faithfulness to you" (Jer. 31:3; cf. Is. 63:9; Hos. 11:1; Deut. 4:37 etc.). But the most profound and significant use of love in the Old Testament is where it is a description of God's abiding, redeeming *presence*: "The angel of his presence saved them; in his love and in his pity he redeemed them" (Is. 63:9; cf. Ps. 69:16-18; Zeph. 3:17; Joel 2:13 etc.). So abundant is the evidence that one cannot escape the inevitable suggestion that for the prophetic Hebrew mind, the fullest extent and intensity of the concept of love is to be found in the *nearness* of this God, whose secret presence crowds in upon the lives of men and women and thereby saves them.

In the teachings of Jesus it is in the fifteen parables where God is pictured that one finds the strongest emphasis upon his love. God is a man who gives a banquet and invites many (Luke 14:15-24). He is a judge who "vindicates his elect who cry to him day and night" (Luke 18:1-8). He is a farmer who delays the destruction of his fig tree for three years and then at the insistence of the vinedresser, for another year (Luke 13:6-9). God is a man who gathers grain into the barn at the harvest time (Matt. 13:24-30), a father who gives good gifts to his children (Luke 11:11-13). "It is not the will of my heavenly father," Jesus said, "that one of these little ones should perish"

(Matt. 18:14); and then he went on to tell a parable of a shepherd hunting in the dark for a lost sheep, and a woman probing in the dirt for a lost coin (Luke 15). God's love is like that. It is his primary purpose, his blessing, his salvation, lifting us out of the dirt of life, returning us to his fold from our darkness and wandering, reclaiming value and meaning in our lives by restoring us to himself, like a lost coin or a lost sheep.

What this implies is that to know God, we must love him, for "God is love" (I John 4:8). Love is the deepest way of knowing persons, and God is person. What this suggests is that to know him, we must return to him, for love is reunion, and the encounter with this God is the profoundest means of knowing him.

God's Justice Is His Wrath

There is, however, a darker side to God's justice which plays a very important part in the Hebrew and Christian concept. In the Old Testament, wherever one finds a reference to the love of God, his wrath is always somewhere in the background. Two major ideas stand out. The first is wrath as God acting to punish or destroy persons for their sin. The Psalmist describes the light of God's countenance in terms of consuming anger: "His lips are full of indignation, and his tongue is like a devouring fire" (Ps. 90:7; cf. Is. 30:27; Jer. 30:24). Jeremiah complains that he is "full of the wrath of God," he is "weary of holding it in" (Jer. 6:11), and then in a provocative passage describes the "storm" of God's wrath as an awareness of his holiness: "My heart is broken within me, all my bones shake; I am like a drunken man...because of his holy words" (Jer. 23:9). Perhaps the most awful picture of this aspect of God's wrath is found in Isaiah: "Who is this who comes from Edom, in crimsoned garments from Bozrah...I have trodden the winepress alone...I trod them in my anger, and trampled them in my wrath...and I have stained all my garments" (Is. 63:1-3).

The major source of God's wrathful activity for the Hebrew prophet concerned man's rejection of God; and so it is that a second and even more profound description of wrath is where God withholds himself from persons, where his wrath is his absence: "How long, O Lord? Wilt thou hide thyself forever? How long will thy wrath burn like fire?" (Ps. 89:46). "Hide not thy face from me. Turn not thy servant away in anger...cast me not off, forsake me not" (Ps. 27:9; cf. Ps. 88:7). One of the most poignant of these references is where the object of God's wrath is compared to a "lonely bird on the housetop...Because of thy indignation and anger...thou hast taken me up and thrown me away" (Ps. 102). The Hebrew never took God for granted, and his knowledge of the love of God was always deepened by the awareness of his wrath.

In the teachings of Jesus, again contrary to popular misconception, the wrath of God played a prominent role. By actual count, there are almost three times as many references in the Synoptic sayings of Jesus to God's wrath as there are to his love. In the parables, God is a king who sends his troops and destroys those who reject his invitation to the wedding feast (Matt. 22:1-10), or throws the wedding guest without the proper garment into outer darkness (Matt. 22:11). "Do not fear those," said Jesus, "who kill the body, and after that have no more that they can do. But I will warn you whom to fear; fear him who, after he has killed, has power to cast into hell; yes, I tell you, fear him!" (Luke 12:4-5). The fear of God, in its largest sense as reverence, awe and respect, and with an element of terror, was an important part of Jesus' teaching about God. And yet, this is one of the great missing elements from most people's understanding of God. We do not like to hear about God's wrath, and so we ignore it, and thereby miss the tension between love and wrath that is the very heart of the mystery of power locked up within the justice of God. Without a full understanding of the awfulness of God's wrath, there can be no full appreciation of the power of his love.

But is God angry? This is often the mistaken notion of those who reject this concept. True, the word anger is used, but only because of the poverty of our language. God's wrath is not anger in some human, peevish sense, but rather an expression of his justice and love, of his eternal spirit and power. In the Bible the wrath of God is a positive-negative. It is the force of positive destruction and negative divorcement. God's wrath is his holiness, his intolerance to sin. It is his reaction to our rebellion. God's wrath is a broken fellowship. It is his confirmation of humanity's self-rejection. It is his love in agony. Ultimately, even as the love of God is his presence, so the wrath of God is his absence: a great aching loneliness in the souls of men and women and in the heart of God. It is the prodigal separated from the father, the servant divorced from the king. It is darkness, alienation and death.

There is a bitterness in such separation from God that is only understandable to one who knows the glory of fellowship with him. The prophet knew this. Jesus knew it. And they wept as they faced

53

the dereliction of men and women. Yet wrath is one of the lost words of this generation. If there is any message that needs to disturb a comfortable and partially committed age that has surrounded the eternal God of justice with a mass of sticky sentimentality it is the awareness that God's love is a consuming fire. It is a presence that pierces our souls with the knowledge of the awful seriousness of his claims. Is our God too small to terrify us? To fill us with a sense of mystery and awe? Is our God too weak to chasten us? Then he is not the God of Jeremiah or of Jesus. Is there an anvil of discipline and wrath against which the hammer of God's love strikes fire to mold the unyielding iron of our personalitites? If not, then our God is too small; and one can understand another reason why our theology has lost its power.

God's Justice Is His Command

The God of the Bible and of Jesus is a sovereign God. He is not a "president" who can be voted out of office, but a king who commands our allegiance. There is a "thou shalt" in the prophetic description of his justice which comes to dramatic vividness in that great acted parable where Moses directed the Levites to read the Law in the echoing valley between Mount Gerizim of the blessing and Mount Ebal of the curse. When Moses summed up the revelation of God, he did so in terms of just such a thundering dialectic: "Thou shalt...thou shalt not." There is good theological reason for the Hebrew to describe the entire Old Testament experience of God as *Torah*, which means Law.

The strongest aspect of God's justice in the teachings of Jesus is that of command and imperative. Here the Kingdom of God comes to sharpest focus. God is a father who insists that his sons go to work in the vineyard (Matt. 21:28f). He is a king who invites persons to his Kingdom feast with an insistence that becomes a royal decree. He is a husbandman and a master of servants who demands that the vines in the vineyard, and the grain in the fields and the servants in the household render the fruits of their special status (Luke 13:6-9; Matt. 13:24-30; 18:23-35). He is a father yearning for his son (Luke 15:11-32), a shepherd searching for his sheep (Luke 15:1-7), a woman probing in the dirt for her dowry (Luke 15:8-10). Throughout the Bible we see a God who lays the imperative burden of his presence upon the prophet, and in a unique way upon Jesus, and this becomes an urgent message that will not be denied, a burning fire that cannot be ignored. This imperative is the inevitable thrust of his justice. The fact that God loves us with a sovereign love is in itself a demand that we love him. The fact that God's wrath burns with unquenchable fire is in itself a command that we beware, for God is not mocked. The fact that God is merciful is a demand that we who would partake of his sovereignty must also be merciful. The fact that God is righteous is a royal decree that we who would be servants of his Kingdom must render the righteous fruits of that servanthood. It is at the point of the imperative that the power of Jesus' message of the Kingdom comes to its greatest concentration; and here we cannot compromise without blaspheming against God.

This great theological insight has one clear implication. In order for us to know this imperative God, we must first obey him; and out of that obedience, as we give our lives to him in faith and service, will come a knowledge of God that needs no intellectual proof, no miraculous support, no institutional encouragement. For obedience is one of the deepest avenues of spiritual knowledge. Our temptation is to say, "prove that this is so, and I will submit." What Jesus is saying throughout his entire theology of the Kingdom is that only as we submit shall we know. For God must be known on his own terms, and those are sovereign terms.

God's Justice Is His Condition

One final dimension of God's justice must be described. Implicit in everything Jesus and the prophets said, and explicit in much, is the fact that God's judgment is conditional upon our choices. The author of Leviticus says of God: "If you do not hearken to me, if you spurn my statutes...I will do this to you" (Lev. 26:14-16). Jesus said, "If you forgive men their trespasses, so will the heavenly father forgive you" (Matt. 6:14). There is an "If" in God's relationship with persons that places us under responsible judgment. "Love your enemies *so that* you may be sons of your father" (Matt. 5:34). Sonship is conditional upon our accepting the love of God and so reflecting this love in our lives. The loving of others is not a good deed that we do in order to become children of God; it is rather the spontaneous reflection of the inner fact that we have *already* become children of God because we have accepted his loving presence in all its imperative power.

What is God's condition? It is an expression of his justice, the "other side" of his command; for we are given a command to obey, the ability to disobey, and the obligation to choose and the promise of reward and punishment conditional upon that choice. It is all a description of the justice of God. The condition is also a kind of divine self-control, and so is an aspect of God's wrath. The condition is a declaration that we are free, and testifies to the divine respect for our integrity. It is God's declaration that we are persons and not animals; and that freedom is one of the most precious marks of our humanity. It is God treating with absolute seriousness both our freedom and his command; and the condition, too, is an imperative. The condition is the environment, the occasion and the area of operation for Christian ethics: as humans we must make choices, and by these choices do we judge ourselves.

God's Justice is All of This in Creative Tension

One of the marks of a thoroughly integrated theological mind is the ability to say it all in a few words. Jesus had this ability in supreme measure, and nowhere is this more evident than in his parables. Again and again in these brilliant pictures he summarized the entire range of his thought.

One of these is the parable of the just king (Matt. 18:23-35) where we see in dramatic form the tension between these four aspects of the nature of God. "Therefore the kingdom of heaven may be compared to a king who wished to settle accounts with his servants." The setting is the judgment chamber of the king. The servants are brought in to render an account of their stewardship. The parable is given to a disciple audience; and in the concluding statement, "So also my heavenly father will do to every one of you...," in one of those short, brilliant interpretations common to Jesus' parables, he identifies the servants as the disciples in the audience and the king as his "heavenly father." It is the God figure who is the center. It is he who gives point and focus to the story, acting in judgment, not at some future final time, but within the lifetime of these servants.

Most of the servants are apparently in good standing; but one is in debt, and this says that there is something wrong with his relation to the king. The debt is enormous — ten thousand talents — a sum far exceeding the taxes paid to Rome by all the provinces in Palestine in one year! It is a completely illogical amount and would have caused a shock to those who heard the parable, like telling a modern story in which someone owed the national debt. This alerts us to an important element, for it is on just such illogical points that Jesus regularly hung the creative new teaching of his parables. What is this debt which calls such dramatic attention to itself? It is the cause of a bad relationship with the king. It is so large that it can't possibly be paid; and it can't even be incurred, for there is a limit to what one can borrow or steal or even overdraw! And yet the debt must be paid. If the king represents God, and being a servant is being a part of his spiritual kingdom, then it is impossible to escape the implication that the debt is some reference to sin as a broken relationship with God. This man is an "unworthy servant," a contradiction in terms, what Jesus often called a "hypocrite," one who pretended to be what he was not, like the wedding guest who didn't have the proper garment (Matt. 22:11), or the five "foolish virgins" who had no oil in their lamps (Matt. 25:1-13). This debt is more akin to a collective debt, like a national debt; or translated into theological terms, it would seem to be a reference to what is called "original sin," our natural condition inherited simply by virtue of our humanity. As the author of Ephesians put it, "You are by nature children of wrath" (Eph. 2:3).

The king takes a serious view of the debt, and both the man and his family must be sold. How true this is of sin. It bankrupts our lives and the lives of our loved ones, because alienation from God is seldom a personal affair. The servant falls down and worships the king. He prays for forgiveness; and the king has compassion on him and forgives him. One sees here another reason for the size of the debt. It underscores the amount of the forgiveness. How true this is of the forgiving love of the prodigal God. Forgiveness can never be earned. We never deserve it. Whatever price we pay, and it takes all that we are, even then it is always sheer gift.

The story moves on, and we see another facet in the nature of the king. His love is a demanding love. The story repeats itself. The servant finds a fellow servant who owes him one hundred denarii, a small sum, and the same dialogue occurs, only this time there is no forgiveness. He throws the other in jail. And so the size of the debt of the first servant underscores the smallness of the debt of the second, and vividly contrasts the forgiving love of the king with the problem of the servant, his lack of forgiveness.

The king hears of the incident and calls the servant back into account; and we see that he is still under judgment, for judgment is not something that happens and then is over. It is going on all the time. It is a continuous relation to God. So the king places him under indictment: "Should you not have had mercy on your fellow servant as I had mercy on you?" Forgiveness, to be accepted, must be reflected; and so by the inability to forgive his brother, he shows

57

that he wasn't forgiven in the first place. He has never really accepted forgiveness because he has not accepted the imperative that goes with it, wanting only the benefits but not the responsibilities. This is all a description of the dynamic tension between love and wrath, command and condition within the justice of God. The servant has the opportunity to forgive, but this free choice is also a sovereign command. "Then the Lord summoned him and said, 'You wicked servant...' And in anger...delivered him to the jailers till he should pay all his debt;" and it was too large to pay. So the parable ends with the confirmation of the servant's rejection and alienation; and we see the wrath of God as his rejected love. God's love is not mocked. It must be obeyed to be received.

And so God's justice is his total relation to men and women, a dynamic interplay between his love and his wrath, his command and his condition. Nowhere is this more beautifully summarized than in the parable of the prodigal father, using "prodigal" here in the sense of complete abundance (Luke 15:11-24). We can see ourselves in the picture of the young man who wants his inheritance. He is headstrong, doesn't like parental authority and wants to do his "thing." And the father knows that the only way for the boy to find the maturity necessary for life is to have the freedom to make his own essential decisions. So he sends him off the way we send our little ones for the first time to school. This is a perfect picture of the life that God has given us as human beings, the crown of his creation: freedom to make basic choices, to say "yes" or "no" to him. He has been prodigal in his indulgence, and this freedom is a demonstration of his love.

But life is hard, and the resources of youth are quickly dissipated; and we see that beautiful son reduced to eating with the pigs, for the Hebrew the epitome of degradation. At this point, he seems to awaken as if from a bad dream, and remembers one very important word: "Father...I have sinned against heaven and in thy sight, and am no longer worthy to be called your son." Wrapped up in this statement is the entire concept of the justice of God. Here is the definition of sin, our rebellion and self-divorcement from a loving heavenly father. Here is the mystery of the wrath of God, a strange, awesome divine self-control. The father did not follow the son to the city like an over-zealous parent: "Don't go there, don't do this!" Instead he gave him the ultimate gift of his humanity, the freedom to destroy himself if he must. This is the meaning and the price of our humanity. We must be free to be human. We must be able to say no to God, and to our own best interests. We must be able to make a mess out of the whole business if we will; for this is the freedom which reflects the justice of God.

And so the son's freedom is also a command that the son live up to his sonship. He had to be "worthy" to be a son, for with every gift goes a responsibility, and the greatest of all is this gift of God's love. Freedom to do our "thing" in the world is never license, but is always governed by the laws of God. The son was still living under the authority of the father, even though his rebellion had taken him far away. He never really broke any of his father's commandments; he just broke himself against them.

But "while he was yet far off," the father saw him. He was watching for his son. He didn't violate his freedom through coercion. He waited; and we see the wrath of God not as anger, but as a divine self-restraint, as love in agony, allowing his beloved sons and daughters to destroy themselves if that is how they insist on using the freedom of their humanness. But in this story, the son returned and confessed the father to be "his" father; and the prodigal father put his arms around him, a cloak on his shoulders, a ring on his finger and ordered the fatted calf to be killed. For his son "was dead and is alive, he was lost and is found."

God's love is like that, all bound up with the wrath, the command and the condition of his justice. Love is God's primary purpose, his blessing, his salvation. Ultimately, in both Old and New Testament, the love of God is his presence: not an idea, or an emotion, or an action so much as the healing, saving, redeeming, liberating presence of God. Reunion is the ultimate mystery of God's love; and what this implies is that to know God we must love him, for "God is love" (I John 4:8). This is the deepest way of knowing persons, and God is person. To know him we must return to him, for love is reunion.

Love, wrath, command, condition: these are the dimensions of the nature of God, the substructure of reality, the warp and woof of all that is. This is the way the universe works, for this is God's way, and it is in the dynamic interplay of these monumental forces that the drama of life is enacted. Throughout the rest of this book we shall see this insight weaving in and out of all that is said. Here, then, is the atomic nucleus of power locked up in Jesus' Gospel of the Kingdom; a God who cannot be ignored because he *must not* be ignored.

PART THREE

HEAVEN, THE DIMENSION OF THE KINGDOM

Chapter V

God's Space Is The Kingdom

But we are a very practical and scientific people, trained to believe what we can see and explain; and the Gospel of the Kingdom falls strangely on our ears. Especially so, when we hear Jesus describing this Kingdom as something *into which* we are called to enter, like a room, or a vineyard, or a king's household. If we take these figures of speech seriously, we are immediately beset by a whole battery of very mundane questions. Just where is this Kingdom of God in time and space? What are its dimensions? How can we possibly relate it to the real world of sticks and stones, of science and mathematics, of all we have learned about the universe in this age of exploding knowledge?

These are difficult questions, and perhaps we would be well advised to leave them alone for another hundred years. But we can't do that, for they are tremendously important in the practical business of the Christian life. For if we cannot think realistically about the Gospel in terms of what we know about the world, then it is going to be almost impossible to take it seriously enough to experience its power; and that is the widespread tragedy of our age. So, with a certain trepidation, I would like to examine the Kingdom of God in terms of the natural world, something seldom done, and perhaps with good reason.

Mythology, the Problem of the Kingdom

The first thing we need to understand is that the early Christians really believed that God acted in history. They really believed that miracles happened, that the spirit of God entered into the lives of men and women, that they lived in an open universe, where with

God all things are possible. And this ability to believe with all their minds was a great source of power to the early church.

The Nature of the Problem

One of the greatest sources of weakness in the twentieth century proclamation of the Gospel is our difficulty in believing that the things described in the Bible could possibly have happened. We live in a closed universe where miracle is regularly dismissed. We can't really acknowledge that the ordinary world is open to the gracious activity of God. We tend, rather, to assume that nature runs according to fixed and immutable laws which, as a scientist friend of mine likes to put it, doesn't "play tricks" on us. Even though we are constantly discovering new facts about the universe, there are few real surprises; and so the very surprising message of the New Testament has difficulty in being taken seriously.

The problem is that the Bible seems to be based on a world view no longer credible in the modern age. The first century view of the universe common to all the Near East was that which was summarized by the philosopher Aristotle. The planet earth was flat and the center of the universe. The sky was a series of solid, transparent domes: some thought there were three; others, at least seven. In these revolving spheres, the stars were fixed like nails, moving only as the great spheres turned on their axes. The sun, moon and planets were free to wander across them. Above the spheres was a great reservoir of water, and below the flat earth was a vast deep, sometimes called hell, or "the water under the earth" (Deut. 5:8). Both Old and New Testament writers seem to have accepted this many-storied heaven; for example in the vision of Paul where he is caught up to "the third heaven" (II Cor. 12:2), or in John's picture of the father's house with "many rooms" (John 14:2). For the authors of the Bible, heaven was "up" and hell was "down." But today we have gone to the stratosphere, and not found heaven; we have drilled into the earth and not found hell; and many are bewildered as to the location of these great realities about which the Bible has so much to say, and wonder if the rest of the Bible is equally incredible.

Ever since theologians tried to stifle Copernicus in the sixteenth century because he taught that the sun, not the earth, was the center of the universe, Christian scholars have been more and more reluctant even to talk about this subject of cosmology. Many continued to cling to what they considered to be a biblical, pre-Copernican view of the universe. Even Martin Luther spoke of Copernicus as a new astrologer wanting to prove that the earth "is moved and goeth around and not the sky," which he thought "the over-witty notion of a fool." He simply pointed to Joshua for his proof that the sun moves around the earth: "Sun, stand thou still at Gibeon; and thou Moon in the valley of Ajalon" (Josh. 10:12). The result of this continuing embarrassment over the relation between the cosmology of the Bible and modern science is that there has been much disagreement, confusion and a great deal of silence on the subject. Most of the systematic theologies of recent years have studiously ignored it. Many who are trained in science, but also have an active faith in the Bible, make an uneasy accommodation to the problem by putting their scientific knowledge in one side of their minds and their religious faith in the other, with a water-tight compartment between; and it is difficult for them to relate the one side to the other. And so for great numbers of people there is a lurking suspicion that science and religion really are incompatible, and we cannot say anything meaningful about the direct relation between God and his created world.

The result is a great loss of power in our experience of the Christian Gospel and in the spiritual vitality of our culture in general. Mircea Eliade, a contemporary historian of religions, makes this point eloquently in his book, *The Sacred and the Profane.* He notes that every civilization in the history of mankind has had what he calls a "Sacred Space," that is, some understanding of where the Deity, or their equivalent thereof, resided: a totem pole, a sacred rock, an ark of the covenant, a temple, or, and this is my adaptation of Eliade's thesis, the revelation of God in the Hebrew-Christian Bible. As long as that civilization knew where its sacred center was, it knew where it was in space and time; and so it knew who it was and what life was all about. But if that civilization ever lost its sacred center, and this has been the story of mankind, then that culture was doomed. As Bultmann points out in his book, *Primitive Christianity Against Its Environment,* this is what happened to ancient Greece. Among other things, it lost its belief in the Olympian Gods as a product of the rise of a skeptical philosophical movement called "Sophistry." The result was philosophical panic in Athens and eventually the demise of the vigorous Greek culture.

Our age is facing one of the gravest crises in its history. As the result of a similar process of "sophistication," we are losing our sacred center. Paul Tillich, Johannes Metz and many other theologians have observed that we have been moving in this century from a God-centered to a man-centered universe; and I would add that since God has been deposed, we don't know where to put him. My shelves are filled with books describing God as a "problem," and detailing our modern loss of transcendence, that is, a sense of where God is. And since we don't know where God is, we don't know where we are in space and time; and the widespread symptoms of meaninglessness and despair are the agonized cries of an identity crisis in an age that has lost its way.

One modern response to this problem which captured the attention of the last generation is again expressed by Rudolf Bultmann, whose image looms large over the last fifty years of Christian history. He called it "De-Mythologizing." In his essay, "New Testament and Mythology," Bultmann focused the discussion for an entire generation upon the problem of what he called "mythology," that is, upon those places in the Bible where the invisible God acts upon the earth in visible ways. According to his definition, God creating the earth in seven days, or the angel appearing to Mary, or Jesus stilling the storm or appearing to the disciples after the resurrection, are all "myths." This does not say they are untrue; but that implication is commonly understood. How to handle biblical mythology was the question Bultmann raised for a whole generation. It was picked up by many others, like J. A. T. Robinson, an Anglican Bishop, in his book, *Honest to God*, and created a considerable shock wave for two decades of Christians. What indeed can we say about the way the Bible describes the invisible God entering the visible world, without losing our intellectual integrity? How can we take the Bible seriously in the twentieth century when it is based upon a world view no longer acceptable? Great amounts of ink have been spilled on this question in recent years, but it has been a fruitful discussion. Out of it have come three types of answers.

Moderate De-Mythologizing

The first and most widespread I will call "moderate de-mythologizing." This begins by recognizing that the biblical writers were not scientists and did not seem to be concerned about the mechanics of how these things took place. They were primarily theologians, interested in making one supreme point in whatever they said about the physical universe: God created it, and he continued to sustain it with his active presence. Being pre-scientific minds, they tended to describe these events in highly simplified ways, and our job as scientific persons is to try to understand what they were saying, but in our own, more modern terms. This seems reasonable, and most people do this automatically in one way or another. For example, one can say that the word for "day" in Hebrew (*yom*) can refer to a period of twenty-four hours, but it can also mean an indefinitely extended period of time, like an age or eon, and so it probably should be interpreted in the Genesis account of creation. Or the name Adam in Hebrew is not a proper name at all, but a generic term that actually means "mankind." Eve means "womankind" and Cain (*cayin*) refers to those who were workers in bronze — that is, bronze-age people. So we need not worry about where Cain got his wife, for we are talking about a vast human process condensed in Genesis into a simple story. Or one can explain the Hebrews crossing the Red Sea, or more exactly "reed sea" (*yom suph*), as a natural phenomenon where an extremely low tide and high wind combined to drain the water from this marshy area. After they got across just in the nick of time, the tide came in and the wind changed so that the pursuing Egyptians were drowned. This is not at all implausible, and God did it, no matter how it is explained. Jesus' stilling the storm on Galilee can thus be moderately "de-mythologized" by explaining that he seized upon a common experience on that lake to make a point about having faith. I have myself stood beside that sea and seen the winds suddenly die, so that within twenty minutes the lake changed from a dangerous turbulence to a placid pond. Or one can "explain" the feeding of the five thousand by saying that the unselfish example of a boy in sharing his lunch prompted others to go into the homes and villages nearby and get enough food to feed the multitude. All of this is perfectly plausible, and permits the activity of God in these events, but in ways more understandable to us than the somewhat magical descriptions found in the Bible.

What we are saying in our "moderate de-mythologizing" is that God indeed does work in human affairs, but he does so *through*, and not against, his natural order. This is comforting, and at times quite convincing, but it also presents problems. It may be just too simple, and this is the very complaint we have leveled against the biblical writers. How do we explain the resurrection? How do we explain the ultimate mystery of creation? Some things in the Bible can probably be explained in these ways; but others leave us wondering if we are not trying to over-simplify, and for what reason? Lack of faith?

Radical De-Mythologizing

A second approach to this problem is that of Bultmann, and a whole school of thought arising around him. One might call this "radical de-mythologizing." Bultmann insisted that if we accept any elements of so-called mythology in the New Testament, we must accept them all, and so he rejected any selective, moderate de-mythologizing. If the truth of the New Testament is to be preserved for this scientific age, we must get rid af all mythology, and that, he insisted, is the way the New Testament was meant to be understood in the first place. What he gives, then, is an "existential" understanding of New Testament mythology; one that focuses upon the "inner" event rather than the "outer" one, upon the faith of those who experienced and described these events, rather than the crude stories that are merely simplified attempts to describe what is ultimately indescribable.

Bultmann claimed that all New Testament mythology is based on language and images taken from Jewish and pseudo-Christian redemption myths. These arose among the so-called Gnostics who lived in the early days of Christianity and tried to blend Christian theology with Greek philosophy and oriental religion. So, the language and images themselves contained in the New Testament are not congenial with the original Christian understanding. The real purpose of these "myths," said Bultmann, where the invisible God is pictured acting in visible ways, is not to present some objective picture of the world, but to express man's understanding of himself. The event of Jesus Christ is the revelation of the love of God, and what it does is to make persons free to be themselves. The Christ event is an act of God through which mankind becomes capable of self-commitment, of faith and love and an authentic life. So here in these mythologically described events we have a unique combination of history and myth, where the crucifixion is historical, but the resurrection is not — at least in the crudely physical ways described in the Gospels. Christ "rose" in the minds and hearts of those who became aware that in the crucifixion God was manifesting his love in a unique way. So, for Bultmann, the crucifixion replaces the resurrection as the center of Christian theology. The risen Christ meets us in the preaching of the cross, and so the history of the resurrection is an "inner" history of faith, not an "outer" event that happened in space and time.

De-Mythologizing Bultmann

Now Bultmann aroused a storm of criticism, as one might expect, and I have spent a good many years trying to sort out this aspect of his thought. There seems little question that he put his finger on the nerve of the problem, and the widespread acceptance of his analysis showed that he spoke for a large number of people troubled about this matter. If the Bible cannot be accepted by a scientific age, then it must either be abandoned, or somehow made acceptable; and his choice of the latter route showed his concern to maintain this focus of Christian doctrine. Perhaps the greatest contribution which Bultmann made through this whole discussion is his stress on the "inner" nature of historical experience, what he called *Geschichte*, in contrast to *Historie*, which refers, for him, to the objective facts of history. Certainly we bring something of ourselves to any observation. As I have already suggested, history must be interpreted in order to be truly understood. The Bible is inevitably interpreted history. The inner history of mind is an important aspect of our understanding of God's activity in the world; and to accept the involvement of God in human affairs at all is to say something about our own faith experience. To believe in divine creation, or in Jesus' capacity to perform miracles, or perhaps most sensitively in the resurrection, is a statement of faith, and so inevitably involves the inner condition of mind and heart.

But the acceptance of these insights does not necessarily point to Bultmann's program of radical de-mythologizing, which has several serious problems. In the first place, his use of the term "myth" to describe God's activity in and upon the physical world tends to prejudice our understanding. Despite his disclaimers, most people tend to think of "myth" as something that didn't really happen, like a fairy tale; and one notes that for Bultmann to call the resurrection a "myth" meant that it simply did not occur as an objective fact, with an empty tomb, and Jesus appearing to the disciples. These are merely symbols to describe what happened within their hearts as they came to believe that God was really in their midst. I shall continue to use the term "myth," but only because I cannot find a better, less prejudicial one.

Another problem is Bultmann's curious insistence that we must accept every biblical myth at face value, or none at all. This is what philosophers call "nothing but" or reductionist logic, and does not follow either from the nature of the case or from the defense Bultmann gives it. Unless we are to hold every word of the Bible equally authoritative, a radically conservative biblical literalism which Bultmann would certainly not accept, then we must be prepared to make critical decisions about biblical mythology as we do about other matters of fact.

Some have objected that what Bultmann has done is to deny modern Christianity the right to have any understanding of the cosmos and God's relationship to it at all. The clear fact is that if we are going to talk about a creator God who has revealed himself in Jesus of Nazareth, then, whether we like it or not, whether it is difficult or not, we must talk about the relation of the invisible God to the visible world in plain, objective, common sense terms which are consistent not with nineteenth century German idealistic philosophy, but with the modern scientific world. Bultmann is right in saying that the Bible must be understood in ways that will not violate the integrity of the scientific mind; but his radical rejection of biblical cosmology and turning inward to existential philosophy not only does not answer the critical questions, but does violence to the Christian faith.

The major problem with Bultmann's program of radical de-mythologizing centers around the very concern that prompted it. It is not so much unscientific as "pre-scientific;" for in the last analysis, Bultmann was a nineteenth century mind. For one thing, his world view was nineteenth century. When he had such difficulty with the relation between the visible and the invisible, between matter and energy, between solid substance and what the Bible calls "spirit," he was showing that his world view was based on the crude nineteenth century physics of Isaac Newton, rather than on the more sophisticated post-Einstinian world view of today. Bultmann was really de-mythologizing the Bible to make it compatible with a scientific world view of slow speeds, mechanical pushes and pulls and large, solid objects that has long since been superceded by the concepts of infinite speed, relativity and quantum physics.

A second scientific problem has to do with method. The biblical methodology that led to Bultmann's extreme historical skepticism is also that which he used to excise or radically reinterpret biblical mythology. As we have already noted, his form critical method is too filled with dubious assumptions, too arbitrarily deductive in superimposing his assumptions upon the evidence, to be relied upon as a support for his extreme historical skepticism. It also requires us to examine his program of radical de-mythologizing with highly critical eyes. As I shall try to demonstrate, a more empirically scientific approach to the Gospels reveals not only that Bultmann's extreme skepticism is unjustified, but that his *radical* de-mythologizing is unnecessary. The application of a more scientific method to Gospel research reveals that Jesus was a far more sophisticated mind than Bultmann gave him credit for being. If one is willing at certain points to distinguish the mind of Jesus from the ideas common to the first century, something Bultmann was unwilling to do, then as we shall see it appears that Jesus already demythologized many of the first century ideas to which Bultmann objects. Furthermore, if one approaches the material in terms of twentieth century science, many of the problems Bultmann had with the Christian story automatically disappear.

Re-Mythologizing

For all its original promise, the process of de-mythologizing, whether moderate or radical, has failed to probe to the heart of the question of God's activity within and upon the created world. There is, however, a third approach which gives genuine promise, what many are calling "re-mythologizing." Recognizing the inevitability of speaking mythologically about God and his creation, and the necessity of doing some de-mythologizing, this approach concentrates upon the re-understanding of biblical concepts in terms of modern science and its language. Some biblical ideas will no doubt have to be abandoned. It is no longer credible that the earth is the center of the universe, or that heaven is "up" and hell is "down" in some crudely geographical way. But this approach also recognizes that the Bible is a sophisticated book, and that at certain points it is our own inadequate understanding of what the Bible is saying that is at fault. As our knowledge of creation becomes more advanced, so do we have a greater ability to understand some ancient ideas, which are strangely very modern.

If, as we have said, the language about God is ultimately that of analogy, then the same is true of the mythology of God's relation to his created world. We are talking analogically, for that is all one can do when discussing that which goes beyond his three-dimensional thought categories. This is what the scientist must do when he describes the ultimate reality of matter and energy: the classic picture of the atom is a ball with a ring around it; light has been described as both a wave and a particle (*photon*). These pictures are ultimately inadequate, however, since what the atom and light are in themselves can only be expressed mathematically, which is another form of symbolism. And as our knowledge of reality increases, so must the language of scientific analogy change, to talk of anti-matter, left-handed electrons or black holes in the universe, all of which are merely symbols for what cannot be exactly described. The same is true of theological language. The language of faith and its analogies gets out of date, and so it must be constantly updated, or re-mythologized, in order to command assent.

There are many today who are working to rediscover the transcendent in modern terms. One interesting illustration is the sociologist, Peter Berger, who finds what he calls "Rumors of Angels," that is, hints of the transcendent, in the commonly observed phenomena of order, hope, damnation, play and humor. In all these ways society reveals its ability to transcend those forces of chaos, hopelessness, injustice and severity within the human scene that threaten to stifle the human spirit. Huston Smith, an M.I.T. philosopher, in his essay, "The Reach and the Grasp, Transcendence Today," holds up the possibility of re-discovering transcendence on two levels. The first is what he calls a "this worldly" level, similar to that described by Berger; and he points to evidences for this in such things as love, hope and commitment. The second is the "ontological" level, which is the way the created world exists. Here he indicates a many dimensioned universe, where at least three worlds exist: a "micro world" of photons and massless reality, a "macro" or middle-sized world wherein we reside as humans, and a "mega world" of the expanding universe. This growing appreciation of the mysterious complexity of our universe is one that is becoming increasingly manifest among philosophers and scientists as well as theologians.

I teach a course at the college wherein I have an unrehearsed dialogue for two weeks each with a Philosopher, a Physicist, a Chemist, a Biologist, a Mathematician, a Psychologist and a Sociologist. We talk about theology, and one thing I have learned very clearly is that we cannot prove anything about religion from science. I discovered this when I was a sophomore in college, but the experience of the years has made this fact even more inescapable. But I have also learned another exciting thing. As each of the sciences approaches the limits of its discipline, what one of my colleagues calls the "mystery," there begin to appear certain hints, or "rumors," using Berger's term, of the transcendent God showing through the boundary between the three-dimensional world and that of the infinite. For example, the old view of the physical

70

universe was based upon the concept of mass and the absolutely predictable laws of motion. In the nineteenth century, many philosophers insisted that from this viewpoint, science left no room for a God who could act upon this mechanically predictable universe. But since the time of Albert Einstein, this old view has been replaced by another more flexible one, where Newton's laws are seen to be limited to large masses, and where matter is composed either of waves or photons of energy, and governed by the laws of structure and the behavior of an electro-magnetic field. The old Newtonian concept of an absolutely predictable cosmos has been replaced by one where predictability is limited to larger masses but where "indeterminacy" governs the smaller units. Einstein showed in his theory of relativity that Newton's laws appear as special cases for slower velocities, but break down when applied to those approaching the speed of light.

It would seem that matter takes many more forms, is more dynamic, changeable, fluid and unpredictable than Newton ever dreamed. It would appear that our old devotion to solid matter, to an absolute distinction between here and there, and now and then, is not so simple as we had thought. Newton has been upstaged by Einstein. Now this does not *prove* anything about theology or the Christian Gospel; but it does give us pause in dismissing some elements of biblical cosmology — like miracles or an empty tomb — as easily as Bultmann and a host of others have done in the name of science. In this modern view of the physical universe there are new analogies for understanding the relation of God to his world, further "rumors" of the God who, although invisible and intangible, is inescapably real. Probe the heart of the atom and the discovery is incomprehensible power. Probe the essential reality of the God of creation and the biblical analogy is the same — power beyond comprehension.

Further help in re-mythologizing the Bible comes from non-Euclidian geometry, where the concepts of dimension and space undergo certain revisions that provide *analogies* for understanding some of the concepts in the Gospels. In this century, the old closed universe has been challenged by the concept that the cosmic space to which our solar system belongs is not limited to the axioms of a flat, Euclidian system. Rather, it demands a new set of axioms to explain Einstein's *curved* system in which light rays, following the shortest path, are bent when passing near large masses like the sun. This means that cosmic space to which our solar system belongs is not

Euclidian, but spherical, curving back to rejoin itself. The problem is that the axioms of Euclid do not apply to the surface of a sphere. The sum of the angles within a spherical triangle amount to more than 180 degrees. The shortest distance between two points becomes a great circle instead of a straight line. This curved universe is really a different "dimension" than that described by Euclidian mathematics, and has axioms and postulates that are unique to itself, and require spherical mathematics for adequate description.

This means that it is possible to conceive of as many dimensions as one pleases, each differing in its curvature, and each possessing its own set of mathematically valid axioms. All one has to do is take a sphere and slightly alter its shape and he has a whole new dimension of reality with its own axioms and postulates that are mathematically consistent within that system. This suggests inescapably that there are dimensions which cannot be observed or even pictured in conceptual form, but can nevertheless be adequately expressed in mathematical terms. As Karl Heim, German philosopher of science, observed, "Reality is evidently very much richer, deeper and more mysterious than it at first appears to us to be."

A classic dramatization of this principle comes from a phantasy written by a mathematician named Abbott some years before Einstein propounded his theory of the fourth dimension. The hero of this story is a square who lives in Flatland, a realm with only two dimensions, depth and width, but no height. All the inhabitants are either squares, triangles, circles or many-sided figures. In Flatland there is a particular square who is given to prophetic dreams. One night he dreams that he goes to Lineland, which has only the one dimension of width. Everyone in this land has to "stay in line." Going to the king of Lineland, the square inquires why his citizens do not get out of line. He is greeted with derision, for everyone knows there is no such thing as being out of line. In his frustration, the square goes in his dream to Pointland, where there is no dimension at all. If one removes the dimension of width, he is left with a point, so everyone here is literally "on the spot." The same dialogue ensues: "Why don't you get off the spot?" and the same derisive response, for everyone knows there is no such thing as "off the spot." In his frustration, the square wakes up.

Soon, however, he has another dream, and this one is truly prophetic. He dreams he goes to Cubeland. He discovers the dimension of height, and in his ecstacy he goes about leaping over things; for life has taken on a new and liberating dimension. At this point he wakes up and rushes to the leader of Flatland with the news that there is more to life than the Flatlanders realize. He is greeted with the same response he received in his dream, derision, disbelief, and finally persecution, and they throw him into a flatland jail. There he languishes, as the story comes to an end, and Abbott leaves his readers hanging on the edge of the realization that life probably consists of more dimensions than the three to which people are so slavishly committed. And then a very short time later Einstein startled the world by showing that by adding the factor of time, there are at least four dimensions to reality. Since then mathematicians have been demonstrating that an infinitude of dimensional systems is not only conceivable, but mathematically probable.

Jesus' thinking was primarily oriented in what I shall now call the "dimension of the spirit." This demands a "supernatural" awareness of a dimension governed by different laws, having different properties, related to and yet apart from the physical world as we know it. It is a realm where ideas and relationships that seem illogical or incongruous or mutually exclusive to us in a three-dimensional world cannot be judged to be so, since the categories of three-dimensional space do not necessarily apply to the dimension of the infinite. We cannot *prove* the existence of this spiritual realm by physical, three-dimensional axioms. But *on its own terms*, there is proof. It is in this dimension of the transcendent that Jesus' thinking was oriented; and the analogy of dimension has important new possibilities for understanding his view of the cosmos. In these and other ways it is becoming increasingly possible to re-mythologize biblical language and so believe rationally in God's activity in the world as pictured in the Bible.

Heaven, the "Space" of the Kingdom

The Uniqueness of Jesus' Message

In getting at the world view of Jesus, one must first understand that his was a uniquely creative mind. He had a way of transcending the ideas of his culture and time that left people astounded, mystified or terribly excited. We must distinguish, for example, between Jesus' teaching and that of his contemporaries, including those who wrote the Gospels, lest we find ourselves canonizing the entire Near East. He just did not think or talk like them. I have given illustrations of this in Chapter II, and will be giving more. Furthermore, he was accustomed to teaching in one way to the disciples, and in another to the opponents in his audiences; and because of this, he was regularly misunderstood, then as now. His disciples consistently failed to understand his message, his person and his purpose, until he cried out in frustration that Peter was on the side of men and not God (Mark 8:33). His opponents did not know what he was talking about, so mired were they in their own dimension of theological legalism. As Jesus said, they did not have "eyes to see," any more than the Flatlanders realized that there was a "higher" dimension to life.

The Dimension of the Kingdom

Jesus' mind was absolutely consumed by the concept of God and this is the basic clue to understanding his cosmology, which was simply another facet of his concept of the spirit. Basically, he viewed the cosmos as two interacting dimensional systems, the spiritual dimension of the creator and the physical dimension of creation, both under the sovereignty of God. As he said, God is "Lord of heaven and earth" (Matt. 11:25). This view was typical of the pharisaic Judaism of his day, and was nothing new. But then Jesus went beyond the crude understanding of this cosmology, where heaven was "up" and hell was "down," in ways that reveal a sophisticated mind that must not be restricted to the misconceptions of his day. If one is careful to distinguish between the statements made by Jesus and those by the Gospel writers and people in his audiences, we see that he went beyond the common first century view in dramatic ways. Jesus de-mythologized and re-mythologized the first century concepts of heaven, hell, satan and a host of other ideas, long before Bultmann ever raised this question.

Let us take the concept of "heaven," which is typical. There are five terms Jesus used to describe this dimension of reality: heaven, spirit, power, Kingdom and angel. The Gospel writers viewed heaven as "up" and identified it with the sky. Heaven was the "abode of God" (Luke 19:38), from whence the angel who announced Jesus' resurrection "descended" (Matt. 28:2). When Jesus was baptized, Mark says the spirit "descended from heaven" (Mark 1:10), and both Mark and Luke describe Jesus "ascending" into heaven.

At times Jesus is recorded employing heaven to refer to the sky (Luke 10:15); but most characteristically it is for him a term used in close connection with the "person" of God: "*Your* heavenly

74

father...*my* father in heaven" (Matt. 5:48; 7:21). In this personal way, his teaching about heaven is always to a disciple audience, the one to which he gave his most characteristic teaching, and always within a context heavy with the judgment of God. One of the clearest examples of this is found in Matthew 18:10 where he refers to the disciples as "little ones," and affirms their immediate spiritual fellowship with God in terms of heaven as a *present* experience: "I tell you that in heaven their angels always behold the face of my Father who is in heaven" (cf. also Matt. 6:20; Luke 10:20). Heaven, in these passages, describes a presently existing dimension where living persons are related to God in a special way. In effect, it identifies the relationship itself, for heaven is where God is.

Jesus pictured the Kingdom of God as the dimension of the spirit into which we are called to enter, where the axioms are not the usual ones of the physical world, although the imagery seems to give to the Kingdom a sense of space. As we have seen and must always keep in mind, most basically for Jesus, the Kingdom is a description of the presence of God as spirit and power. Here, then, in this usage, the spirit and power of God is described in the analogies of space. This is demonstrated in those places where the Kingdom is something to be entered within history, like a vineyard where two sons are told to go and work, and one says he will, but doesn't, and the other says he won't, but does (Matt. 21:28-32). In the parable of the laborers, some enter the vineyard in the morning, others late in the day, and time is passing. This is an historical scene, and the Kingdom exists to be entered within the lifetime of those invited (Matt. 20:1-16). As Jesus said to the pharisees: "Woe to you...for you did not enter yourselves, and you hindered those who were entering" (Luke 11:52). The Kingdom of God in this sense is not some far-off goal, but the dimension of God's presence, to be entered *now*.

The Crisis of the Kingdom

For Jesus, the cosmos stands under the judgment of God. The earth is the stage whereon is acted out the drama of mankind's confrontation by the "fire" of God's presence. The world is in a state of tension between creator and creation. This is dramatically seen in a series of contrasts where these two systems or dimensions are placed in drastic opposition. "Everyone who acknowledges me *before men*, The Son of man also will acknowledge *before the angels of God*" (Luke 12:8-9). In Mark, he compares the sins of the "sons of men and their blasphemies," presumably against him, on the physical level, with their blasphemy against the Holy Spirit, which is un-forgivable in the sense that such rebellion against God is the ultimate meaning of sin (Mark 3:28-29). This is what I shall later call, the sin against the *aion*, which is the dimension of God. Jesus rebuked Peter in the same vein: "You are not on the side of God but of men" (Mark 8:33). The disciples are told to let their lights shine "before men," that they may glorify their father "who is in heaven" (Matt. 5:16). Jesus seems to have considered it his mission to call persons out of the dimension of the physical into that of the spirit; to call them from the realm of the sovereignty of self, into the Kingdom of the sovereignty of God.

We are now in a position to ask again the question, "where" is God? and perhaps crystallize some kind of answer in these new re-mythologized terms. God is in heaven, and heaven is where God is; and that is not a location that can be pointed to in some crude three-dimensional way, for God transcends these three dimensions in which our thinking is bound. So the word "where" explodes when used to talk about God, and we are left with a series of analogies from the three-dimensional world, like wind and light and vineyards and dimension. I think what Jesus is saying, in its simplest terms, is that God is very near to us, and so heaven is very near. As he said to his disciples in describing their preaching of the Gospel of the Kingdom: "The Kingdom of God has come near to you" (Luke 10:9). The heaven of God's presence is as near as the vineyard to the laborer invited to enter it, as near as the air to one who would breathe it, as near as the dimension of height to that of width, the dimension of time to that of space.

And as we say this, we must be prepared to abandon even these analogies as our understanding of this mysterious universe expands, and as we see more and other kinds of "rumors" of the mystery of the Kingdom in the life around us. The analogies of post-Einstinian science will surely be replaced by those of later ages. But know this, that a Christian can talk about the dimension of God just as realistically in this scientific age as the scientist can talk about the atom or the nature of light, or any other aspect of this physical universe which he can describe ultimately, in its most essential aspects, only in terms of analogy. When the scientist comes to the limits of his discipline, he begins to talk the same language as Jesus. He becomes a philosopher, a theologian or a poet.

76

Chapter VI

God's Time Is Eternity

But if God is spatially near, he is also temporally near; and Jesus' teaching was filled with a sense of the fullness of God's time, which gave it a peculiar urgency that is an important element of its power. Yet this is a very difficult subject to analyze, for Jesus seems to have viewed time and history from two decisively different points of vantage. He would talk about the time of the Kingdom from what would seem to be a normal, mundane point of view; but then baffle us by speaking from a plane of reference that cut across the human scene from a strange, oblique direction beyond the human. In order to understand his teaching about time and history, we must be prepared to see these in terms of the same physical and spiritual dimensions that formed his view of the cosmos, and were the heart of the very mystery of his incarnate person.

Horizontal Time

Jesus' interest in time was, first of all, what we might call a "horizontal" interest. This is time viewed in terms of the three-dimensional world, where the ticking of the clock separates one moment from another; where past, present and future are distinct. This is "created time," and depends on the physical world for its existence. The left side of the time-line is creation, and the right is the *eschaton*, the end of physical time; and in between are all the high and low moments that make up our daily lives. Jesus was interested in them all. He talked of the past history of the Jews in terms of Moses, the prophets and the traditions of the elders (Matt. 5:21; 5:12; Mark 7:5-23). He spoke of the future as a time when lost sheep would be found (Luke 15:3-7), when Jerusalem would be destroyed (Luke 21:24), when the Gospel would be preached to all nations

(Mark 13:10; Matt. 24:14), and ultimately as a time when history, as we know it, would come to an end (cf. Chapt. XIV). This linear process as Jesus viewed it is essentially the same as that presented by modern science where the creation of our universe is seen as beginning at a point in time, and moving toward a conclusion where matter and energy will reach a stable state and life as we know it will end.

But Jesus was primarily interested in the present. He saw the past as that which yearned for the advent of "this day" (Luke 4:21), a very special moment in history for which the prophets longed (Matt. 13:17) when God's redeeming purpose came to incarnate expression in his own fulfilling life: "Go and tell John what you have seen and heard..." (Luke 7:22), "Can the wedding guests fast while the bridegroom is with them?" (Mark 2:19). For Jesus, and then for the Christian Gospel that came from him, the norm of time is the redemptive significance of the historical Jesus, which Oscar Cullmann, a Swiss scholar, has called "the midpoint of time." This means that something has happened in Jesus Christ that is decisive in the history of God's plan for human redemption; and henceforth, this historical event has become the fulcrum of human history.

Jesus pictured his advent as the time when the Kingdom of God was "at hand" (Mark 1:15), like a field that is "white for harvest" (John 4:35; cf. Matt. 9:37), like the "finger" of God coming upon them (Luke 11:20). This was not in some horizontal sense, as if the Kingdom came at that time like a long awaited train which finally arrived. If the Kingdom is the spiritual presence of God, then we cannot restrict his saving activity to any linear segment of human history. What Jesus was referring to here is the fact that at that moment in history, in him God's Kingdom was especially near in a "spatial," and so a temporal sense. In what he called "the time of your visitation" (Luke 19:44), the power of God's presence was at work, as never before, in his redemptive life and word; and ever after, because of his advent, the Kingdom which had always been available, as God has always been available, was now infinitely *more available* in the new and very special ways we shall be describing throughout the remainder of this book. And because of that fact, the time of Jesus' coming was a moment of unique judgment upon men and women, a time (*kairos*) that had a special place in God's plan of salvation. This is vividly expressed in a word credited to John the Baptist, but probably more valid as a word of Jesus: "*Even now* the axe is laid to the root of the trees" (Luke 3:9; cf. Matt. 7:19;

4:17; Luke 6:43).

Vertical Time

But the time of the Kingdom is God's time, and this transcends the horizontal ribbon of human sequence. God's judgment is the expression of his nature, which cannot be bound by human events. And these times of judgment (*kairoi*) which give ultimate meaning to the history of a human life and to the entire span of created time, are ultimately God's time, compressed and delimited by the finite mind of man. And our experience of his presence becomes an experience of his time, which Jesus called "eternal life." So we must turn any linear, human view of time *on end* if we would follow Jesus into the most characteristic aspects of his thought, where he applied his intense awareness of the dimension of the spirit to his concept of time. This is time seen from the *vertical* point of view of God for whom *all time is present*.

Mankind stands not only in the "valley of decision," between the mountain peaks of creation and *eschaton*; he also stands within this flow of horizontal time being drawn "upward" toward eternity. There is an absolute, qualitative distinction Jesus makes between the temporal and the eternal that is the chronological expression of the tension between the physical and the spiritual dimensions of the cosmos. It is the application to time of the doctrine of God, what Nels Ferre, a contemporary theologian, has called "the mystery of God's time." This upward tug of eternity is completely characteristic of Jesus' concept of the Kingdom and represents the essence of his creative addition to the Jewish view of time.

This is a difficult concept to understand, and we need to re-mythologize Jesus' cosmology by finding new analogies for his teaching about the "vertical" time of the Kingdom that are more compatible with the present age. From the new science come two analogies that can be helpful in getting us "unstuck" from our old concepts of "solid time." The first is the speed of light. The basic problem of time is that of finding a fixed base from which to calculate. The firmly rooted point system which we need in order to make spatial or temporal measurements is actually something created by the human mind. It is a necessary fiction, which we need in order to describe motion in space or time. In the history of science, there have been various attempts to find such a fixed, stable point. In antiquity, the earth was considered such a point, but the astronomer Copernicus showed that this was false. Then it was thought to be the sun, but Giordano Bruno destroyed this idea. Later something called the "ether" was proposed, but Michelson and Morely disposed of that concept. Sir Isaac Newton talked about what he called "absolute time," but Neuman and Vorhinger showed the inadequacy of this. In our contemporary science, we now look to a deeper level of objectivity based on the speed of light, which has both mass and speed, and is described in the seemingly contradictory terms of both a particle (photon) and a wave (quantum). According to this view, whatever moves with the speed of light is theoretically moving infinitely fast and can cover any distance in a moment of time, although in actual practice such speed can be measured. Now supposing that instead of the speed of light which is a measurable 186,000 miles per second, I could really go infinitely fast. For the purposes of the *analogy* that would mean that theoretically, if not actually, the intervening space would disappear. It would no longer have any practical meaning. With infinite velocity, time and space would become one in the *event* of light.

Now when Jesus spoke of time, in what I have called a "vertical sense," he was describing eternity in terms of the nature of God who dwells in "everlasting light" (Is. 60:20; cf. Luke 16:8). The implications of this analogy are fascinating. As the German theologian Karl Heim observed, "It must therefore be conceivable that there is a being whose time-rate reaches the upper limit of probability." This would mean that for such a being the whole universal history, which at our time rate stretches over millions of years, would be compressed into a moment. For such a being there would be no time at all. Everything would be compressed into an eternal moment. Time and space would become one in the eternal "event" of his radiant presence. What this analogy of light suggests is that God is the infinitely fast one, and our problem in experiencing him is that we humans are simply too "slow." Science fiction? No, just the remythologizing of an old biblical analogy that is strangely modern.

A second analogy from the new science that provides us with another "rumor" of God's transcendent time is that of relativity. In time measurement, as in space measurement, the calculation is dependent upon the standpoint of the observer. To the three spatial coordinates of the physical world, Einstein added the coordinate of time. And in this four dimensional situation, space and time depend on the state of motion of the observer. In relating this to the Christian Gospel, what it suggests is that time must be viewed in terms of the state of motion of both God and man. One might draw an analogy for this statement in the following way.

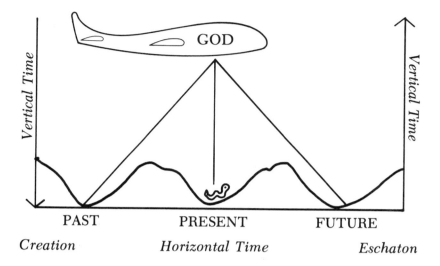

PAST   PRESENT   FUTURE

Creation   *Horizontal Time*   *Eschaton*

In the above, we have a picture of time. The horizontal line represents three-dimensional time, where each moment is a separate tick of the clock, bounded on the left by creation and on the right by the final consummation. Along this line I have drawn a series of mountain peaks divided by deep valleys. These represent the past, the present, and the future, each separated from the other by a mountain peak that keeps them implacably distinct as long as three-dimensional time continues. In the central valley of the present, there is a worm crawling along from left to right, who is always in the present. He cannot move to the past, nor can he call up the future. We humans are like that worm, trapped in the valley of the present. But flying high overhead is an airplane, and within the cockpit is seated the God who eternally "Is," from whom all time is equidistant. As he looks down upon the scene from that dramatically different point of view, he can see the valleys of the worm's past, his present and his future, all at the same moment of time, because he is "higher" than the worm. He dwells in a different dimension, where all time is present. This is the "vertical" time of God, and it means that for God to know ahead of time what we will do, as Paul implies in his concept of predestination, does not in any way deprive us of our freedom of choice. It only says that the phrase "ahead of time" is

81

a human, horizontal concept that has meaning on a three-dimensional level, but does not limit the activity of God whose experience of time is eternally "vertical." "For as the heavens are higher than the earth, so are my ways higher than your ways and my thoughts than your thoughts" (Is. 55:9).

Now it is highly significant to see Jesus viewing the relation between space and time in terms of what I shall call "spiritual continuum," where coordinates of space and time operate according to the axioms of the spirit, and all is viewed from the "observer-point" of God, who is Lord of time. Of all the Synoptic expressions pointing to Jesus' "vertical" conception of time, the one that does so most clearly is the word *aion* (Hebrew, *olom*), translated "age" or "eternity." It sometimes occurs horizontally as an "everlasting" continuation of events, but mostly it is used in a vertical sense to describe the time of God's eternal presence. As the German, Gustaf Dalman, pointed out years ago, *aion* is closely related to the Kingdom of God. For example, in the conclusion to the incident of the rich young ruler, the phrase "enter the Kingdom" is paralleled (v. 30) with "the age (aion) to come" (Mark 10:24). This term is also closely identified with the Holy Spirit in Mark 3:28-29, where "blasphemy against the spirit" is called an "eternal sin," that is, a sin against the *aion* — a sin against the eternal realm of the spirit. In these Gospels, the *aion* is eternity as the presence of God to whom all time is immediately related, for whose justice all time is the revelation, and from whom all time and eternity are equidistant. When persons are confronted by this God, there opens up for them a new dimension of time, a new life in the radiant presence of God, where the experience of time is but the fleeting fullness of those who are in love. For the creator God, the "infinitely fast one," who dwells in "unapproachable light," whose axioms are not limited to those of the three dimensional world, horizontal duration has no meaning except as an aspect of creation. In the last analysis, the *aion* is a description of the Holy Spirit, and so of the Kingdom of God in terms of time. In this eternal reality, space and time are one.

When is the Kingdom?

Let us now try to crystallize our answer to this question in terms of Jesus' teaching about the Kingdom of God. There are, first of all, many parables where the Kingdom of God is presented as something into which men and women can enter now, in this life. In the parable of the two sons (Matt. 21:28-32), the father tells the one son to go to work in the vineyard, the symbol for the Kingdom, and although he agrees, he does not go. Then he asks his other son, who rejects the request, but *later* does what his father wants him to do. The point is that time is passing, and minds are changing, and the Kingdom is available for entrance at any time, a working experience that continues throughout the passage of horizontal time. The same is true of many other parables about the Kingdom, for example that of the laborers in the vineyard (Matt. 20:1-16), where the call to enter comes and laborers enter the vineyard at different times of day; or where the Kingdom is pictured as a narrow door to be entered (Matt. 7:13-14; Luke 13:24), and Jesus criticizes the scribes and pharisees for not entering this door, and for hindering those "who were entering" (Luke 11:52). In all of these passages and many more, the Kingdom is a present experience of entering into the "space" and "time" of God which is available for us *now*, during this horizontal stream of three dimensional history.

But this Kingdom is also pictured as a future, final event at the "end" of the horizontal time-line. In the parable of the ten virgins, for example (Matt. 25:1-14), Jesus pictures the Kingdom as a wedding feast into which the bridesmaids enter only at some future final moment when the bridegroom returns, and together they go in with him. Elsewhere it is pictured as a great judgment scene where sheep are divided from goats (Matt. 25:31-46), or a closed door (Luke 13:25-30), a wedding feast (Matt. 22:11-14), or an experience of two people grinding corn, where one is taken and the other left behind (Luke 17:22-37). In these passages, the Kingdom is a dramatic, once-for-all, climactic event, beyond which there is no passage of horizontal time, but only reward or punishment.

Most characteristically, however, and this is what is becoming more widely appreciated these days, Jesus talked about the Kingdom of God as *both present and future*, both historical and eschatological, in ways that transcended the "now" and "then" of horizontal time in the eternal present, or presence, of God. That Jesus talked about the Kingdom as present, and then as future is not a contradiction. These are rather complementary ideas, and this point is clearly made in many of his parables. In the parable of the wheat and the weeds (Matt. 13:24-30), the Kingdom is pictured as a field of growing grain wherein there are also weeds. Time is passing, and one over-zealous servant wants to "prune the roles" by rooting out all of the weeds the owner has not planted. He is dissuaded and told to wait until the harvest; and all the while we are moving along the linear stream of time. But then the harvest comes, a climactic and decisively terminal moment, and there is no more growing side by side, but only the gathering of the wheat into the barn and the throwing of the weeds into the fire. The *eschaton* has come. In the same parable we see these two references to Kingdom time as an ongoing stream, and as a final moment of judgment. They are not contradictory, but complementary ideas. The same is true in the parables of the net (Matt. 13:47-50), the two houses (Matt. 7:24-27), the unforgiving servant (Matt. 18:23-35) and a host of others.

This means that for each life, the Kingdom has two points of special significance: 1) the point at which the particular individual enters the Kingdom; and 2) the point, at the end of the age, when for all mankind the Kingdom is consummated. Both of these are what Jesus called *kairoi*, times that are heavy with the tension of God's imperative. At such times God's judgment is especially "near." Jesus' cosmology was therefore not just an impersonal discussion of the relation between space and time, but rather another extension of his overwhelming concern for the fire of God's judgment in our midst. Space and time are charged with decision. Men and women are called to live in two worlds at once: the physical world of persons and the spiritual realm of the Kingdom; in the horizontal times of human history and in the vertical time of God. The space and time of God are always near in the valley of decision, always about to come; but they are most uniquely and powerfully near in the person and word of Jesus Christ.

PART FOUR

PERSONS, THE CHILDREN OF THE KINGDOM

Chapter VII

The Psychology of the Kingdom

The most central and agonizing point of impact for the Kingdom crisis is the human mind and heart. Jesus' teaching about the personal God was primarily concerned with individuals and their inner relationship with this God who reaches out to us person to person. It is in this dimension that the power of the Kingdom is most dramatically experienced. So in this chapter I want to take another look at the Kingdom of God, but this time from the point of view of persons as Jesus saw them, with infinite potential and in desperate need.

Inattention to the Psychology of the Kingdom
The curious thing is that this, too, has been an aspect of Jesus' teaching strangely missing from most of the recent major statements of New Testament theology. There are those who have insisted that Jesus' concept of the Kingdom had little or nothing to say about the personal lives of men and women. Some years ago I reviewed a book entitled, *The Kingdom of God in the Teaching of Jesus* by Norman Perrin, the distinguished professor of New Testament at Chicago Theological Seminary. He had summarized everything being written about the Kingdom of God, but I noted that he had entirely omitted any reference to what I called the "Anthropology of the Kingdom." Some time later I met him in the cafeteria line at Union Seminary in New York, and he asked me what I meant by the "Anthropology" of the Kingdom. It was therefore reassuring to note that in his next book, written just before his death, *Rediscovering the Kingdom of God*, Perrin corrected this oversight by putting his primary emphasis upon just this personal element in Jesus' teaching about the Kingdom.

Because of this strange silence, I find myself often preaching and lecturing on this subject, and sometimes people will come up and ask me why their ministers do not have more to say about their personal spiritual needs. I am not sure I know the answer to that question, but I suspect it has something to do with the shift in Christian emphasis in recent years toward social problems, or our absorption with the failure of the church.

And so the individual has become the "forgotten man" in the theology and preaching of many churches. There are, of course, notable exceptions to this, but I am convinced that generally speaking, this has been true. Mainline Protestants especially have discussed the "modern man," the "post-modern man," the "secular man," the "suburban man," the "inner city man," the "organization man," and we have even rediscovered "the new woman," but the personal, spiritual needs of the individual within the church have been drowned in a sea of sociological abstraction. Particularly during the 1960s it was considered somehow improper for theologians or clergymen trained in the "better" seminaries to talk about the individual. This is called pietism, and for years has been the subject of much suspicion, perhaps because of what some would call a "false piety."

Now this is a curious situation in view of what seems to be the clear fact that Jesus spoke primarily to and about individuals. Certainly the Kingdom of God involves an intense social concern, and I shall deal with this at length in a later chapter. But as far as I can see, in the teachings of Jesus, the center of power lies in the interaction between God and persons. God must redeem individuals first before he can redeem their structures. He commands us to serve as persons first, before we serve as groups. The "ground zero" for the atomic impact of God's Kingdom power is the human mind and personality. But Laodicea is still holding to the form of religion and denying its power; and the center of that problem is not a group called "Church." It is the single human heart. It would seem that one of the greatest needs of the Christian church in these days is a mission to itself, to rediscover the relation of the individual to the Kingdom of God.

What is a Man or a Woman?

You would think that by now we should know who we are. But the strange thing is that we don't, and this confusion is another cause of our reluctance to say too much about the subject of persons. I ask my colleagues in the Psychology Department, "What is a man or a woman?" and about all they feel they can legitimately say is that there are many conflicting views. The experimental psychologist has insisted that man is an aggregate of conditioned reflexes, and this conception has held a virtual tyranny over departments of psychology for many years. But as James Deese points out in his book *Psychology as Science and Art*, in more recent times this tyranny has been breaking up, with the result that many new clinical approaches to psychology have become popular, like Transactional Analysis, or Logotherapy, each with its own view of the nature of man.

The same confusion is found in the physical sciences. In his book *The Naked Ape*, Desmond Morris writes that there are 193 living species of monkeys and apes, 192 of which are covered with hair. In other words, man is a clever animal, and this view is widespread in biological circles today. In a book entitled *The Mechanical Man*, Dean Wooldridge has described man as a machine, a view not uncommon among those who would reduce persons to the observations of the physicist. Some chemists are tempted to describe humans as complex fluid systems. But whether it be psychology, biology, physics or chemistry, there seems to be general agreement among physical scientists on at least one thing: there is nothing absolutely unique about men and women. We differ from animals only in degree, and for some scientists this is a very moderate degree. Now the point is that this radically contradicts the Christian view that man is made in the image of God, and so it is difficult for Christians to reconcile their concept of man with what they learn about him from the physical sciences.

Within Christian theology there is also considerable confusion: over whether or not man is naturally immortal; whether or not the soul is a substance; whether salvation is conditional or universal; over the origin and destiny of the soul. There is surprising conflict about these matters, and this causes confusion among secular psychologists in understanding what the Christians are saying about man. Lindsay and Hall, in their book *Personality Theory*, long a standard text for college courses, describe the "Christian" view of the soul as immortal, free and of divine origin, a substance that is different from the physical body. This, they say, must be firmly rejected. So in terms of this text, there is really no basis for agreement between Christian theology and secular psychology. The point I would make is that this view so firmly rejected by modern psychology, is neither universal with Christian theologians, nor is it true to the teachings of Jesus, as I shall try to show. Lindsay and Hall are rejecting a "straw-man;" but what can we expect, since Christians can't agree among themselves on the nature of man? So we have a lack of attention within Christianity to the nature of persons, coupled with an aversion to personal religion, all within a general context of conflict and confusion concerning this subject. It would seem that there are many reasons for a weakness in Christian theology at this point.

Current Interest in Personal Religion

But the pendulum of popular interest has been swinging back, and a return to a concern for persons has become clearly visible in the last decade. The so-called "consciousness circuit," described by Theodore Rosack in his book *The Unfinished Animal* (with a mirror on the cover), reveals a fascinating and wide-spread reaction to this ignoring of our individuality. Transcendental Meditation, Essalon, Consciousness Raising, these and so many others, are cries of outrage against the swamping of human personalities within structures. The "Jesus Freak" movement, coming as it did right out of the drug sub-culture, with its extreme fixation on "inner space," was, I believe, a clear reaction against the Christian church's inattention to the individual. Personal religion, personal morality, personal discipline are the things stressed by this "new breed," and their more moderate successors, who turn up in our classes with a very positive desire to study the Bible. They are highly motivated to serve society, but they want to do so in terms of single human beings: visiting the sick, ministering to those in prison, or fighting for the liberation of persons who are caught in the ghettos of their sex or their age or their circumstances. The great social focus of the sixties has shifted in the seventies and eighties to the individual.

One of the most visible illustrations of this trend can be seen in the various movements for charismatic renewal within most denominations, augmented by a steadily increasing literature on personal religion. In my own denomination there is a current revolt among many laymen and ministers against bureaucratic stifling of personal religion on the part of an over-organized and over-socialized church. This is evident in the movement of "Presbyterians United for Biblical Concern," chiefly a clergy group, and among those who publish "Presbyterian Laymen," who appear almost like a denomination within a denomination. All of this shows a hunger for a ministry to persons that is manifesting itself in many ways, both in secular society, and in every sector of the Christian church. My concern is that this renewal be more than just the temporary reaction to another tired swing of the theological pendulum. The ingredient that is desperately needed in this mix, to stabilize and confirm it for the strengthening of the church, is a coherent Christian understanding of the nature of man that is carefully based upon critical biblical study and is at least conversant, if not consistent, with what we know about contemporary science. Again, there is only one place to begin, and that is with the Holy Word of Jesus, who had much to say about this subject that is clear and compelling, if only we will allow him to speak in his own way.

The Psychology of the Kingdom

"What is man that thou art mindful of him, and the son of man that thou dost care for him?" (Ps. 8:4). This word of the psalmist directs us to the beginning of the search for what I shall call "the Psychology of the Kingdom." Jesus' many statements about human need and potential were based upon a consistent view of man that shines unmistakably through them all; and before we can see the impact of the Kingdom at work within the lives of persons, we must know something about his answers to a few basic questions: What distinguishes us from the beasts? What are our most basic needs and how can we satisfy them? What is true humanity? What is the human soul? What is the meaning of life after death? As we approach this subject, an enormous number of questions rise to greet us.

These questions are actually all tied together, and the key lies in the nature of the soul itself. Throughout hundreds of years of discussion, many answers have been given to this question, and one way to clarify Jesus' answer is to place it against the background of these other views. Basically they tend to cluster around three alternatives.

Monism: Soul and Body are One Substance

This is the simplest. The soul and body are of the same substance. Man is essentially physical. This view was clearly presented by a group of ancient Greek philosophers who agreed that soul and body were a unity, but disagreed on the nature of its substance. Democritus, for example, taught in the fifth century B.C. that the soul was a cluster of atoms that were round and smooth and very mobile. For the Stoic philosophers, who dominated the thought of Athens in the three centuries before Christ, the soul was physical (*phusikos*), composed of a kind of fiery breath — literally hot air — which seems particularly appropriate for some of us! Whether atoms, hot air, or whatever, the insight is the same. Soul and body are physical and of one substance.

Hebrew psychology has much in common with this ancient Greek view and antedates it by several hundred years. In the Old Testament, man is an animated body. He is body (*basar*) and spirit (*nephesh*), which is the essence of life, and essentially physical. Man does not *have* a soul, but by the creative act of God, he *becomes* a living soul (*nephesh haya*, Gen. 2:7). The soul is a general term describing the life principle of any living thing, animal, vegetable or human (Is. 1:14). In man it resides in the breath and the blood (Lev. 17:11; Deut. 12:23) and is centralized in the heart. The soul, then, is the life of the body, and death is the result of their separation.

At times the Old Testament goes beyond this basically physical view of the soul, especially where it uses the term "heart" (*leb*) to refer to the emotional lives of persons, or "spirit" (*ruach*) to identify the more exceptional endowments of their human nature (Num. 5:14; Job 32:18; Ex. 28:3, etc.). In these places, the soul or spirit is that aspect of man which sins, responds to God, and is capable of a special relationship with the Holy Spirit: "the high and lofty One who inhabits eternity," and revives the spirit of the humble (Is. 57:15); "I will give them one heart, and put a new spirit within them" (Ezek. 11:19). At these times it seems that the Old Testament has a full-fledged concept of the separate identity of the soul, until one realizes that there is here no real doctrine of the survival of the soul after death. Salvation, in the Old Testament, is still the preservation and extension of physical life which is the unity of body and spirit (cf. JGTJ-156-158; Deut. 5:33; Ps. 33:18-19). In the many ways in which it is being expressed, this is probably the common view today among physical scientists. Man is a completely physical being.

Dualism: Soul and Body are Radically Different

A more complicated view of man is usually identified with the philosopher Plato who was born in Athens in 427 B.C. For him the soul is the very likeness of the divine. It is immortal and unchangeable, and differs sharply from the body which is just the opposite (Phaedo 78b). The soul is without beginning or end and existed at first in the highest heavens; but some souls fell and were forced into bodies where they were condemned to a series of re-incarnations for ten thousand years. At the end of this time, if they have sufficiently purified themselves, they will return to their heavenly home. The soul is perhaps best described in this system in terms of life as idea, and its main characteristic is that it is non-material and radically different from the body. It is therefore naturally immortal, and thus automatically pre-exists and post-exists the body.

Christian theology for many hundreds of years talked of man in such Platonic terms. The soul is naturally immortal, eternal and in-destructable, and so the doctrines of hell, purgatory and limbo were developed to provide a home for all souls before birth and after death. Only man has a soul which is made in the image of God, and herein lies his uniqueness from the animal from which he differs radically and in "kind." This is still the popular view of what Chris-tian theology has to say on this subject, and is what modern psychologists, like Lindsay and Hall, feel they must "firmly reject."

The question as to whether or not this is an accurate view of Christian theology has been raised insistently in recent years. It depends, I think, on where one goes for his theology. My own research leads me to the conclusion that this is not a completely "Christian" view, because in some ways it is contrary to what Jesus is saying in the Gospels. Rather, it reflects the influence of Plato upon the theology of the early church, as it rolled like a great snowball through the first few centuries of the Christian era. This "intrusion" into Christian theology has created enormous and un-necessary difficulties ever since, and especially today as we try to reconcile Christian theology with what we know about biology and psychology. One of the large tasks of the modern biblical theologian would seem to be to recover the primitive Holy Word of Jesus, which, as I am going to try to show, avoids the problems of Plato's psychology and has a peculiarly "modern" ring.

Qualified Dualism: Soul and Body are Both the Same and Different
Jesus' view of man has similarities to both the above conceptions, but strikes off in new and creative directions that show his applica-tion of the Kingdom of God to the person of man. His understanding of the soul hinges on his abundant use of the word *psuche* (Hebrew *nephesh*), which is our modern word "psyche." He employs this term in three ways, and in doing so gathers together insights from

the Old Testament and Greek Platonic thought and blends them with his own creative addition, producing what he called "new wine."

1) *The Psyche in its Physical Dimension.* First of all, the psyche is to be identified with the body (*soma*). Like the Hebrew *nephesh*, the soul is essentially the physical life force which animates man's body and ceases to exist with its destruction. In one especially clear passage, he parallels psyche with the physical body and then contrasts them both with the Kingdom of God: "Do not be anxious about your life (*psuche*) what you shall eat...nor about your body (*soma*), what you shall put on. Is not life (*psuche*) more than food, and the body (*soma*) more than clothing?...But seek first his Kingdom" (Matt. 6:25, 33; cf. Mark 10:45; Luke 6:9). At this point Jesus is just being a good Hebrew in his use of the term *nephesh* and would, I believe, agree with the modern biologist that the soul of man is naturally and basically physical.

2) *The Psyche in Its Psychological Dimension.* He then goes on to refer to man's psyche in ways that describe his higher qualities, his thinking, feeling, emotional life. A term more often used at this level is heart (*kardia*) which is the locus of the self, where doubt or faith reside (Mark 2:8; 11:23). The heart is the focal point of man's will wherein dwells the devotion to physical things that destroys service to God (Luke 16:15). The heart, or psyche, is the seat of the emotions from whence come the quickening fires of love for the risen Christ (Luke 24:34). In these and other ways Jesus describes this higher capacity which men and women share to a degree with animals, but which completely outstrips them in the escalating genius of their humanity. But still, so far, Jesus is giving us standard Old Testament psychology. All this is ultimately physical and tied inextricably to the body.

3) *The Psyche in its Spiritual Potential.* But now we must begin to think in new ways if we are to follow him in his theology of the Kingdom. It is only here that we begin to part company with those psychologists and biologists who would reduce man exclusively to the level of "Naked Ape," however clever, or "Machine," however sophisticated. At this level Jesus goes beyond both Old Testament Judaism and modern secular psychology into the realm of the spirit, where the psyche actually experiences the new dimension of the Kingdom of God. I am not talking about the concept of a separate soul, naturally immortal, which one finds in Platonic dualism, although there are some similarities. This is rather what I would call

a "conditional dualism" that reflects in Jesus' psychology that very condition which is essential to the justice of God. This third dimension of soul is a *potential* dimension that represents men and women's highest *capacity* and depends on their own choices and commitments.

For Jesus, persons are physical beings who possess the capacity and the terrible need for the spiritual realm of God. They are creatures whose souls are naturally one with their bodies, but who possess the wonderful potential for a new dimension of life, both in and apart from the body. Jesus holds out this possibility to Peter in a statement which attributes to the soul (*psuche*) its potential separation from the body. Peter has been rebuking Jesus for teaching that it is necessary to suffer and die (Mark 8:31); and Jesus replies that Peter is "Satan" because he is "not on the side of God, but of men," a very serious charge (Mark 8:33). It was at this juncture that Jesus made the point which the editors felt crucial enough to report rather fully. "For whoever would save his life (*psuche*) will lose it; and whoever loses his life (*psuche*) for my sake and the gospel's will save it" (Mark 8:35). A tremendous statement! For in this brilliant play on words, he crystallizes his whole message of the judgment of God upon the souls of men.

There is a contradiction in this passage which gives us the clue to its meaning. You can't lose your physical life and save it too. So Jesus is using the word "life" (*psuche*) in two ways; first as the physical psyche, which Peter is so desperately afraid of losing; and second as that higher aspect of *psuche* capable of being saved through him and the Gospel. He is calling Peter and the others to follow him to the cross, promising them that even though they might lose their physical lives, they would thereby save that spiritual capacity for life which is not tied inevitably to living or dying. "For what does it profit a man (Peter), to gain the whole (physical) world and forfeit his (spiritual) life?" (Mark 8:36).

Capable of being saved or lost, with or without the conditions of physical life: this is what he was saying to the disciples when he urged them to endure persecution to the "end" in order that they might be saved (Matt. 10:22), or when he instructed them not to "fear those who kill the body but cannot kill the soul (*psuche*); rather fear him who can destroy both soul (*psuche*) and body (*soma*) in hell" (Matt. 10:28). The soul and the body are capable of being destroyed together, or are potentially separate, with the one being destroyed and the other "saved." This is the soul in its spiritual potential which formed such an essential part of Jesus' addition to the psychology of his time, and such an important element in his theology of the Kingdom of God.

Throughout chapter VIII we will see Jesus' intense concern for his "inner" dimension of the souls of men. He never tried to localize or describe it in detail. In this regard he was a poet rather than a scientific psychologist. He tells us what it is like: a seed that was dead and is now alive; inert soil that has received something potentially life-giving from the outside, and in the mystic union of soil and seed rises into the "higher" dimension of the new plant. It is like an idle worker, all potential until he is fulfilled in the new vocation of the Kingdom vineyard. The soul is like dough transformed by the bursting energy of the leaven, like a poor man who discovers a treasure in a field. He is the same old person, but now with the new wealth of the Kingdom, his soul's spiritual potential has become actual through the power of God.

Whether one can refer to this fulfilled soul potential in terms of "substance," any more than we can call the "psychic" a special kind of matter, is impossible to answer. I don't think Jesus would have done so; and in the light of modern psychology and biology, any concept of a crudely physical soul separate from the body would seem to be impossible. But perhaps in the new physics of non-solid matter, where one can conceive of an indefinite number of spatial systems, one can indeed catch a "rumor" of the soul fulfilled in the spiritual dimension.

Chapter VIII
Our Need for the Kingdom

But now let us bring the full impact of Jesus' teaching about the Kingdom to bear on the crisis of humanity, upon persons and their needs. This is where he put his emphasis: not on men and women as psychological creatures, but on persons as we stand under the judgment of God. The individual psyche is the point of sharpest impact of God's judgment. The burden of his love, the terror of his wrath, the insistence of his imperative, the warning of his condition, all come to most agonizing focus, like some cosmic laser beam, upon the inner human condition. Man's basic need is to reconcile himself with the imperative of God's love, to resolve the fragmentation of the cosmos and make the two realms of heaven and earth one within him; to transcend the old horizontal, temporal dimension of the physical and begin living in the eternally new, vertical dimension of the spirit. So it is that these absolute distinctions between love and wrath, heaven and earth, eternity and temporality, are for Jesus most characteristically expressed in more personal terms: "He who is not *with me* is *against me*" (Luke 11:23).

The Vocabulary of the Human Crisis
Jesus was interested in the psyche in its physical state. For him it was infinitely precious. "Even the hairs of your head are all numbered...You are of more value than many sparrows" (Matt. 10:30-31). He was also interested in the psychological dimension, and so laid claim to our affections, and commanded us to love God with all our hearts and souls (Mark 12:30). But it was to this third dimension of the psyche in its spiritual potential that he seems to have been most attentive. In describing this locus of God's special concern, there are three terms he regularly used.

The first, and surprisingly the least typical, is the word spirit (*pneuma*), referring to the spirit of God. Surprising, because one of Jesus' chief contributions to Old Testament thought was his emphasis on the reality of the Holy Spirit. But we must allow him to do this in his own terms, and they were unusual ones. The Old Testament taught that the spirit of God comes upon and within men at certain times and for certain special purposes (Is. 59:21; Micah 3:8; Ezek. 2:2, etc.). This spiritual incursion, however, is exceptional and temporary. Jesus, on the other hand, describes the coming of the spirit not only at certain times and for special purposes, but in an abiding and eternal way that re-creates the human psyche and constitutes the essence of salvation.

He had a vivid concept of the spirit of God as a presence external to the human soul, but capable of acting upon it. For example, he described his spiritual baptism in the metaphor of a dove, and Luke underscored its objective nature by adding "in bodily form" (Luke 3:22). The spirit of God acting to heal the human body was pictured as a "finger" (Luke 11:20), and he told the disciples of his experience of being "driven" by the spirit into the wilderness (Mark 1:12), and being "anointed" by the spirit in terms of Isaiah 61:1-2 (Luke 4:18). He identified the spirit as a "gift" of God to persons (Luke 11:13), as the source of the words they would speak in their own defense (Mark 13:11), and as an inner "treasure" of the heart out of whose abundance the mouth would speak (Luke 6:45). In these and other ways, Jesus portrayed the spirit as an objective presence that stood in most powerful opposition to the entire satanic realm (Mark 3:29-30); and as I shall show later, this demonic battleground is the human soul.

Another term employed to describe the presence of God within was power (*dunamis*). Three times the evangelists use it to refer to that which accompanies the Holy Spirit, and for all practical purposes can be identified with its action in a human life: "Jesus returned in the power of the Spirit" (Luke 4:14); "Stay in the city until you are clothed with power from on high" (Luke 24:49; cf. 1:35). For Jesus, power is that which accompanies the Son of Man as he returns at the end of time (Mark 13:26), and in Mark 9:1 is that which attends the coming of the Kingdom within an individual life: "There are some standing here who will not taste death before they see that the Kingdom of God has come with power." The essential being of God himself is power; and the life of the Kingdom is one filled with the power of his presence.

This points to the most typical description of the third dimension of the soul, which is Jesus' language of the Kingdom of God. In its most elemental meaning, the Kingdom identifies the spiritual presence of God. We have seen it as the eternal, vertical dimension of the cosmos into which we are called to enter. Now we come to that part of his teaching where, as we respond to the claims of God's justice, this same Kingdom enters into us, and re-creates us in the fullness of our spiritual potential. In its highest capability the human soul is a chapel which is only bricks and mortar until it becomes a place of worship. Then it is transformed into a living house of God which transcends its physical condition. As we try to gather together what Jesus said about this drama of salvation, there are at least six ways in which human need is expressed, and these are all variations on the single theme, our need for the Kingdom. The word "need" is used advisedly; for Jesus' theology of the Kingdom is intensely practical. It is not directed to some scholarly understanding of theological doctrine, but to the urgent needs of men and women.

Persons are Empty and Need to be Filled

"Being asked by the pharisees when the Kingdom of God was coming, he answered them, 'The Kingdom of God is not coming with signs to be observed'; nor will they say, 'Lo, here it is!' or 'There!' for behold the Kingdom of God is *within* you" (Luke 17:20-21). We must begin by understanding one thing clearly. For Jesus, the Kingdom of God was an experience of God's sovereign presence *within* the human psyche. It is this dimension that has been most studiously ignored by those writing books on the Kingdom in the last two generations; but it is exactly here that Jesus locates the most practical focus of his entire message. I have used the King James translation of this passage, because the phrase "Within you" avoids the ambiguity of other more recent translations, and because it is, I believe, more accurate. Without going deeply into this complicated discussion (cf. JGTJ-169-176), let me just summarize it.

The problem is whether to translate the Greek preposition *entos* as "within" or "among." In the one case, we have a clear reference to the locus of the Kingdom within the secret recesses of the human heart. In the other, one could see this as a more external, social phenomenon. It is a very important point, and this passage tends to be a kind of fork in the road for one's understanding of the Kingdom. There is some possible confusion in the translation of the Greek *entos*, although I find this confusion much exaggerated. The hard facts are these: In biblical Hebrew, primarily a written language, there is a possible confusion in the preposition (*beqereb*) which can mean both "within" and "among;" but in Aramaic, the spoken language of Jesus' day, there is none whatever. The words are distinct, and if one were translating the Aramaic for "among" into Greek, he would have to use *en*, and not *entos*, and that is what Luke avoids. In the formal Attic Greek of pre-Christian times, again there is possible confusion over the use of *entos*, which can mean either "*within*" or "*among;*" but in the Greek Old Testament, the New Testament and the spoken Greek of Jesus' day, there seems to be little or no confusion in the use of *entos*, which consistently means "within." Since the Greek of Luke 17:21 is clearly *entos*, since Jesus spoke Aramaic and not classical Hebrew, and since the Gospels were written in the common Greek of the first century, not the literary Greek of hundreds of years before, there would seem to be little choice but to translate this as "the Kingdom of God is *within* you."

This rendering is further supported by a wealth of evidence showing Jesus' concern for the Kingdom as an active presence within the souls of men. There is, for example, that intriguing statement in Mark 9:50, "Have salt in yourselves, and be at peace with one another." For the Hebrew, salt had a special religious significance in the making of an enduring covenant. To "eat of his salt" was a sign of lasting friendship. As a symbol of incorruptness salt was offered along with the sacrifices (Lev. 2:13). So salt came to symbolize a covenant relationship with God, and F. C. Grant made the creative suggestion some years ago that Jesus is making here a play on words. The Hebrew word for salt, *melakh*, sounds much like the word for "rule" or "sovereignty," *malak*. What he would be saying then is that men are to have the covenant, the sovereignty, literally the Kingdom of God, *within* them, if they would be at peace.

It is in such metaphorical ways that Jesus most characteristically expressed this inner dimension of the Kingdom. It is like a seed growing secretly within the human soul (Mark 4:26-29), like leaven expanding within the dough of life (Luke 13:20-21). It is the "word" of the Kingdom sown within the good soil which bears the fruits of the spirit (Mark 4:3-8; 13-20). In an extension of this metaphor, the good seed are the "sons of the Kingdom" who are wheat growing alongside of weeds (Matt. 13:24-30); and elsewhere it is a gift (Luke 12:32) or a valuable treasure that comes into a man or woman's life as a personal possession (Matt. 13:44-45). "For out of the abundance of the *heart* the mouth speaks. The good man out of his good treasure brings forth good, and the evil man out of his evil treasure brings forth evil" (Matt. 12:34-35). So "Give for alms those things which are within; and behold, everything is clean for you" (Luke 11:41). It is in giving of the inner fruits of the spirit — love, joy, peace — that we demonstrate the essential cleanliness of our souls, for "you will know them by their fruits" (Matt. 7:16; cf. Mark 7:14-23; Matt. 23:25-28). There is an abundance of evidence that for Jesus man is evil and in desperate need *within*; and the remedy he proposed is the filling of that needy soul with the only thing that can "save his life" (Mark 8:35): the spirit, the power, the Kingdom of God.

The problem is that the house of man's soul is empty; and even when cleansed of the demons, like the dumb man Jesus has just cured (Luke 11:24-26), however swept and garnished the house, if it is empty, then that banished demon will go and gather others more evil than himself, "and the last state of that man becomes worse than the first." The great aching need of the human soul is that it is empty, void of the only power in the world that can crowd out the demons.

Nowhere does this message come to more graphic and poignant focus than in Jesus' use of the metaphor of light and darkness. "The eye is the lamp of the body. So, if your eye is sound, your whole body will be full of light; but if your eye is not sound, your whole body will be full of darkness. If then the light in you is darkness, how great is the darkness!" (Matt. 6:22-23). The eye here is a metaphor of the human soul as an organ for the receiving of light. The lamp is a similar metaphor describing the psyche in the complementary activity of emitting light, a common figure of speech for Jesus, who describes the disciples as lamps set upon a hill proclaiming the word of the Kingdom (Mark 4:21; Luke 8:16). The metaphor of light is a typical reference to God who is the "light of Israel" (Is. 10:17), and to the children of the Kingdom whom Jesus calls to be the "light of the world" (Matt. 5:14).

In contrast to this, darkness is the symbol for anguish and death (Is. 9:2), for evil (Is. 45:7), for God's punishment (Is. 5:30; 47:5), for alienation from the light of God's presence (Is. 49:9; 60:2), in effect, for the *absence of God*. Elsewhere it describes the day of God's wrath (Zeph. 1:15; Amos 5:18-20), and has an especially powerful use in referring to the inner lives of persons: "We look for light, and behold darkness...We look for justice, but there is none" (Is. 59:9, 11). Jesus picks up this same imagery and contrasts the "sons of light" with those whose inner lives are like tombs, filled with darkness and "all uncleanness" (Matt. 23:27). They are destined to be cast into "outer darkness," which is exclusion from the Kingdom of God (Matt. 8:12; 25:30).

So, in this cryptic little parable, Jesus seems to be saying that the soul, like an eye, is that through which the light of God enters one's life. Like a lamp, it is also that from which the light of God's inner presence shines forth. If one's soul is sound, then the whole self is filled with this light, but if one's soul is not sound, he or she is filled with the darkness of God's absence, which is the very definition of an evil (poneros) soul. And if this potential light is darkness, how great is the darkness!

This is the ultimate tragedy. There is nothing so dark as that which stands in opposition to the light of God. There is nothing so empty as the soul from which the light of God's presence has been excluded. For the terrible fact about darkness is that it is pure nothingness, the condition of non-light, and in this parable it represents a spiritual vacuum. It is like one of those great, gaping "black holes" astronomers have discovered in the universe, caused by the collapse of matter, and into which other matter is sucked, only to disappear in the disintegrating blackness. The absence of God is an awful, destroying emptiness penetrating into the very heart of man. Our need is for God, and darkness is the symbol of that need. As Emil Brunner used to put it, we are made in God's image, but it is an "empty image" until it is filled with the only power that "fulfills" the human condition: the spirit, the power, the Kingdom of God.

Persons are Estranged and Need to be Reconciled

Our human condition is further described by Jesus as a tragic alienation. In the Genesis story, man's primitive fellowship with God has been broken by his wilfullness and pride, his desire to be his own God and to eat of the fruit of the knowledge of good and evil. And so we have been cast out of the garden, and our continuing need is to recover this primeval fellowship with him.

This is the real meaning of what later theologians called "original sin:" not something that each of us has done, or some blame that we inherit because of a mythological Adam; but rather sin is something we *are*, or better, *are not*, because of our humanity. It is a need that is built right into our human condition as God's incomplete creation. We are *originally* and naturally in need of God and his Kingdom, estranged from that to which we have been originally called. As Paul put it, we are by nature "children of wrath" (Eph. 2:3). Jesus brings this alienation to sharp focus in a series of contrasts which reflect the sword of judgment cutting across the human situation, separating what for him are the two essential conditions of mankind. We are children of darkness or children of light, children of the evil one, or children of the Kingdom. We are bad fish or good fish, tares or wheat, goats or sheep. What he is doing is calling us from our condition of alienation into a new condition of fellowship with God.

This alienation is our existence outside the Kingdom. It is the present experience of the wrath of God, a very important element in the power of that driving concern which was the broken and bleeding heart behind Jesus' teaching. This is the tragedy behind the refusal of the invited guests to come to the wedding feast (Matt. 22:1-10), and the motive that prompts the king to send to the highways and byways compelling people to come. But they are too busy; and this self exclusion from the Kingdom is the justice of God giving to us the freedom to reject his invitation if we will, to spurn the Kingdom feast of his loving presence, and choose instead the wrath of his absence, if we must. "Woe to you lawyers!" he said, "You did not enter yourselves and you hindered those who were entering" (Luke 11:52); "Unless your righteousness exceed that of the scribes and Pharisees, you will never enter the kingdom of heaven" (Matt. 5:20); "How hard it will be for those who have riches to enter the kingdom of God!" (Mark 10:23). There is a great and terrible loneliness to which men and women condemn themselves when they reject God's sovereignty; and this plumbs the very depths of hell.

Jesus did not usually refer to hell except to describe the end time (*eschaton*), but there is a consistent logic within the Kingdom to identify it as a completely tangible and present reality. On one occasion he calls the pharisees "children of hell," describing their present condition as children of satan (Matt. 23:15, 33). Another time the phrase "powers of death" has a certain present force (Matt. 16:18); and we see hell casting its shadow into history; for hell is where God is not. The cult of despair, so strong in the 60s, gives us a very real insight into the nature of present hell, into what the Jesuit, Gleason, calls the damned soul's tension between love of self and love of God. One of the most powerful illustrations for re-mythologizing hell as a state of infinite loneliness comes from the research of the psychologist, Frieda Fromm-Reichmann: "In the last analysis anxiety and fear of real loneliness merge where they are an anticipation of

101

the fear of ultimate isolation and separation, of the inconceivable absolute loneliness which is death." As one patient put it, "I don't know why people think of hell as a place where there is heat and where warm fires are burning. That is not hell. Hell is if you are frozen in isolation into a block of ice. That is where I have been." In such psychotic agony one can gain a new and terrible insight into the even more abysmal loneliness of the "children of hell" who are rejecting God: "O Jerusalem...How often would I have gathered your children together!...Behold, your house is forsaken and desolate" (Matt. 23:37-38); "But he will say, 'I tell you, I do not know where you come from; depart from me, all you workers of iniquity!'" (Luke 13:27). Man's problem is that he is in hell, which is the human experience of the wrath of God.

So it is in reunion that God meets this crying need, and the most beautiful picture of the resolution of our estrangement is still the parable of the prodigal son. Here is the rebellious son, in the far city wasting his substance, ruining his life, pouring out his inheritance, until he becomes aware of one awful fact. He is separated from the father; and in that shocking realization that is like peering over the precipice into the abyss of hell, he becomes aware of his estrangement. So he turns around, in every way that one must when he or she is reduced to an animal level, and he returns to the father. And in that marvelous reunion scene, we see the love of God reaching out to the alienated, refusing to violate the freedom of the son, but waiting for the prodigal to return. Our problem is that we are estranged; and Jesus' preaching of the Kingdom is his invitation, direct from the heart of God, to come home to the father's house.

Persons are Sinners and Need to be Forgiven

Jesus further sharpened the Kingdom dilemma in terms of the contrast between the righteous and sinners: "I came not to call the righteous, but sinners" (Mark 2:17). "There is more joy in heaven over one sinner who repents than over ninety-nine righteous persons who need no repentance" (Luke 15:7). The righteous are the "blessed ones" whose allegiance to righteousness is an indication of their present possession of the Kingdom (Matt. 5:10). They are the well as opposed to the sick (Mark 2:17), the secure as opposed to the lost (Luke 15:7), the sheep as compared to the goats (Matt. 25:31 ff.).

But once one has recognized Jesus' use of this terminology and his concern for persons offending against the law of God, one must observe that his teaching was more radical than that of John the

Baptist. John preached repentance from the sins committed against God's law; and this was typical of Old Testament Judaism. But Jesus went more deeply to the root, the "radix," of the problem. Only thirteen times is he recorded using the word sin (*hamartia*) or its correlates. His stress was more on what caused these symptoms of rebellion against God, what he called the "eternal sin," which is blasphemy against the Holy Spirit (Luke 12:10). This is the sin against the *aion*, against the eternal dimension of God. Blasphemy in this case means the taking lightly of the Holy Spirit, which is the severest form of rejection. What cannot be forgiven is not some act of rejection which, having been done is forever done; but rather it is the condition of soul that prompts the blasphemy which is the sin against the eternal. For Jesus, the most serious sin is not the breaking of a law or the doing of an unrighteous act, but the blasphemy which is our confirmation of that alienation which already exists between ourselves and God.

What Jesus did was to emphasize God's forgiveness for the sins that we commit. There is no debt too large that cannot be resolved, no act of rebellion too awful for the father's forgiveness; and this is one of the most liberating words of his teaching. If there were no soap in the world, if we could not get the stains off our hands, the dirt from our clothing, in the course of time our bodies would become black with smut and our clothing heavy with grime. The cleansing action of soap and water is not a luxury but a desperate necessity. Forgiveness is like that. It is the provision within the spiritual economy of God for the removal of the stains of guilt and shame, of memory and regret, of evil thoughts and motives, of the bitterness and despair that cover our lives, weigh us down and threaten to bury us beneath their weight. Forgiveness is God's provision for the creation of new motives and new desires within, so that it is realistic for Jesus to say to the forgiven woman, "Go and do not sin again" (John 8:11). Forgiveness is the knowledge that if God can forgive us, then we can forgive ourselves; for it is our own self-recrimination that fixes the stains of guilt within. We clutch our stains to our breast, as if we know we must be punished and are determined to do this ourselves. Forgiveness is another chance. It is the renewal of God's invitation to the feast. It is the intense awareness of the love of God. It is knowing that God does not hold against us the record of our misdeeds. Now this inner cleansing is not a luxury, but an absolute necessity; and the escalation of suicide in our time reveals the terrible weight of this unresolved burden.

Ultimately, for Jesus, forgiveness is the restoration of a relationship, and so it is in the reconciliation with the father that the ring and the shoes are restored, the fatted calf is killed — all symbols of the renewal of the worth, dignity and status of the prodigal son.

Persons are Bedeviled and Need to be Cleansed

This leads us to one of the most interesting, most searching, and also most controversial tensions through which Jesus views the Kingdom of God. Persons are bedeviled and need to be cleansed. This is the language of the demonic: Satan, and a galaxy of terms like beelzebul, devil, evil one, demon, viper and enemy. There is a revival of interest today in this subject. As Hal Lindsay has put it in the title of his book, *Satan is Alive and Well on Planet Earth.* We need, therefore, to re-examine the matter in terms of the Holy Word, because Jesus had a lot to say about the subject, and this, I think, is not well understood.

Let us begin with the Old Testament where there seems to have been a development in the idea of Satan. In its simplest form, the concept refers to any adversary, whether an angel on the Lord's business (Num. 22:22), or a man like David (I Sam. 29:4) who is called an "adversary," literally a "Satan." Then Satan assumes individual nature as a "lying spirit" (I Kings 22:22). Finally, in its highest expression, Satan becomes a proper name for one of the angelic sons of God who, as the servant of the Lord, acts as the accuser of men, the tempter to sin, the source of sin and physical ailments, the one who tries men's loyalty to God (Job 1, 2; Zech. 3:1-2; I Chron. 21:1).

It is not, however, until we come to the Jewish literature produced between the time of the completion of the Old Testament and the writing of the New, that we see the elevation of Satan to the position of a rival God (Assumption of Moses 10:1; Enoch 54:6). It is important to note that despite his objective existence, in this literature, Satan is thoroughly tied to man and the Jewish doctrine of sin. He is the personification of sin, the sum total of all that is sinful, and as such, exists as a rival God; but only so long as sin is possible, so long as man lives in a mortal state. When physical death ceases to have meaning in the final judgment, then Satan and his demons are automatically cast into hell. Satan's very being would seem to be somehow linked with the physical existence of persons before the final judgment.

But Jesus' Gospel was a "new garment;" and in his creative

104

teaching we see an approach to demonology that is grounded in Judaism, but reaches beyond his first century moorings in a strangely modern way. This is, of course, a highly debated matter, and what I am going to suggest makes no claim to inerrancy. To some it may sound very radical, to others quite natural.

While lecturing on this subject to a college class one day, there was a knock at the door. Since this was unusual, I opened it with interest, and in came a figure dressed in a red suit, with horns, a tail and a very business-like pitchfork. He, or it, walked to the front of the room and began to harangue the class to the effect that this foolish professor didn't know what he was doing when he denied the existence of an objective devil. Finishing his speech, he went out, slamming the door behind him. I do not know to this day who was behind the red mask; but someday perhaps I will, and then it may be too late!

What I am suggesting is that Jesus' view of Satan has only a superficial resemblance to this satanic visitor or to what Hal Lindsay and so many others are confidently presenting as the Christian view of the demonic. In my own research into this tangled subject, there are five propositions which describe what I find Jesus saying about Satan.

1) *Jesus talked of Satan as the representative of all that is in direct opposition to himself, to the Kingdom and to the spirit of God.* In the wilderness scene, Satan is described as the tempter of Jesus (Mark 1:13). In the parable of the sower (Mark 4:3 ff.), he is that which takes away the "word" sown in the soil of men's soul — the word which is intimately linked with the spiritual presence of the Kingdom "within." In the parable of the wheat and weeds (Matt. 13:24 ff.), Satan is the "enemy," the author of those weeds within the historic dimension of the field, destined to be burned, which stand in direct contrast to the true wheat of the Kingdom. In the parable of the strong man (Mark 3:27), we find the same opposition. The "house" of the parable is the man in the historical context who has been ruled by the dumb demon. There are at least two indications that the cleansing force, the "stronger than he" (Luke 11:22) who drives out the demon, is the Holy Spirit. The pharisees have charged that the power Jesus uses to exorcise this demon is none other than that of Beelzebul, and Jesus takes this accusation to be blasphemy against the Holy Spirit (Mark 3:29). Furthermore, the so-called "Q Source," where Matthew and Luke agree, clearly indicates that it is the "finger," the spirit or Kingdom of God, which

has entered that house and spoiled the goods of Satan (Luke 11:20). *2) Jesus speaks of Satan in close connection with physical man or woman whose body or mind is sick.* When the paralytic is lowered through the roof, Jesus identifies his paralysis as "sin" (Mark 2:5, 7, 9-10). He calls what appears to be epilepsy an "unclean spirit" (Luke 9:42), exactly what Beelzebul is called in Mark 3:30. After he has healed the dumb man, he identifies this physical (or psychosomatic) ailment as "Satan" (Mark 3:23), and one is reminded that demonology was the language of first century medicine and psychology.

3) Jesus used this vocabulary to describe persons whose inner natures are sinful because they are opposed to God. In two instances he is reported to have identified the pharisees as "offspring of vipers" (Matt. 12:34; 23:33), the viper being a traditional Jewish metaphor for Satan. In Matthew 12:34, the reason for this identification is that they are inwardly "evil," like a corrupt tree, like a man whose heart is evil. In Matthew 23:33 this charge is part of a series of parallel accusations which describe their inner natures as being evil to the point of death: "full of dead men's bones and all uncleanness." Demonology was the language of sin.

4) Jesus seems strangely reluctant to identify Satan as a separate, individual personality. His recorded use of the word "spirit" *(pneuma)* gives us an illuminating insight into the difference between his view of Satan and that of his Jewish contemporaries. When one separates the use of *pneuma* as it occurs on Jesus' lips from those times it obviously originates with someone in his audience or with the Gospel editor, a striking fact emerges. In the words of his contemporaries *pneuma* occurs sixteen times on nine occasions to refer to Satan or his angels. When the term occurs on the lips of Jesus, however, we see a curiously different usage. Eleven times on nine occasions it refers to the spirit of God, but never once does he use it clearly and unequivocally to refer to Satan or his demons. True, it occurs thus in four instances, but each is a special case. In Mark 6:7 it is the Gospel editor who attributes this language to Jesus. Mark 9:25 shows Jesus using this term for Satan, but he is quoting the child's father. In Luke 10:20 he is merely reiterating what his disciples have told him (v. 17), and correcting them: "Do not rejoice in this, that the spirits are subject to you" (v. 20). The word occurs in Luke 11:24, but as a parable where it is likely to be more symbolic. In Jesus' day the word *pneuma* had two main uses — to describe the spirit of God, and to identify that aspect of the human personality capable of relating to God. For Jesus' contemporaries, Satan had identity as a separate personality and partook of the same spiritual nature as God. This was their justification for using *pneuma* for Satan; and if Jesus had agreed with them, one could expect him to have done the same. But he didn't, and this is the crucial point. The startling absence of *pneuma* for Satan in Jesus' teaching suggests a reluctancce on his part to view Satan as either a rival God or a separate personality.

There are several passages that seem at first glance to negate the force of the above, but which in reality need not do so. In the temptation scene (Mark 1:13), there is no need to posit a rival God tempting Jesus. He would seem to be describing an inner experience of moral-spiritual struggle involving the desire for physical, temporal things, like turning stones to bread or gaining political power or being saved from death. We can expect him to use language his contemporaries could understand. The statement, "I saw Satan fall like lightning from heaven" (Luke 10:18) is a figurative way of saying what is the theme of this whole passage: "Lord, even the demons are subject to us in your name!...I have given you authority to tread upon serpents and scorpions, and over all the power of the enemy...the spirits are subject to you." Jesus has sent the disciples out to heal *sick men and women* and bring the word of the Kingdom of God *to men and women* (Luke 10:9), and this is the rephrasing of their reported success in contemporary terms. Jesus' statement to Peter in Luke 22:31, "Satan demanded to have you," when balanced by his other, "Get thee behind me Satan" (Mark 8:33), probably has a similar meaning. He is talking about the weakness of a soul not yet dominated by the spirit of God. In the parable of the sower (Mark 4:3 ff.), Satan is a separate personality, but in the explanation to that parable (vv. 14-20), he symbolizes the "birds," as only *one* of the figures that account for the failure of the seed to grow. The others — the rocky ground, the sun, and the thorns — represent tribulation, persecution, the cares of the world, delight in riches, desire for other things. Satan is just one of the *many* ways Jesus describes the sins of the flesh that get in the way of the entrance of the seed of the word of God into the soil of the soul. In similar fashion, in the parable of the wheat and weeds (Matt. 13:24 ff.), Satan is not a rival God, but "*all* causes of Sin" (v. 41).

5) All of this points to the conclusion that for Jesus, Satan is the representative of, and at times the very personification of men and women in a state of opposition to God. He desribes persons in

rebellion against the Kingdom as "evil" (*poneros*) (Luke 11:13, 34; Matt. 18:32, 13:49). Satan is "the evil one" (*ho poneros*, Matt. 13:19). The man who rejects the Kingdom is "an enemy" (*echthros*, Luke 19:27; cf. Acts 13:10). Satan is "the enemy" (*ho echthros*, Matt. 13:25; Luke 10:19). The clearest identification of Satan as sinful individuals comes in those passages where they are actually equated. In Matthew 23:33 we find the pharisees described as "offspring (or brood) of vipers," and then identified as the serpents themselves. In the Beelzebul controversy, Jesus is identified by his opponents as Beelzebul (Matt 10:25). This would be the greatest of insults, for they would be linking him with that which stands in the most direct opposition to the very heart of his life, message and person. He calls Peter "Satan," and then explains with an illuminating phrase: "For you are not on the side of God, but of *men*" (Mark 8:33). Not of principalities or demonic powers, but of *men*. Peter is still rejecting the dimension of God in his efforts to save his physical life, and running the risk of losing his soul in its spiritual potential. Finally, in the parable of the sheep and the goats (Matt. 25:31-46), the poetic balance requires us to equate "the devil and his angels" with the goats, which must in all probability be a reflection of those in his audience who "did it not to one of the least of these." Satan is linked throughout this material with the physical world of men and women in opposition to God.

I have developed the evidence for this point at some length because of the veritable barrage of demonic literature with which we are being inundated, some of it in the name of the Christian Gospel. Again, it all depends on where one goes for his sources of Christian theology. The Apostle Paul had a common first century belief in the demonic realm. I think Jesus did not. Many Christian theologians through the centuries have taught the existence of Satan as a separate personalitiy. I think Jesus did not. Rather, the Holy Word as it is found in what I consider to be its most primitive, Synoptic form presents Satan as the personification of the force of the physical as it stands in natural opposition to the spirit of God. Satan is the epitome and mythical representation of the darkened psyche excluded from the Kingdom of God. Satan is a certain natural force of rebellion against the spirit of God that resides in each soul. Satan represents the sin of men and women in all that Jesus meant by that concept. In this present age, where theologian and psychologist are trying to understand one another, we might identify what Jesus called Satan as the force of basic urges that are flesh-begotten and flesh-centered, or as a certain egocentricity that resists the sovereignty of God. And so it seems legitimate for Christian theology to de-mythologize and then re-mythologize Satan, because Jesus did so two thousand years ago. Thus Jesus brings the judgment of God to focus upon the human soul in another terrible antithesis. Persons are either sons of the Kingdom or sons of Satan.

And that is our dilemma. Satan is indeed very much alive and well on the planet earth. As the comic book theologian Pogo has said, "We have met the enemy, and he is *us*." There is only one power on earth that is capable of restraining and redeeming the demonic souls of men and women. As Jesus said, "If I by the finger of God cast out demons, then the Kingdom of God has come upon you." The sovereignty of God is our only defense against the hellish force of the demonic human self let loose upon the world.

Persons are Uncommitted and Need to be Enlisted

We come now to a very important phase of this discussion, where Jesus views the Kingdom of God as a vocation. At this point, he sets up a tension between a purposeless and a purposeful life, recognizing our need for commitment to someone or something that gives our lives meaning and direction. This is particularly clear in the first part of his parable of the laborers in the vineyard (Matt. 20:1-16): "For the kingdom of heaven is like a householder who went out early in the morning to hire laborers for his vineyard."

There are several indications that the figure of the vineyard represents the Kingdom of God as an experience within the present, historic lives of persons. They are called to labor within it at various times, some early, some late. It is a state of special favor with the householder, and people are rewarded for merely being in it. They are allowed to enter simply by responding to the call of the householder, and not by any special merit of their own. Furthermore, the strange economics of the parable reminds us of Jesus' practice elsewhere of illustrating a significant teaching about the Kingdom with some bizarre element, inconsistent with physical reality, but quite consistent with the dimension of the spirit (cf. Matt. 18:23-25). The unusual factor here is the giving of equal reward for unequal service. They all receive the same denarius, however long they have worked. It would seem that it is not the economic needs of the vineyeard, but rather the needs of the laborers, the nature of the householder, and some other subtle fact about the vineyard itself that prompts the householder to continue to hire laborers at the last moment, when they could not possibly be of real service, and then to pay them all the same wage.

The point is crystallized in the householder's question, "Why do you stand here idle all day?" Theirs is a double need: for something to which to commit their lives, and for the Kingdom of God. And in this dramatic call to a new vocation, Jesus brings together the driving imperative of the sovereign God of justice and the desperate predicament of the laborers. They are persons whose lives find meaning in work, and they are idle. They are those whose souls are made to be spent in the service of God, in this highest of human vocations; but they are standing outside, uncommitted in some common marketplace. Meaninglessness is one of the greatest contemporary sources of powerlessness in an overly affluent society, where our abundance of possessions has rendered us "idle" in terms of the sources of power we most desperately need.

And so, in the curious economy of the Kingdom, we are called to a working responsibility, where the rewards are absolute, one denarius for all, and where the greatest reward — the very definition of the reward itself — is simply being within the Kingdom vineyard. This is the end of the idleness, the waking of that sleeping potential within us, to which Jesus' call to the Kingdom vocation appeals with an insistence that sends the householder back to the market place again and again and again.

There is a "mustness" about this Kingdom experience that reflects the imperative of God's justice, and makes the image of the laborer or the servant most appropriate. Jesus constantly made use of this figure to describe the children of the Kingdom. He often referred to his disciples in his parables as servants (*douloi*); and the laborers in the vineyard, who later complain that they have borne the heat of the day, probably represent those like Peter in Jesus' audience who asked the question about the rewards of discipleship. "Lo, we have left everything and followed you. What then shall we have?" (Matt. 19:27). The servant, for Jesus, is the one who stands in a uniquely close relation to God (Matt. 13:27-28, 22:3; Luke 14:17). To be a servant is itself God's reward, and this is the most natural explanation of the parable of the unthanked servant (Luke 17:9). "Does he thank the servant because he did what was commanded?" The implication is that he deserves no thanks because it is reward enough to be allowed to plow the master's field. The servant vocation is such a redeeming privilege that nothing more can or need be added.

110

Persons are Dead and Need to be Made Alive

The judgment of God comes to its most agonizing impact upon the souls of men and women in the terrible contrast Jesus draws between those who are alive and those who are dead. This is not just a metaphor, but his most essential description of that condition of being or non-being identified by the contrasts between the empty and the filled, the estranged and the reconciled, the sinners and the righteous, the bedevilled and the cleansed, the uncommitted and the enlisted. Here is Jesus' ultimate statement about the love and wrath of God within the human situation.

The word "life" (*zoe*) is a technical term for Jesus, referring to the presence of the Kingdom of God within. It describes physical persons living in the vertical dimension of the eternal (*aion*). It is therefore a special quality of life that comes with the fulfillment of our highest potential, the quickening of the spiritual dimension of the soul. Jesus called it "eternal life" (*zoe aionios*). This is clearly seen in Mark 9:43-48, where the alternatives of "life" or "hell" are dramatically emphasized: "If your hand causes you to sin, cut it off; it is better for you to enter life maimed than with two hands to go to hell, to the unquenchable fire." The parallelism of "enter life," "enter the kingdom" (v. 47), clearly identifies the two in Jesus' mind. Hands and feet are the things people think they need within their present physical existence. They stand for those things which apparently get so out of proportion at times that they hinder entrance into the Kingdom of God. They are in and of themselves not necessarily a hindrance, but only when they cause us to sin, when they assume greater importance than the Kingdom.

There is a striking similarity between this metaphor and many other teachings of Jesus where such spiritual stumbling blocks are located within men's lives. In Luke 14:26-27 he warns that one's relatives or one's very life must not stand in the way of the Kingdom. In the parable of the wedding feast (Matt. 22:1-14), it is a farm or merchandise that prevents those invited from attending. In Mark 10:21, 23, a passage especially reminiscent of Mark 9:43-47, Jesus tells a rich young ruler that he must sell all he has and give to the poor, for it is hard for those with riches to enter the Kingdom. All of these hindrances represent some aspect of physical life. When parents, riches, farms, merchandise, hands, feet, eyes, and life itself receive more importance than they deserve, they must be cut off; and we see the radical nature of Jesus' teaching, and the terrible importance of this matter. This is all presumably going on in the pre-

111

sent, where it is possible to enter the Kingdom life "maimed," without those aspects of physical life which seem overly important, but *with* the other hand or foot or eye that have not become a hindrance. This is what Emil Brunner used to call "the eternal life in love" which God bestows on us, which is the essence of his own being. God's love is ultimately his presence with men, and this is the meaning of salvation: partaking of the very life dimension of God.

The antithesis of life is death, and humanity's greatest problem is that it is spiritually dead. Even as life identifies the soul's new being within the dimension of God, so death describes its spiritual non-being without the Kingdom. As Nels Ferre put it, man's non-being, his spiritual death, is the condition for, and the occasion of, love as the being and presence of God. It is to such "dead men" that Jesus directs his message: "Woe to you, scribes and Pharisees, hypocrites! for you are like white-washed tombs, which outwardly appear beautiful, but within they are full of dead men's bones and all uselessness" (Matt. 23:27). Jesus called them a "breed of vipers" (Matt. 23:33) and "children of hell" (Matt. 23:15), and warned the disciples of the "leaven of the Pharisees" (Mark 8:15) which is the "anti-leaven" of death. This would seem to be what Jesus was saying to those potential disciples who asked first to go bury their own dead before following him (Matt. 8:22; Luke 9:60): "Leave the dead to bury their own dead." He called them away from death to the proclamation of the Kingdom message of life.

In Matthew 10:6, Jesus sends the disciples to "the lost sheep of the house of Israel" and commands them to heal the sick, cleanse the lepers, and cast out demons, and "raise the dead" (v. 8). Those to whom they are to go are ones who deny him (v. 33) and will lose their souls (v. 39). In this context it would seem that there is more reason for taking this as a command to raise the spiritually dead, the lost, the demonic, the rebellious, and make them "sons of the resurrection" (Luke 20:35, 36), than as a command to raise the physically dead. When Jesus reports to the disciples of John that "the dead are raised," he is saying the same thing as "the poor have good news preached to them" (Luke 7:22). These are the "blessed ones" who take "no offense" at him (Luke 7:23), who are being brought from spiritual death to spiritual life. This would then be more compatible with the shock and surprise over the raising of Lazarus or the resurrection of Jesus than if the disciples themselves had been accustomed to bringing physically dead men back to life.

Life and death are the awesome alternatives which form the

aching heart of Jesus' concern for persons. In the parable of the lost son (Luke 15:11-32), he brings to a climax a series of parables, contrasting those who are "lost" with those who are "found," with the revelation that to be "lost" is to be "dead," and to be "found" is to be "alive again" (Luke 15:24, 32). In sone sense the boy was very much alive, but his riotous living is described as rebellion against the father, being in want, unworthy to be a son, sinning against heaven, lost and perishing. What seemed to be life was really death.

The parable of the rich fool is another that makes this awful point (Luke 12:13-21). The key lies in the dual contrast between two kinds of "life" and two kinds of "treasure," both of which cast into bold relief man's involvement in the judgment of God. There is a play on words here in the significant distinction between life (*zoe*, v. 15) and soul (*psuche*, v. 19), which can also be translated, life. The ideal life (*zoe*) "does not consist in the abundance of his possessions," but in being "rich toward God;" and we note that Jesus uses "treasure in heaven" elsewhere (Luke 12:33) to describe the Kingdom. The terrible alternative is the situation of the man (v. 19) who has much produce stored in his barn, but is not "rich toward God"; and in this complaisance of death, he plans to take his ease (v. 19). The shock of the tragedy comes in the shattering word, "thou fool," the same indictment Jesus levels against the five virgins who have no oil (Matt. 25:8) and the pharisees who are unclean within (Luke 11:39). This man's physical wealth has suffocated his spiritual potential, and this very night his soul is required of him. The question, "The things you have prepared, whose will they be?" suggests the non-being of death found elsewhere (Matt. 25:12) and we hear an echo of his warning to Peter, "For what does it profit a man, to gain the whole world and forfeit his life?" (Mark 8:36).

The curious and sinister thing about it all is that this hell of life without God is pictured, at least on the surface, as a very pleasant existence. Spending life's resources wantonly, taking one's ease in the castle of one's self-indulgence, could be a very comfortable way of life, and we are reminded that death, too, must be very comfortable. Spiritual death is symptomized by the complete indifference to God, to his justice and righteousness, that characterizes the true atheist, who simply does not care. An easy, uncomplicated, unagonizing style of life; but Jesus is saying that, in fact, it is a terminal illness. It is like the strangely comfortable process of freezing to death. The deepest night, the extent of alienation, the vacuum of emptiness is spiritual death.

The awful predicament of the human situation is this: without the radiance of God's presence, we live in the shadow of approaching doom, with the promise of death at the end of time, and the reality of that death in the present. We are weeds destined for the fire (Matt. 13:24 ff.); we are bad fish (Matt 13:47-50), virgins without oil (Matt. 25:1-13), unproductive servants (Luke 19:12-27), sons of Satan (Matt. 23:33), salt without savor (Luke 14:34), all destined to be "cast out" into outer darkness. This present living death is seen most vividly if one overturns the sermon on the mount and concentrates on the negative side, on Jesus' Ebal of the curse. This woeful, cursed life-in-death is comfortless; it is empty of God's righteousness; it is merciless; it is blind to the presence of God, poverty-stricken, anxious over much, bad fruit, evil treasure; it is the life of a fool whose soul is founded on dissolving sands. And we see the hell of God's wrath, the heart-broken absence of his loving presence, shrouding mankind in the dark night of the soul. And we hear Jesus' cry from the cross, as he participates with suffering and rebellious humanity in the very pit of hell: "My God, my God, why hast thou forsaken me?"

But Jesus did not leave us in darkness and death any more than God left him on the cross. The life to which we are called is life in the radiant presence of God. It is the immediate possession of something new, that we did not already possess — the spirit, the power, the Kingdom of God. It is the promise of life at the end, and the reality of that life in the present. The Kingdom is Jesus' victorious answer to the death of the soul. As Paul and the author of John beautifully summarized Jesus' Holy Word: "I came that they may have life, and have it abundantly" (John 10:10). "For the law of the Spirit of life in Christ Jesus has set me free from the law of sin and death" (Ro. 8:2). Hugh Ross Mackintosh pointed out years ago that an easy doctrine of sin is one of the marks of the age of "enlightenment," and also a sign of religious degeneration. I would add that this is often based upon a sentimental doctrine of God and a failure to bring his judgment to bear directly upon the souls of men. It is also, I think, the result of failing to base one's theology upon the Holy Word of Jesus.

Two world wars and a half century of continual crisis have shattered our confidence in inevitable progress, and brought a renewed sense of man's sin and weakness. This has been aided by clinical psychology, focusing attention upon the unhappy forces within the human psyche, and by the writings of certain philosophers and literary artists. European existentialists, like Sartre, Dostoevsky and Camus, with their concern for the inner man, have dramatized and popularized an agonizing concern for the abysmal tragedy of life. In a way this has all led us back to the place where we can more readily understand Jesus, who had such a sense of this heart-rending situation that the Gospels preserve a vivid picture of a man of sorrows, weeping over Jerusalem. His radiant difference from these despairing existentialists, however, is that he was committed to the *full* awareness of the justice of God, and herein lay the power of his message. He knew the hell of God's wrath in its complete and bitter darkness, *but he also knew the heaven of his love, the radiance of his redeeming presence.* And in this there is a measureless abundance of power.

PART FIVE

JESUS CHRIST, THE REVEALER OF THE KINGDOM

Chapter IX

Jesus' Self Portrait

It is in the person of Jesus that God's Kingdom becomes most available. As the Holy Word is brought to focus within the person and life of "The Holy One" (John 6:69), we see that Jesus' message about God cannot be separated from what he did, who he was, and what he said about himself. So the teaching of Jesus and the biography and identity of Jesus must go together. To separate them is to lose the historic point of greatest power in the revelation of the sovereign God. In this chapter I want to take another look at the Kingdom and its power in terms of the one who proclaimed it, to see how Jesus himself was involved in the Holy Word of the Kingdom.

A Reddish Beard?

What did Jesus look like? I have a painting on my wall which pictures him as a handsome man with steel gray eyes, long reddish hair and a reddish beard. And lest one think this is too fanciful, we must know that my painting is supported by a letter from a man named Lentulus to the Roman Senate, dated in the third century, describing Jesus as a "man of noble appearance, with curled hair, parted in front, falling dark and glossy over the shoulders, with a smooth high forehead, a strong reddish and irregular beard." That ought to prove the validity of my painting and settle the matter, except that the letter is probably spurious and is to be dated not from the third, but from the fourteenth century.

Actually, there are no known portrayals of Jesus primitive enough to be considered authentic. The early Christian theologians are silent on the subject. The closest is perhaps a bronze statue of Jesus which the historian Eusebius claims to have seen at Caesarea Philippi, picturing him as "an upright figure, clothed in a double cloak," but this comes from the fourth century, and the statue has long since disappeared (H.E. III:18). What we do have, however, is even more important than any authentic painting might be. That is a series of word portraits where the evangelists, and then Jesus himself, give us a clear picture of what he was like, who he was, and how he fitted into the proclamation of God's Kingdom. But first, we must get this discussion in perspective within the contemporary scene.

A Variety of Pictures

Modern history appears to have turned several decisive corners that have made recent decades radically different from the past. We have been experiencing a rapidity of change in every area of life that is leaving us all breathless, and driving some into pathological states of mind. Albert Toffler documented this chillingly in his book, *Future Shock*. The field of religion is not immune to this phenomenon, and we find ourselves today in a period of great theological change. Nowhere is this more true than in the area of Christology, the formal discussion of the person and nature of Jesus Christ. At no time since the first six centuries when the church fathers were hammering out the creeds of the church, has there been such widespread and vital ferment in this field.

One result is a growing pluralism among Christians in their understanding of Jesus Christ. Along with an escalating variety of life and thought styles in politics, economics and other areas, it is becoming apparent within the church that there is a growing independence of thought and increasing variance of view with regard to this important question. It is becoming harder for Christians to recite the Nicene Creed with complete honesty, and some churches are substituting in their worship locally generated creeds for these historic affirmations.

The changes to which civilization has been subjected in the last few decades are so extreme that there are many things that have probably gone beyond immediate recall. One of these is the luxury of orthodoxy, that is, of large groups of people agreeing within certain clearly defined limits on what they collectively believe about almost any subject, whether it be politics, economics or religion. The orthodoxy of the Nicene Creed, the first ecumenical creed, adopted at Nicea, near Constantinople in 325 A.D., wherein Christ was declared to be of one substance with the Father, but of two natures, fully God and fully man, is under serious attack, and may very well be on its way out as a vehicle for uniting the church. The current Christological ferment is well documented in a collection of essays edited by John Hick, entitled, *The Myth of God Incarnate* (1977), wherein we see a number of British theologians having great difficulty with the historic creedal statements about Christ.

Another side-effect of this pluralism is a series of quickly changing moods in Christian theology. Because of rapid communication, and what might be called "media overkill," we can go in a matter of months from one collective mood to another. When one thinks of the passage of various segments of American theology from the Social Gospel of the 1920's to the Neo-orthodox rebuttal of the 40's, to Existentialism, the Death of God, the New Humanism, Secular Christianity, Process Theology, a return to the Social Gospel in the 1960's, and Liberation Theology in the 1970's, one is reminded of a swiftly escalating stream as it plunges faster and faster toward some imminent cataract. Where it will lead no one knows; but one thing is certain: In the last five decades we have gone through enough theological movements to last any civilization several hundred years. The spin-off from this is that many who are involved in these various theological moods retain their stance as the currents of popular interest flow elsewhere; and in their wake more and more people are left with widely divergent views about religion in general and Jesus Christ in particular.

There are so many different pictures of Jesus being presented these days that a new type of book is making its appearance which gathers up the various modern portraits into a kind of comparative collage. The most vivid is perhaps *Son of God to Superstar*, by John Hayes, a paperback with a psychedelic cover. Christology seems to have made the popular bookstands!

And no wonder, with the fascinating variety of portraits being produced. S.G.F. Brandon, for example, in his book, *Jesus and the Zealots*, has pictured Jesus as a radical social activist, a member of a political group in the first century who attempted to overthrow the Roman government by murder and violence. Albert Cleage has described him as a black revolutionary in his book, *The Black Messiah*. Hugh Schonfield, a Jew, has disturbed many Christians in his book *The Passover Plot* by picturing Jesus as a scheming political figure who planned his apparent death and resurrection as a clever hoax to gain power and influence. Morton Smith's book, *The Secret Gospel*, portrays him as the founder of a secret society. Several, like A. Dupont Sommer and A. Powell Davies, have insisted that Jesus was an Essene, whose life was patterned after the Teacher of

Righteousness, an early leader of the community that transcribed the Dead Sea Scrolls. With our special fixation on sex, others have given us a picture of a very human Jesus, like Kazanzakis, whose book, *The Last Temptation of Christ*, describes him as a rather confused young man who seduced Mary Magdalene, was subsequently converted, and spent the rest of his life trying to make it up to her. This kaleidoscope of images is described by John Wick Bowman, in a little book appropriately titled, *Which Jesus?* One might ask, "Will the real Jesus please stand up?"

One of the major causes of this creative instability has been a lessening of the authority of the Bible, and in this case, the Gospels, as a source for theology. And many, like Bultmann, have turned inward for their theology, to the spirit of existentialism, where all kinds of subjects, from art to religion, are examined in terms of one's own inner life, one's own opinions and points of view; and one is encouraged to see himself in what he is examining, whether it be a painting, piece of music, a novel, or the life of Jesus Christ. A recent student of mine did a study project where she examined many contemporary images of Christ. She discovered that there was a positive correlation between the picture any particular author painted of Jesus, and what she was able to discover about that author. Albert Cleage's picture of Jesus as a black revolutionary, for example, looks strangely like Albert Cleage.

Each With His Own Brush

But this is not necessarily sinister. In my library I have a book entitled, *Each With His Own Brush*, in which the editor has gathered paintings of Jesus from the four corners of the globe. The immediately apparent fact is that each artist has pictured Jesus in terms of his or her own culture. The Chinese artist sees him with slanting eyes. The black artist sees him as a black man. To the white artist he is a white Anglo-Saxon. What this says to me is that there is validity in accepting the fact that each one of us is inevitably going to see something of himself in his image of Christ. Such existential freedom can constitute a serious distortion of the picture; but *if disciplined*, and if understood and accepted on those terms, this phenomenon can also greatly enrich our collective and total understanding of this figure who looms so large in history that it would appear no one mind, no one point of view, can encompass him in his entirety.

So, I am not going to attempt to give "the" definitive picture of

Jesus in this chapter, but only a few major guidelines for Christology, induced from the Synoptic Gospels in general and his Holy Word in particular. What I am going to suggest is that it is the biblical Jesus who provides the check on extravagance, the standard against which any one picture must be judged. The exciting thing for me has been to see the strange way this Synoptic Christ has of both embracing and transcending so many of these "mood images" of Jesus. For me to direct our Christological attention back to the historical Jesus is therefore to direct us outward, beyond our own frame of reference, our own point of view and theological "mood" into an area where most moods find some substance, and all stand under judgment.

Keeping One's Hold on History

The record is this: His name was *Jeshua Ben Joseph*, Jesus son of Joseph. Born approximately 5 B.C. in Bethlehem, the ancestral village of his parents, he had four brothers, or half-brothers, and at least two sisters, or half-sisters. Raised in Nazareth, he began his ministry at about the age of thirty. He was baptised by his kinsman John, and his ministry lasted from one to three years, at the end of which he was illegally crucified by the Romans under the procuratorship of Pontius Pilate. Three days later his followers ecstatically proclaimed that he had risen from the dead. This basic narrative gives us a clear and realistic picture of a human being who actually lived in a particular place at a particular time. This much is documentable, not only in the Gospels, but in the writings of such secular historians as the Roman Pliny (65 A.D.), and the Jewish general-turned-historian, Josephus, who was born about the time of Jesus' death. There are also ancient references in the Jewish Talmud to the antipathy to this one who claimed to be God. There is actually more written documentation for the life and teachings of Jesus than for any other figure of antiquity, and this despite the fact that in the first three centuries Rome deliberately tried to burn every Christian document it could find.

Jesus was an historical person and these are actual places. Galilee, where he made his headquarters, is today a lovely fresh water lake, and one can go water skiing where Jesus is recorded stilling the storm. Calvary remains as an outcropping of rock just inside an old church near the Jaffa Gate of East Jerusalem, and one can sift the dust of his life through one's fingers as he walks about modern Palestine. So the archeologists dig, and find the stones that he knew, and the bones of his friends, and perhaps the foundations of his old home. Not a God incognito, not a mystical legend, but a man in the flesh. Whatever else one affirms about him, this much must be said.

Jesus himself is recorded giving us the same picture. Someone said to him, "Good Teacher, what must I do to inherit eternal life?" and he responded, "Why do you call me good? No one is good but God alone" (Mark 10:17-18). He became tired and hungry, angry, and at times exasperated with his disciples. He didn't want to die, and was tempted to give up the whole wretched business. His teachings reveal the ability of a first-rate lay theologian, who thought and taught in certain consistent ways that give us a surprisingly clear profile of his mind. He had a few favorite illustrations, like vineyards, and light, and fathers, and growing things which he used in many different ways; and there were certain typical expressions, like the Son of Man, or The Kingdom of God, that are the signature of his thought. All of these are the natural characteristics of a fully human individual.

If one takes Jesus' humanity seriously, then whatever else one says about God's revelation in and through him must somehow be related to plain, ordinary, everyday history. One of the most important elements in the power of the Christian Gospel is that it is not only a set of ideas about God and his relation to men, but it is all wrapped up with an event in history. God's word has become most understandable and available to us in the humanity of him who proclaimed The Holy Word. The mystery of the eternal God who is spirit, glory and power, has become incarnate in thirty years of time and fifty miles of space, in the very human life of an individual who spoke words we can understand and analyze and verify. It is at this point that we three-dimensional creatures are most able to come to grips with God, to find a "handle" that we can grasp and hold onto in common ways that are consistent with our own humanity.

What Did Jesus Think About Himself?

The question is, who was he? Was this fascinating man just another charismatic teacher like Apollonius of Tyana who lived at the same time as Jesus very close to Palestine and whose teachings were recorded by his pupil Damis? Or do we have in Jesus one who towers above all mankind in some strange colossal majesty? The early church called him "The Holy One" (John 6:69; Acts 13:35; 4:30; I John 2:20); and the Apostle Paul and the authors of the Gospel of John and the book of Hebrews called him the image of the invisible

God (Col. 1:15), the incarnation of the eternal word of God (John 1:1-18), the son of God who upholds the universe by his word of power (Hebrews 1:3). Very extravagant language! The question of Jesus' uniqueness has been a troublesome one to the modern age, especially in the light of our growing knowledge of the many other religious leaders of antiquity and the biblical revolution that has raised the question as to whether or not the divine stature of Jesus was a mythical creation of an over-enthusiastic church. Was he after all only a particularly charismatic religious teacher who would be shocked and perhaps offended by the adoring worship of twenty centuries?

The temptation at this point is to leap to a defensive sermonic answer, and simply load the response with the elaborate statements of the later New Testament. My suggestion is that we begin with Jesus and open ourselves to his message about the Kingdom of God which is inextricably involved with a clear and compelling understanding of himself. This is a more risky approach, and demands that we place the exalted language of Paul, John, the author of Hebrews and the entire creed-creating church under the scrutiny if not the judgment of Jesus' own self-understanding. But if we are to take the Holy Word seriously as a source of Christian theology, this is what we must do; for Jesus had a great deal to say about himself. As far as I can see, it was this awareness of identity and mission that was the most unique element of his message. It was this that made his enemies want to crucify him as much as anything he did or said. Witness the reaction to his sermon at Nazareth (Luke 4), where he said that in himself the prophecy of Isaiah was even that day being fulfilled.

As I suggested in Chapter II, there are really three levels from which one can derive Jesus' theology, and this becomes particularly productive when looking for his understanding of himself, and his relation to God. There are first of all his direct words about himself, and this is a surprisingly large body of material. Then there are the theological assumptions which underlay what he said. These are not too difficult to detect, but one must examine all the Gospel sayings of Jesus in order to do this. Thirdly, there are his actions and attitudes apparent in the narrative, especially in those acts which are deliberate and repeated. This third source is the most difficult to confirm because it is so obviously dependent on the editors. But by identifying patterns of repeated action, like his intention to place his life in jeopardy, and by constantly testing the compatibility of the editorial narrative with the Holy Word, one can have some check on authenticity.

A Man with a Unique Mission

The usual way to approach this aspect of theology is to deal with the titles which were applied to Jesus. I count fifty such titles used in the New Testament to identify him (JGTJ-238). Among these there are six which occur often enough in the Synoptic Gospels to lay claim to being part of his own primitive self-awareness.

He called himself the Son of Man, Son of God, Messiah, prophet and Lord, and seems to have seen his mission in terms of the Suffering Servant of God, as found in Isaiah 53. It is the Son of Man that was his favorite. These titles, however, are so filled with ambiguity, and so highly controversial in their meaning, that we would do well to follow Jesus' lead, and not base our understanding of his sense of mission too heavily upon them. Going more deeply, there are four roles which the Gospels attribute to Jesus: judgment, authority, suffering and preaching. The chief one on which we shall concentrate here is the judgment role. It is quite apparent that the dominant note in the early church's understanding of Jesus' self-consciousness is that of his involvement in the judgment of God (cf. JGTJ-237-253).

Casting Fire Upon the Earth

The depth of Jesus' own thought comes where he pictured himself and his mission in terms of a series of graphically vivid metaphors. It is here that we find the most valuable raw material for Christology that is more immune to the excesses of a myth-creating community. It is here that Jesus' self-awareness is too subtly imbedded in all types of teaching, too regularly recurrent in all underlying sources, to be the creation of community or editor. This is the most defensible source for a Christology without extravagant myth, and is another of those great reservoirs of power within the Holy Word of Jesus.

"I came to cast fire upon the earth; and would that it were already kindled!" (Luke 12:49). There is abundant evidence that Jesus' use of fire in this passage is a description of his mission to cast before mankind the very judging presence of God. It was so used regularly in the Old Testament, in sections with which Jesus identified. Fire is that which accompanies the appearance of God (Ex. 3:2), and symbolizes his judgment against sin (Is. 66:16). Fire is equated with God's jealousy (Ezek. 36:5), his wrath (Ezek. 38:19) and his word (Jer. 23:29). It describes God's separation between the good and the bad (Is. 33:14). Out of thirty-two uses of the word fire (*esh*) in Isaiah, a book Jesus often quotes, nineteen refer metaphorically to God's judgment against sin. It is therefore especially pertinent to discover that in all probability Jesus is borrowing here from Isaiah: "For behold...by fire will the Lord execute judgment" (Is. 66:15-16a). The language, imagery and literary context of these two passages are so similar, that Jesus would seem clearly to be referring to Isaiah where God is offering his people either "a new heaven and a new earth" or the flames of his anger (Is. 65:13-66:24).

This impression is further strengthened by Jesus' use of fire elsewhere. On the ten recorded occasions, every one, if we include the case under disscussion, deals with the judgment of God upon sin. At one point he mixes the metaphor of fire with another which we have already discussed: "For every one will be salted with fire" (Mark 9:49). Like Mark 9:50, "Have salt in yourselves," the metaphor describes the incursion of the Kingdom of God into the human life, and this is a disturbing, refining experience — like fire, which also strangely preserves, like salt. This message of the Kingdom is not a set of intellectual ideas which are offered for our consideration. It is rather the very selecting fire of God's judgment, the crisis demand for a decision that always attends his presence, with the resulting separation of those for whom this fire means salvation (life, the Kingdom) from those for whom it means destruction. It is difficult to avoid the suggestion that the words attributed to John the Baptist are actually paraphrasing Jesus' own self-reference: "He will baptise you with the Holy Spirit and with fire" (Luke 3:16; cf. Heb. 12:29).

"Do you think that I have come to give peace on earth? No, I tell you, but rather division; for henceforth in one house there will be five divided...father against son" (Luke 12:51-52). The continuation of this long discourse in Luke and its Matthew parallel pursues this shocking theme. The Prince of Peace did not come to bring peace in the sense of preserving the self-righteous, inbred, narrow, nationalistic peace of the Hebrew status quo. He came rather to cast the refining and separating fire of God's judging presence upon the earth, and create a radical division within the Jewish family and even within his own disciple group, between the sheep and the goats, the wheat and the weeds, the sons of the Kingdom and the sons of the evil one, as they respond to the fire of God within his challenge.

Interpreting the Present Time

"You hypocrites! You know how to interpret the appearance of earth and sky; but why do you not know how to interpret the *present time?*" (Luke 12:56). Hypocrite seems to be one of those special terms Jesus reserved for audiences other than his disciples, almost always to warn of the judgment of God. So here he is speaking to an audience containing many scribes and pharisees, warning them of God's impending judgment. And the burning focus is upon "the present time." This use of the word time *(kairos)* here is consistent with our discussion of it elsewhere (cf. pp. 78 f). It is a limited period of decisive significance associated with some crisis act of God (cf. Jer. 10:15; 6:15), and is not infrequently used in the Synoptics to describe Jesus' coming (Mark 1:15; Luke 19:44; 18:30). If we compare Luke 12:56 with the only other Synoptic utterances having any similarity to it (Luke 19:44; 18:30), one is led to conclude that "the present time" referred to here is the crisis of Jesus' ministry, which in one way is the unique event in the history of God's redemption; but in another way is the same crisis always present when persons are confronted by a strong revelation of the Word of God. And so Jesus wept when he entered Jerusalem that last week, for they did not know the time of their "visitation" (Luke 19:44, cf. JGTJ-242).

Issuing the Call to the Kingdom

It is in the parabolic material that Jesus' mission sayings take on a special urgency. He pictures himself casting before men and women the selecting, dividing thrust of a call to enter the Kingdom of God, and that call separates the world into two basic realms. In the parable of the laborers (Matt. 20:1-16) he sees himself as a "householder" who goes again and again to the marketplace of the uncommitted world, inviting men and women to come and take their places within the vineyard of God's sovereignty. In the parable of the dragnet (Matt. 13:47-50), the metaphor changes to that of an uncommitted sea of fishes, and his call to the Kingdom becomes a net cast into the sea, gathering those who respond into the fellowship of the net. He pictures himself as the fisherman, casting the net of the Kingdom into the sea (cf. JGTJ-138). He said to his disciples, "I will make you fishers of men," and here he is telling a parable about fishing for men, even as through the parable he is casting the net of the Kingdom itself into the sea of faces before him. Some are caught up in it. They are attracted, and so they respond. Others swim away like fish who are frightened, or are diverted by the cares of their own little world.

In the parable of the wicked husbandmen (Mark 12:1-12), Jesus is the "beloved son" who reminds the servants of their obligations to the lord of the vineyard, and warns his opponents that they are not really residents of the spiritual fellowship if they do not accept the imperative burden of the lord of that fellowship. In one the most provocative of his self-portraits, Jesus takes the part of a sower who goes forth to sow (Mark 4:3-9; 13-20), and the seed that he casts upon the various types of soils is the "word," which is not only a word about the Kingdom, couched in parables that are hard to understand (vv. 10-12), but is the very Kingdom itself sown in potential life-giving power within the souls of men and women. If properly received, it grows up into the new spiritual individual. The crisis demand is that the soil of man's soul be prepared and so receive the Kingdom in word and fact. Here is a parable about the telling of parables, where the parable itself, the word *about* the Kingdom, is identified with the word which *is* the very Kingdom presence of God. Indeed, the parable is an instrument of crisis, sifting those who hear and understand this "mystery" (Mark 4:10-12) from those who hear but do not have the ears, the soil, the souls prepared to receive the deeper reality which is the Kingdom itself as spirit and power.

A Man with Unique Authority

In Chapter II we looked at the oracular quality of Jesus' teaching. There was a peculiar heaviness, a ponderous significance and power that accompanied his message and came out with particular force in statements beginning, "Truly I say to you..." This quality made his teaching stand out from that of all other charismatic, phrase-making teachers of antiquity. No one, they said, spoke like this, "for he taught them as one who had authority, and not as their scribes" (Matt. 7:29). This is an observation that can be verified by a comparative study of ancient religious literature (cf. UG). Literally, no one has spoken like this. The closest approximation I have found to the way Jesus spoke is in the sayings of Ezekiel where God himself is speaking.

Now this oracular quality seems to have been the product of several factors that can be identified. For one thing, it was a product of the content of his saying. The Holy Word of the Kingdom of God contains within it a profundity of meaning, an importance and urgency that was the essence of its authority. This quality seems also to have been a product of the way those who remembered and recorded the material conceived of him. They believed he was the Son of God, and certainly this must have caused them to present his words in this portentious light. But ultimately, the evidence points to Jesus himself as the most original source of this oracular mode, of this element of authority in his word. He had a conception of himself that was part of the authority of the Kingdom, and the initiator of that image in the minds of his hearers.

This is clearly seen in the parable of the pounds (Luke 19:12 ff.). A certain nobleman went into a far country to receive kingly power and then return. Calling ten of his servants, he gave them ten pounds, about twenty dollars, each, and told them to trade with these until he returned. When he did, he discovered that one servant had made ten pounds, another five, but a third had hid his money and made no increase because he was afraid of the "severity" of the nobleman. There are at least three indications that the nobleman was Jesus' own word picture of himself. In the first place, the words "went into a far country...trade with these till I come..." are typical of Jesus' insistence that he would go away, and after some delay return again. The parables of the returning bridegroom (Matt. 25:1-13), the returning "beloved son" (Mark 12:1-12), and the master returning to the waiting servants (Luke 12:35-40) are cases in point. Secondly, the receiving of "kingly power" (v. 15) in this far country is strongly reminiscent of Jesus' comment to the High Priest that he would be exalted to the right hand of God (Mark 14:62). Thirdly, the giving of the pounds to the servants is strikingly similar to the ways Jesus pictured himself in other parables, for example, sowing the seed in the parable of the sower (Mark 4:1 ff.).

Here we seem to have Jesus portraying himself as the nobleman who is leaving his servants a wonderful gift, and who will return to judge the manner in which it has been received and its burden of responsibility obeyed. There is a wealth of meaning here, but I want to underscore just one thing: the commanding authority of the nobleman. "Trade with these till I come...he commanded these servants...I was afraid of you, because you are a severe man; you take up what you did not lay down, and reap what you did not sow." The word "severe," or literally "austere" (*austeros*), is an interesting insight into the self-conception of this Jesus. One is reminded of his severe criticism of the opponents, of Peter and the twelve disciples: "Woe unto you, hypocrites," "Get thee behind me Satan," "How long am I to bear with you?" Severity would seem to be one ingredient in Jesus' sense of authority. He demanded everything from those who would follow him, even as he gave to them everything of himself. There could be no half-way measures, no fence sitters; they were either for him or against him, they either took up their crosses and followed, or they did not. The "austere" road he followed was a "narrow gate" that many would approach, but few would enter (Matt. 7:14).

This sense of authority comes out in other ways where we see Jesus viewing himself as greater than all the cherished institutions of the Jews: "Something greater than Solomon is here" (Luke 11:31); "Something greater than the temple is here" (Matt. 12:6); "You have heard that it was said to men of old...But I say to you" (Matt. 5:21); "The Son of man is lord of the sabbath" (Matt. 12:8). Greater than Solomon, or the temple, or Moses, and even the sabbath itself. Who is this who makes such claims to authority? No wonder they complained — or were shocked — or impressed!

One day in his home town of Nazareth, he was invited to preach in the synagogue. He was known to them all, and they were impressed by the reputation he had been acquiring in Galilee. So he read from Isaiah, where it says, "The Spirit of the Lord is upon me, because he has anointed me to preach good news to the poor...to proclaim the acceptable year of the Lord" (Luke 4:18-19). Luke summarizes the sermon he preached that day in one sentence: "Today this scripture has been fulfilled in your hearing." And those old friends, who had been initially so pleased at his "gracious words," were "astonished," and "took offense at him, " and tried to throw him off a cliff. An amazing story! What would it take to make one's old friends, his boyhood playmates and neighbors, so incensed they would want to kill him?

Let us not miss the compelling force of this scene. No doubt, as Luke suggests (4:30), he was critical of their narrow Judaism; but the sharp, penetrating point of the matter is what is stressed by all three evangelists. The passage he read said two important things. One was that God would judge Israel with an "acceptable year of the Lord" (Is. 61:2). This described the coming upon Israel of the love and wrath of God. The other was that God would send his "anointed" to bring the "good tidings" of his word. This was a familiar messianic passage, and all would have known it to be such.

129

Jesus brings both ideas to shocking intersection in himself; and Luke's brief summary of his sermon, "Today, this scripture has been fulfilled in your hearing," points to the awesome significance of his own coming with such authority — or such barefaced bravado — that one can indeed understand the violent revulsion that seized the congregation of old friends and neighbors. We must never underestimate the electrifying power with which this Jesus intruded into the luke-warm religious lives of his contemporaries. "I am not come to bring peace, but a division...to cast fire upon the earth." This was evident that day in Nazareth, and raised the question, who is this who speaks with the very judging authority of God?

A Man with a Unique Function

To examine this question we must go even farther, beyond the pictures of Jesus in a preaching-teaching role, casting the message before men and women, to the place where in a strange way he himself has become that message. In these sayings, Jesus brings the fire of the Kingdom to flaming focus in his own person, and we are on the brink of a more subtle dimension of Christology. In Mark 8:35 he is comparing two kinds of men. One is going to save his soul; the other will lose it. The sufficient extra for salvation is whether or not the self is denied "for my sake." His person and his message coalesce and are both together the criterion for the entrance of the Kingdom "with power" into the human soul (Mark 9:1). The same idea occurs in reverse fashion in Mark 8:38: "Whoever is ashamed of me and of my words...of him will the Son of man also be ashamed." The rejection of Jesus is tantamount to the rejection of the Kingdom and the power of God. In Luke 12:8-9 the same thing is said in both positive and negative fashion: "Every one who acknowledges me before men, the Son of man also will acknowledge before the angels of God; but he who denies me before men will be denied before the angels of God." In the missionary charge to the seventy disciples, he again identifies himself as the focal point of the crisis: "He who hears you hears me, and he who rejects me rejects him who sent me" (Luke 10:16). The same phenomenon continues in the parable of the ten virgins (Matt. 25:10), where it is only in company with the bridegroom (Jesus) that the invited guests are able to enter the Kingdom feast.

The parable of the sheep and goats (Matt. 25:31-46) presents one of the most unique illustrations of this close connection between the person of Jesus and the Kingdom crisis: "For I was hungry and you gave me food, I was thirsty...I was a stranger...I was naked...I was in prison...You did it to me...You did it not to me." The identifying criterion of the blessed ones is their service to others, which is in effect a service to, and obedience to, Jesus, who is present in this act of love. It is upon such involvement with him that the final issues of Kingdom judgment are to be decided. This figure of Jesus with his awesome self-consciousness, forbids us to take lightly his call to the Kingdom, and his personal involvement in that call. John would seem to be an accurate interpreter of this Synoptic Holy Word, when he describes Jesus as the incursion into a darkened world of the very judging radiance of God: "This is the judgment, that the light has come into the world, and men loved darkness rather than light" (John 3:19).

So his enemies were right: "You preach yourself" (John 8:13), and John further presses this function in calling him the door, the way, the truth, the life. There is abundant testimony to Jesus' consciousness of being the very crux of the issue in accepting or rejecting God. So he functions in a practical as well as profoundly theological way, in providing a means of entrance into the Kingdom that is visible, tangible and understandable to our human minds.

Is He the Only Way?

But this raises a large question: can one find access to the Kingdom apart from Jesus and the historical Christian faith? At times in the New Testament it would seem there is no other way. In John, Jesus is recorded saying, "I am the way, and the truth, and the life; no one comes to the Father, but by me" (14:6). The author of Acts records Peter saying, "There is salvation in no one else, for there is no other name under heaven given among men by which we must be saved" (Acts 4:12). This strain of exclusivism is clear in the later New Testament, and has come to be the generally accepted answer to this question. But it has caused great anguish to many through the years who have become aware that Christians do not seem to have a corner on brotherly love, or social concern, or even devotion to the presence of God in their lives. And they are reluctant to condemn to hell all men and women throughout history who have not known about the historical Jesus of Nazareth. Many of my students have rejected Christianity because they feel it is too narrow and exclusive, and not realistic in terms of the way things are in the world.

On the other hand, there is evidence that this exclusive strain represents neither an adequate statement of the Holy Word of Jesus, nor the full substance of the faith of the early church. There are many indications that the Kingdom of God transcends the first century, and has been available through the ages wherever men and women have been confronted by God, whatever they may have called him. In the parable of the wicked husbandmen (Mark 12:1-12), the vineyard, representing the Kingdom of God, is inhabited by unfaithful servants throughout a long period of time, and it was not until after they had beaten one messenger, and wounded another, and treated others shamefully, that the "beloved son" finally came. One is reminded here of Jesus' indictment of Jerusalem: "killing the prophets and stoning those who are sent to you! How often would I have gathered your children together...and you would not!" (Luke 13:34). Here is God's Kingdom presence available long before Jesus of Nazareth. In the continuation of that discussion with the opponents, the Sadducees try to trap him with one of those tired theological conundrums. A woman had seven husbands, and the standard question of those who did not believe in the resurrection was, "In the resurrection, whose wife will she be?" (Mark 12:23). Jesus' answer goes to the heart of the matter which is their misunderstanding of and their disbelief in the resurrection: "Have you not read...'I am the God of Abraham, and the God of Isaac, and the God of Jacob?' He is not God of the dead, but of the living." In other words, Abraham, Isaac and Jacob are *already* sons of the resurrection. In his response to his mother and brothers who wish to speak to him, Jesus' answer seems to go beyond a narrow parochialism: "Whoever does the will of my father in heaven is my brother, and sister, and mother" (Matt. 12:50). Jesus' concept of the Kingdom was never so restricted, never so parsimonious as to limit the sons of that Kingdom to those who were his contemporaries or their descendents.

I suppose the major defense of this larger view of the Kingdom comes right out of the nature of this concept itself. If we are talking about the spiritual presence of God, then, paraphrasing something T. W. Manson said years ago, there is no need to ask whether the Kingdom of God is past, present or future, any more than whether God himself is past, present or future. God and his Kingdom are eternal. What Jesus is saying about his particular function is that in him the Kingdom is particularly available. At that momentous time, the Kingdom was especially "near." But it had always been available wherever men and women loved God and accepted his sovereignty.

This is exactly the point Paul and John were making in their great Christological statements, probably to counteract this very kind of exclusivism that has unfortunately become identified with the New Testament. For Paul, Christ was the image of the invisible God, *first born* of all creation (Col. 1:15 ff.); and this eternal Christ was with Moses in the wilderness as what he called "the supernatural Rock" (I Cor. 10:4). John talked of Christ as the eternal Word of God, *from the beginning*, who in the fullness of time became flesh and dwelt among us. For Paul and John, and I think for Jesus in the Synoptics, the activity of God in redeeming men and women in the Kingdom and through the Christ who is his eternal Word, has been going on as long as persons have been available to respond, in every age and every civilization. What Jesus and others in the New Testament are saying is that in him God's love is uniquely available, God's Kingdom presence especially near, the issues of God's judgment particularly crucial.

What this says is that wherever men and women have found God, in whatever way and by whatever name, they have found Christ. So, indeed, he that is the eternal Christ, the eternal Word of God, who is now incarnate in Jesus, is the only way; for union with him is the meaning of salvation. To incarnate the eternal Christ in Jesus of Nazareth, for John and Paul and the early church, was certainly not to limit him to 30 years of time and 50 miles of space.

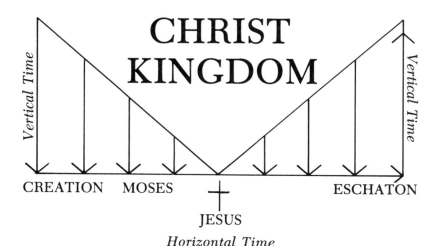

Horizontal Time

133

As the diagram attempts to show, the eternal Christ of the ages is available throughout history, but in and through the historical Jesus, this Christ — what Jesus in the Synoptics called the Kingdom of God — becomes peculiarly available. This one insight, more than almost any other, helps to clarify New Testament theology. What Jesus called the Kingdom, John called the eternal Word, and John and Paul both called the eternal Christ. All are references to the spiritual presence of God. So when Jesus sees himself performing this crucial function in bringing the Kingdom presence of God near, we are on the brink of the profoundest of all theological mysteries, the doctrine of the trinity, which he did not develop, but which the church has been trying to understand ever since.

This opens up the possibility for salvation in any context, wherever men and women are genuinely claimed by God. It does not denigrate Jesus, but rather exalts him; for the Jesus Christ that the New Testament is talking about is not just a lone Palestinian rabbi. He is rather the incarnation of the eternal Word of God, who acts where and when he wills. What the historical Jesus does is to give us a visible standard by which we can judge what is or is not the revelation of God — whether in the Old Testament, the New Testament, or completely outside the Judeo-Christian tradition.

A Man with a Unique Identity

But the age-old question continues: "Who is this Jesus?" Can we not be more exact in terms of his relation to God? It has been a great temptation for theologians through the centuries to sharpen the focus of Christology; but Jesus was noticeably restrained, even when pressed by his enemies. Nevertheless, he did offer two phrases in identifying himself that went beyond his usual practice of simile and metaphor.

The Son of Man

The first of these is the Son of man. The question is often asked, "Did Jesus refer to himself as the Messiah?" This has been a matter of considerable debate, because the Gospels record a strange reluctance on his part to use this term for himself, or even to have others use it of him. A German scholar, Wilhelm Wrede, made much of this at the turn of this century in his book, *The Messianic Secret*, where he insisted that Jesus did not see himself in these terms, but that it was superimposed upon the material by the early church. Wrede's thesis was based upon a thoroughgoing historical skepticism, and this permitted him to take the recorded material more casually than I am able to do.

He is, of course, right that the word "messiah" is resisted by the Synoptic Jesus. It does, however, occur in all four Gospels. In Mark 14:61, Jesus is asked, "Are you the Christ, the Son of the Blessed?" and Jesus said, "I am." There is an oblique reference in Matthew 11:14; it occurs in one of Jesus' resurrection appearances in Luke 24:26; and in John 4:26 he says, "I who speak to you am he." But the word "messiah" obviously doesn't occur very often, and I am prepared to agree with Wrede to the extent that the use of the term is mostly, if not entirely, to be attributed to the early church.

More characteristically, and less open to the intrusion of post-resurrection vocabulary, are those places where Jesus speaks of himself as the fulfillment of Old Testament prophecy (Matt. 5:17). This he does on eight separate occasions (Matt. 5:17) and some of these are clearly messianic; for example, the sermon at Nazareth, where he reads about the Messiah from Isaiah 61, and then announces that "Today this scripture has been fulfilled in your hearing" (Luke 4:21). The violent reaction of his friends and neighbors is described by Luke to show the seriousness of his claim.

But this is still not exactly to the point, and here I think is where Wrede's whole discussion misses the issue. Jesus was a creative mind. We have seen this constantly throughout our study. He used his own vocabulary, and when describing himself this became especially apparent and important. He talked of himself not as Messiah, but rather as the Son of man. On 43 separate occasions he is recorded using this term, and any assessment of Jesus' own self estimation must somehow come to terms with this phrase. There are two critical questions one must face. 1) The first is whether or not this was a messianic title, or simply a reference to "a man" in some generic sense. Gustav Dalman pointed the way to an answer years ago when he showed that when this phrase occurs without the article "the," it refers to any man; but when it includes the article, as in "the Son of man," it is a title, and thus it always occurs in Jesus' vocabulary. Since Dalman, an enormous amount of research has gone into this question, and although there is still no general consensus, it would seem that certain things are becoming clear. F. N. Borsch has recently shown in his book, *The Son of Man in Myth and History* (1967), that there is a growing acknowledgment that the background of this messiah-like title is the widespread occurrence in Middle Eastern theology of a myth of the Heavenly Man, who is son of God and savior of men. He is indebted to Sigmund Mowinckel, whose book, *He That Cometh*, is still the classic summation of the evidence that the concept of the Heavenly Man did have messianic significance, and was available for Jesus' use in the first century. According to Mowinckel, the most primitive roots of the Heavenly Man lay in the widespread oriental idea of the divine 'primordial man," the God "*anthropos*" (Man) which was of mixed Iranian and Chaldean origin. This divine man is the cosmos itself in human form, and the world is thought to have arisen from him in one way or another. He is a pre-existent heavenly being who will come at the end to judge the world. The Jewish conception of the Son of man is a variant of this oriental myth, mixed with many other elements. It was used in certain circles to denote a person who in many ways corresponds to the Messiah. In Daniel, the Son of man is a pictorial symbol of the people of Israel (Dan. 8:17), but the chief Jewish source from this period (c. 300 B.C.) is the Similitudes of Enoch (I Enoch 37-71). There is much evidence therefore that this was a title with messianic overtones.

2) The second critical question has to do with whether or not Jesus referred to himself as the Son of man in some special sense. If the Gospel records are any indication, he certainly did. He used this phrase as a synonym for "I" (Mark 9:31; Matt. 17:22). He described himself in a parable in these terms (Matt. 13:37), and employed it on occasions to imply special authority (Mark 2:10; Matt. 9:6; Luke 5:24). In this way he spoke of his own mission (Luke 19:10); and seems to have used the title at least once in the corporate sense of Daniel 7:13-14 (Matt. 10:23). Despite its abundant occurrence, two generations of scholars have been reluctant to see this as anything more than what Philipp Vielhauer has called a post-resurrection development. It was the early church that attributed this messianic title to the Jesus who had no such pretensions. It is regularly pointed out that the Son of man sayings often seem to be referring to a third person, "You will see the Son of man...coming" (Mark 14:62); and as Vielhauer maintains, the teaching about the Son of man is incompatible with what Jesus said about the Kingdom of God.

This is a highly technical discussion, and as I have suggested, far from settled; but there is a growing body of evidence that supports the conclusion that in most cases, we are justified in seeing Jesus using this title for himself in both an historical and eschatological (end-time) sense. For one thing, the discussion of the last thirty years has shown that these highly skeptical treatments of the Son of man are usually based more on the presuppositions and methodology of classic Form Criticism than they are on the evidence of any particular passage. (cf. Chapter I). The debate then needs to be conducted on this deeper level. One of the most impressive bits of positive evidence is the clear fact that although the concept of the Heavenly Man was fairly widespread, the title, the Son of man (*ho huios tou anthropou*) occurs almost exclusively in the words of Jesus. It is found once in Daniel, a few times in Jewish intertestamental literature, but never in the New Testament except on the lips of Jesus. It is one of those signature phrases, like Kingdom of God, that all of the Gospel sources attribute to Jesus. As Borsch points out, if the early church invented this as a title for Jesus, we would have to assume that between the time of his death and the hardening of the earliest strands of tradition, an intervening group of disciples became so captivated by the Son of man idea, and were so persuasive, that they managed to get all of the Gospel editors not only to agree to use the unfamiliar Son of man instead of Messiah, but to do so in ways that would fail to make it crystal clear that it was Jesus to whom this phrase referred. One would further have to suppose that the early church allowed this Son of man group to pass out of sight without a trace, and then imposed a complete restriction on the use of this term so quickly that no one else is recorded using this phrase within the Christian community. All of this seems so highly unlikely that one wonders that the point even needs to be argued.

As far as I can see, Jesus borrowed this phrase from his Jewish environment, and for his own reasons used it to refer to himself in ways that otherwise would probably have required the more familiar Messiah. One can conjecture that Messiah was so variously understood by his contemporaries, and in ways with which he would not want to identify, that he chose the more unfamiliar title into which to pour his own content.

What was the Messiah?

In the Old Testament there are two great images of this special emissary of God's salvation, the Messiah, or the Christ — its Greek translation. The first is a kingly image: "His name will be called 'Wonderful Counselor, Mighty God, Everlasting Father, Prince of Peace'" (Is. 9:6b), essentially a heavenly figure. The second is a thoroughly human, suffering image, where the Messiah appears as a strange, poignant figure who takes upon himself the agonies of men and women in order that they might be redeemed: "He was wound-

137

ed for our transgressions, he was bruised for our iniquities; upon him was the chastisement that made us whole" (Is. 53:5). Normally these images were kept separate, and it was as a king that the Messiah was commonly understood.

Now Jesus did a very unusual thing that certainly must have puzzled his hearers. For the first time, as far as anyone has yet been able to determine, Jesus united these two images into one: the heavenly king and the earthly, suffering Messiah were the same figure. "They will see the Son of man coming in clouds with great power and glory," "The Son of man must suffer many things...and be killed" (Mark 13:26; 8:31). No wonder Peter and others were puzzled and even offended (Mark 8:32). No one had ever talked this way before, and here is another of those signature phenomena that identify the creative mind of the historical Jesus. So I think it is quite defensible to say that Jesus thought of himself as the Messiah, if one keeps in mind that he described this in his own way and on his own terms.

The Son of God

The early church often referred to Jesus as the Son of God, and it is here that Christology comes to a particularly sharp focus. Although this was not a common phrase with him, there is running throughout his teaching an awareness of a very special relationship to God which this phrase accurately expresses. We have seen this in his use of such intimate expressions as "Abba, Father" (Mark 14:36), and in the familiarity with which he talked about God, something no Hebrew would have presumed to do. It comes to vivid expression in his parable of the wicked husbandmen (Mark 12:1-12).

> "A man planted a vineyard, and set a hedge around it, and dug a pit for the wine press, and built a tower, and let it out to tenants, and went into another country. When the time came he sent a servant to the tenants, to get from them some of the fruit of the vineyard. And they took him and beat him, and sent him away empty-handed. Again he sent to them another servant, and they wounded him in the head, and treated him shamefully. And he sent another, and him they killed; and so with many others, some they beat and some they killed. He had still one other, a beloved son; finally he sent him to them, saying, 'They will respect my son.' But those tenants said to one another, 'This is the heir; come, let us kill him, and the inheritance will be ours.' And they took him and killed him, and cast him out of the vineyard. What will the owner of the vineyard do? He will come and destroy the tenants, and give the vineyard to others."

This is an especially interesting parable, for here Jesus seems clearly to be borrowing from the Old Testament, and then adding certain new elements typically his own. The background and probable origin is the parable of the vineyard in Isaiah 5:1-7:

> "Let me sing for my beloved a love song concerning his vineyard: My beloved had a vineyard on a very fertile hill. He digged it and cleared it of stones, and planted it with choice vines; he built a watchtower in the midst of it, and hewed out a wine vat in it; and he looked for it to yield grapes, but it yielded wild grapes. And now, O inhabitants of Jerusalem and men of Judah, judge, I pray you, between me and my vineyard...When I looked for it to yield grapes, why did it yield wild grapes?...I will remove its hedge, and it shall be devoured...For the vineyard of the Lord of hosts is the house of Israel, and the men of Judah are his pleasant planting; and he looked for justice, but behold, bloodshed; for righteousness, but behold, a cry!" (Is. 5:1-7).

There are many similarities between these two parables not readily apparent on the surface. Eighteen Greek words in Isaiah are closely paralleled in Mark: for example, "dug a pit...built a tower,,,hewed out a wine vat." The general content is the same. Here is an area of God's special favor where the Lord has required the servants to be faithful. When they are not, punishment is to follow. When one sees that the historical and literary contexts of the parable in Mark are quite similar to those in Isaiah, it is hard to avoid the conclusion that Jesus saw his own relation to Israel in the same way. It was a common thing for him to come across a situation in his own life that mirrored something in the Old Testament, and for which the prophet's words were particularly appropriate. So he used Isaiah's parable to make his point.

But now note what he did to it. There are three innovations in Jesus' version that tell us something essential about his mind. First, he added the figure of the husbandman, which Mark identifies in verse 12 as the Jews in Jesus' audience. This is of profound significance, for in one incisive stroke, Jesus cut the Jews out of the place of special favor in Isaiah's parable, and put them in their place as husbandmen rebelling against the requirements of the Lord of the vineyard. The second thing he did was to change the meaning of the vineyard symbol. It is no longer a metaphor for the nation of Israel, but rather for the spiritual Kingdom of God within which reside those of any race who render the fruits of obedience. In one brilliant stroke of his parabolic brush, he took the realm of God's favor out of the local and national, and transformed it into the realm of the eternal and spiritual.

There is one other change which is of supreme significance. Jesus has added the figure of the beloved son. Note the historical setting. This is the last week of his ministry, and he is in Jerusalem. He has already predicted his own death (Mark 10:32), and has been constantly challenged as to the authority of what he says and does. He has been reminding the Jews that they are hypocrites who are not bringing forth fruits worthy of repentance (Luke 13:15; Matt. 3:8). Then, in verse 12, we see that the Jews understand him to be directing the parable against them, and it becomes apparent that here again Jesus is picturing his historical situation in the parable. Here is the beloved son, bringing the reminder of the requirements of the Father's love to these unfaithful servants of the Kingdom, and seeing murder in their eyes even as he tells the parable. The beloved son is none other than Jesus himself, who brings the challenge to accept the sovereignty of God, and offers to give himself as a sacrifice to that cause. Here is Jesus' brilliance at its best, taking a familiar Old Testament parable, and changing it at crucial points in ways that must have been breathtaking, or completely maddening. Those opponents in his audience must have been infuriated, because they got the point: the sharp, damning point.

Chapter X

The Living Parable of the Cross

A Man with a Unique Method

So they crucified him; and the crucifixion became one of the most important aspects of the Gospel as it developed in the history of the Church. The cross became its marching standard, the celebration of the Lord's Supper the heart of its liturgy, Good Friday and Easter the hub of the Christian year and the atoning death of Christ the focus of Christian theology. And the question arises, was this part of Jesus' deliberate plan, or was it all just the early church turning its experience of Jesus' death into theology in order to rationalize a mystery that first shocked them and then gradually asserted the kind of hold that the sacrificial death of any good man would have upon those for whom he had died? Did Jesus have a clearly developed conception of the cross?

As far as I can see, Jesus did not make as much of his death as did the early church. The center of his message was life, not death. The heart of his theology was the Kingdom, not a cross, as this entire book should document. I do not think Jesus would have anticipated the pivotal significance which the cross was to have in Christian history. But he did see the significance of his coming and its relation to the "coming near" of the Kingdom; and the cross was an integral part of that total picture. So, in that sense, he did have a concept of the atonement, although to call it a "doctrine" is probably too formal. I would say that the raw material for the later doctrine was thoroughly implicit in the conscious life and teachings of Jesus.

Choosing the Lonely Road

One of the important introductions to the ministry of Jesus is the temptation in the wilderness (Matt. 4:1-11; Luke 4:1-13). Here Mat-

141

thew and Luke describe him wrestling with his own human nature (cf. p. 121), trying to decide how to use the abilities he must have known he had. In this scene of inner struggle, the evangelists summarize the three alternative roles that various of his contemporaries wanted him to adopt. These were the messianic roles of popular expectation. "If you are the Son of God, command this stone to become bread." Some wanted him to be an economic messiah and feed the hungry; and the miracle of the loaves and fishes dazzled the disciples with this possibility, as it continues to do to those who want the Christian church to put its primary emphasis on the important task of feeding the starving multitudes. But Jesus warned the disciples to "beware of the leaven of the Pharisees" (Mark 8:15); and in the sermon on the mount he clarified the priorities as he had worked them out in his own mind. "Do not be anxious about...what you shall eat...Is not life more than food...But seek first his kingdom" (Matt. 6:25-33). The temptation here would seem to have been to pursue the popular route of economic aid and reform; but he rejected this and chose a lonelier road.

Then he was taken to the brow of the hill overlooking the cities of the Jordan valley: "To you I will give all this authority and their glory." Be a political messiah. Throw off the yoke of Rome! — a glorious mission; and many in his own disciple band wanted him to choose that route. This brilliant, charismatic figure was a natural, and James and John were already working it out that they would sit at his right and left hand when his power was established. And through the centuries, as today, people have tried to turn the Kingdom into a political program. But Jesus rebuked the sons of Zebadee, "it shall not be so among you" (Mark 10:45), and corrected the misconception of Pilate, "My kingship is not of this world" (John 18:36). And again he chose the lonely road.

Then in his mind's eye he climbed to the pinnacle of the temple in Jerusalem, the top of the high stone wall forming the southeast corner of the temple area. "If you are the Son of God, throw yourself down from here." The ancient tradition was that the Messiah would come at the end of time from the sky in just such spectacular fashion, and there were many who confidently expected Jesus to fulfill this apocalyptic role. "Tell us, when will this be, and what will be the sign when these things are all to be accomplished?" (Mark 13:4). Then, as now, there were many people who saw Jesus as an apocalyptic Messiah; and they interpreted his teaching about the Kingdom as a blueprint for the end of the world (cf. pp. 225 f). But again he disappointed them: "Of that day or that hour no one knows...only the Father" (Mark 13:32). Again he chose the lonely road of misunderstanding, of suffering and death; and the shadow of the cross fell over his entire ministry, from Calvary back to the temptation in the wilderness.

He Knew He Was Going to Die

If we take the Holy Word seriously as an adequate expression of the mind of Jesus, then we must concede that he not only was aware of the necessity for his death and intended to see it through, but that he had thought deeply about it and was concerned to relate it to the rest of his teaching. There are fourteen occasions where he is recorded predicting his own death. He prayed that this "cup" might be removed (Mark 14:36), but accepted it as God's will and seemed "constrained" that it be accomplished as soon as possible (Luke 12:50; cf. Mark 10:38; Matt. 26:54, etc.). The intensity of his rejection of Peter who was objecting to this line of teaching ("Get behind me, Satan!" Mark 8:33) suggests how determined Jesus was to accept the way of the cross. The validity of Mark's summary is seen in the way in which all three of the Synoptic Gospels reveal patterns supporting his generalization that Jesus began to teach "his disciples" that he must suffer and die. Eleven of these fourteen predictions are given to an audience of the twelve disciples (Mark 8;31; 9:12; 10:32-34, 38; 14:21, 27, 36; Matt. 26:54; Luke 12:50; 17:25; 22:37).

But Peter's mystification is also ours: why was it "necesary" for him to die? This is one of the most disturbing assertions to come out of these Gospels. Why this terrible necessity that seems to be such an important part of Jesus' sense of identity and mission? If one examines these passion sayings, there are at least three basic answers that seem to be true to the Holy Word. These approach the matter from three different angles and cover the entire range of his thought.

It Was Necessary Because God Is God

In the first place this necessity says something about the nature of God, and here we see Jesus viewing the atonement from God's point of view. He believed that the purpose of his death lay in the intention of God; and that night in the garden he put it very clearly: "thy will be done" (Mark 14:36). This is seen in the ways in which he viewed the cross as the fulfillment of Old Testament prophecy. He was the "shepherd" smitten for the sheep (Mark 14:27; Zech. 13:7), the suffering servant "wounded for our transgressions" (Luke 22:37;

Is. 53:5), the "corner stone" which the builders had rejected (Mark 12:10; Ps. 118:22). It would seem that for Jesus the cross was not a bribe offered to change the mind of an angry God, as some classical theories of the atonement have suggested. The cross was rather an expression of the will of God, revealed to the prophets and fulfilled in him.

This means that from God's point of view, the cross is a reflection of the nature of God himself. All four elements of God's justice subtly permeate these passion sayings of Jesus. The love of God is clearly reflected in the images of the shepherd smitten for his sheep, and the body broken for his disciples, a love that forgives his murderers from the very cross itself (Mark 14:27, 22). The wrath of God is apparent in the comparison of Jesus' death with the drinking of the cup of God's fury, and the payment of a ransom for those in bondage (Mark 10:45; cf. Is. 51:17). The command of God emerges insistently in the constant reference throughout these sayings to the necessity that this death must take place, and in the reminder it gives that men and women must produce the fruits of the vineyard (Mark 12:1-12). Finally, the conditional nature of this sacrifice is revealed in those places where Jesus invites the disciples to take up their own crosses, to eat those symbols of his body and blood — in other words to accept the burden of participation and choice for him or against him which this event lays upon them (Mark 8:34; 14:22 ff.). The cross was necessary because this is the nature of God's justice; and in his life and death Jesus' supreme intention was to reveal the person and nature of God. The cross describes something that is objectively true, apart from us, which resides in the very nature of God.

It Was Necessary Because Man Is Man

But there is another angle from which he viewed the necessity of the cross. It was necessary because people are the way they are. We must not separate the atonement in Jesus' mind from his concern for humanity and its sin. The cross is an indictment of the entire human race. His classic description of this is the parable of the unfaithful servants (Mark 12:1-12). God has called men and women to be servants in the vineyard of his Kingdom; and with their response went the command to produce the fruits of the vineyard. But the servants wanted the benefits without the responsibility, for such is the quality of the human ego. So the Lord of the vineyard sent one special emissary after another to remind these unfaithful servants of the obligations which attend his blessing. Some of these they beat, others they killed, and finally he sent his beloved son. So Jesus, facing his opponents during the last days of his life, aware of their intentions and his own mission, adds this crucial change to the familiar Isaiah parable. The servants say, "come, let us kill him and the vineyard will be ours." Then we can have the benefits once and for all without the constant insistence of the Lord of the vineyard. Here is the ultimate rejection of God's claims, the rejection of his beloved son. And so the cross is an indictment, not only of the degeneration of the noble religion of the Jews in the first century, but of all men and women who in their erotic self interest are rejecting God. For this is our way; and if he had come today instead of the first century, would we, whoever we are, have been any different?

What Jesus is saying is that in the mystery of human sin and God's redemption, love must go all the way before men and women can have true liberation. The cross is God's unique method of salvation, for such love is the most compelling force there is, and this is what it takes. Abelard was expressing such an understanding in his twelfth century theory of the atonement, wherein the cross was seen as a "moral influence," a means of deepening our repentance, of shattering our pride, of driving us to our knees before such love. This is what it means for God to create us as humans and not animals, to give us the supreme ability to make essential choices, the most fundamental of which is the acceptance or rejection of his love. His respect for our freedom makes him vulnerable to our sin; it makes it possible, nay, inevitable, for Christ to be crucified. And so this vulnerable God must woo us. He must make us want to obey him; and his way is love, where he gives himself through his beloved son to meet the harsh conditions of his own justice.

It Was Necessary Because Jesus Was Jesus

We must never separate our doctrine of the atonement from Jesus' sense of personal identity and mission. In these passion sayings there are three types of self image controlling Jesus' thought. 1) The first is a series of metaphors where he sees himself and his death as that of a special person in close relationship to God, whose death derives its significance from that fact. He identifies himself with God's "Shepherd," who stands next to God himself and is destined to be smitten in response to the will of God: "For it is written, 'I will strike the shepherd and the sheep will be scattered'" (Mark 14:27; Zech. 13:7). The death of the shepherd is the occasion for God's judgment

145

upon Jerusalem. He is God's suffering servant messiah who is to be wounded for our transgressions (Is. 53:12), the beloved son sent to remind the unworthy servants that their claim on the vineyard of his special favor was unjustified (Mark 12:1-12), the corner stone which the builders rejected, but which through that rejection was to become the head of the corner (Mark 12:10). There is a richness and consistency to these images and their Old Testament meaning which points to a coherent pattern in the mind of Jesus.

2) He also saw his death in prophetic terms, as he commented in the ironic style typical of him: "It cannot be that a prophet perish away from Jerusalem" (Luke 13:33). His concern to "cast fire upon the earth," to present men and women with the judgment of God, is articulated within his conception of the "baptism" of his death, which he is impatient to have accomplished (Luke 12:50). The prophetic proclamation of God's Kingdom was his chief concern, and to this was inevitably attached an awful price.

3) But did he see himself in sacrificial terms, as theologians through the ages have insisted? I think he did, and the pattern of his thinking is especially clear and well documented at this point. There are ten passages which describe his awareness of death in these terms, and they are all given to the twelve disciples, as Mark generalizes: "And taking the twelve he began to tell them...that the Son of man must...give his life as a ransom for many" (Mark 10:35-45; cf. Mark 8:31; 14:22-25; Luke 12:50; 22:37). This sacrificial conception is all tied up with his view of himself as the suffering messiah who pours out his life to make "intercession" for the transgressors (Is. 53:12), and is given in language filled with the priestly imagery of sacrifice: drinking a cup, being baptised with a special baptism, like a lamb that is led to the slaughter as the agent of our redemption (Is. 53:7; Luke 22:37).

And so one cannot examine the teachings of Jesus carefully without being aware that built into his understanding of God's Kingdom and his own person and mission was this tragic necessity. It could not have come out any other way, for that is the nature of God; that is the nature of human sin; that was the nature and intention of Jesus.

The Living Parable of the Cross

All the above points clearly to what may for some be a shocking conclusion. The cross was Jesus' ultimate teaching. It was an acted parable in the best tradition of the Old Testament prophets. The evidence I think is clear. He went to his death deliberately. We have seen that. During the last week he performed several acted parables. One was the triumphal entry where he was acting out the prophecy in Zechariah 9:9, "Lo, your king comes to you; triumphant and victorious is he, humble and riding on an ass." The cleansing of the temple was a dramatic demonstration of the need for a thorough housecleaning within first century Judaism. He seized upon the sight of a fig tree in leaf, but without figs, to predict the destruction of an unproductive Jerusalem (Mark 11:12-14, 20-26). The last supper was an acted parable from start to finish, with its imagery of poured out wine and broken body, all within the elaborate symbolism of the ancient Jewish passover. The crucifixion occurred within a circle of acted teaching wherein several times Jesus used this ancient technique of the prophets (cf. Jer. 13:1 ff; 18:1-7; Hos. Chs. 1-3; Zech. 6:9-15 etc.).

But this was not just another parable, whether verbal or acted, with a contrived story and symbolism which teaches us something about God. The cross was more than that because it was a real event in the history of God's salvation. It was a "living" parable of all that Jesus believed about God and man and himself; and we see that the crucifixion is an integral part of the Kingdom itself, which is all atonement. The cross is a living story where Jesus' theology of the Kingdom and the active love of God reaching out to men and women come together in this rending experience and produce the profoundest message of all.

Here on the cross was the wrath of God in all his intolerance to sin; the awful declaration that sin is serious, that there is a sternness in the God of justice belying the efforts of every age to sentimentalize his love. And we hear the tragic cry from the cross that gathers up all the hopelessness of men and women lost in the dark night of their own souls: "My God, my God, why hast thou forsaken me?" And the earth shook, and the veil of the temple was rent, and we seem to have here the darkest afternoon of all creation when we see the fearful demands of God's wrath and the awful gulf of rejection that yawns between God and man.

In this compassionate figure is the love of God reaching out to save men and women from the tragedy of sin, and giving himself to satisfy the demands of his own wrath. There is within the nature of God a love that is universal, eternal and unchanging; a love that redeems his wrath, and makes the cross not a symbol of anger, but a symbol of love so great that it is able to stoop to earth and encompass

147

within it the thorn of man's rejection, the pit of hell and Christ on the cross.

Through the cross is revealed the yearning imperative of God's justice, emerging from the tension between his love and his wrath. "You shall love the Lord your God with all your heart, and with all your soul, and with all your mind, and with all your strength" (Mark 12:30). The Christian church has always found God's condemning, saving, commanding power most overwhelming at the foot of the cross. Whoever said that salvation was easy? Whoever said that great love was a comfortable experience? It is rather compounded of great longing, great expectation, great sacrifice, great heartbreak.

And so from that awful sight, the condition of God's justice pierces the hearts of those who in their freedom dare to behold and see. At the foot of the cross, the saving burden of that love, the searing abrasion of that wrath, the awesome force of that imperative, become a question, a choice, a responsibility, a judgment upon persons. He who looks long and hard at the cross faces the command to carry his own cross and take his own place beside the suffering figure. And in that transfixing experience, the cross and the figure upon it become a door into the Kingdom of God. For Jesus is not alone. His agonizing disciples who hang with him there are not alone. God hangs with them on that cross. And in this redeeming fellowship, the cross becomes a throne of Grace.

So the cross was a pivotal event in the history of God's redemption. It really did change things decisively in human history; for ever since that awful afternoon God is more available to us because we are more available to him.

A Man with a Unique Future

But Jesus must not be left on that cross; for there is a vertical dimension to his teaching, as to his life, that transcends such a tragic end. This comes out in two dramatic predictions that reach into the future: his resurrection and his return as eschatological judge. Jesus' thinking about his death always concluded with the resurrection. There are at least six sayings where he seems to have anticipated this event (Luke 17:24-25; 22:18, 29; Mark 8:31; 9:31; 10:33-34). But more important than these, and less open to post-Easter reflection, are the many sayings where he talks of himself as the returning Son of man and eschatological judge. Out of a total of 43 occurrences of the phrase "the Son of man," seventeen refer to Jesus as judge at the end time. In the parable of the sheep and goats, it is the Son of man who is seated upon the throne, separating the sheep and goats (Matt. 25:31-46). In the parable of the closed door Jesus pictures himself as the householder who closes the door and orders the wicked ones to depart (Luke 13:23-30). In the parable of the ten virgins, it is only in company with the bridegroom, a symbol Jesus uses elsewhere for himself, that the waiting virgins go into the eschatological feast (Matt. 25:1-13; cf. Matt. 9:15; Mark 2:19; John 3:29).

The nobleman in the parable of the pounds, who returns from the far country and rewards the servants, is another of Jesus' eschatological self-portraits. This will be discussed more fully in Chapter XIV. The point here is that the life and death of Jesus as he views it contains this vertical dimension of the eschaton, which is the dimension of the spirit; and it is here that his involvement in the Kingdom of God finds its consummation. What this means is that the crucifixion is more than just the death of a good man. It is an open door into the larger realm of the spirit where the messianic career of Jesus is seen to be part of God's eternal plan.

Jesus intended to go to the cross, but he did not intend that to be the last word. His own conception of his messianic career seems to have transcended this awful experience in the certainty of his resurrection, exaltation and coming again as eschatological judge. It is at this point that Paul and John and the early church picked up the Christology of Jesus and developed it into the highly sophisticated theology of the incarnate word, first born of all creation, the image of the invisible God in whom the fullness of God was pleased to dwell (John 1:1 ff.; Col. 1:15 ff.). This certainly goes beyond the teaching of Jesus; but it would seem that in the more primitive words of Jesus the seeds of this later cosmic Christology are clearly visible.

The Power of His Uniqueness

And so the uniqueness of Jesus manifests itself in many ways. It is not something created by the later church, but springs spontaneously from his person and message in the Synoptic Gospels; and it is here that we find the sources of power in the Christology of the church. He was a human being who walked the very streets one can see in the excavations of ancient Jerusalem. As I have pointed out (Chapter II) he had a brilliant theological mind, a stunning ability to teach and preach, and a charismatic spirit that drew to him large crowds of adoring disciples. But there was so much more that led people to sanctify his words and clutch at his garments and call him the Holy One of God. He had a sense of mission that went far beyond the old prophetic concern to proclaim the word of the Lord. He seemed to assume that in his teaching he was casting the very fire of God's Kingdom presence before men and women, bringing them to judgment in a way that made his coming the day of God's visitation. There was an awesome authority to his words that possessed the oracular holiness of God himself. The prophets proclaimed the divine word of God; but Jesus proclaimed the Kingdom of God as *his own word*. No one who could be taken seriously has ever talked this way before or since. He saw in his own life and teachings, in his own person, the issues of salvation. So closely did he identify with the eternal purpose of God that the crux of the choice for or against God's Kingdom was the choice for or against himself.

There was a consciousness of supreme personal identity in everything he said which caused him to insert himself into material he borrowed from the sacred words of the Old Testament, and which found peculiar expression in his references to himself as the Son of man, and the beloved Son of God. And so out of this shocking self-awareness, pregnant with Christological significance, he saw the climax of his mission in that terrible symbol of the cross where the love and wrath, the command and condition of the justice of God could find such profound expression; and then in the resurrection which gave eternal, vertical, eschatological meaning and validation to his holy life and word.

At every point, we are faced with a uniqueness which directs us to the more highly developed Christology of Paul, John and the early church. The heart of it is not a particular title, or some special claim to divinity such as occurs in John where he says quite clearly, "I and the Father are one," or "He who has seen me has seen the father" (John 10:30; 14:9). In the Synoptics it is the sense of identity with God and his Kingdom which pervades everything he said or did that is the ultimate source of his Christological power. He was literally consumed by his conscious oneness with God. In his Holy Word, he came to cast the fire of God's presence upon the earth; and in a strange, incomprehensible way that will always challenge our understanding, that fire was and forever is himself.

PART SIX

THE CHURCH, THE FELLOWSHIP OF THE KINGDOM

Chapter XI

Jesus' Concept of the Church

Within the judgment drama of the Kingdom of God, there are three principal actors: God the sovereign, Jesus Christ the revealer, and the man or woman who is called to become a child of the Kingdom. In Chapter VIII we discussed persons outside the Kingdom as being in great need — as sheep lost in the darkness, as the prodigal far from home. We come now to another role Jesus gives to men and women in this drama of salvation. This time it involves those who are *within* the Kingdom of God. These are the sheep within the fold, the prodigal returned to the father, the growing grain within the field, the fish within the net — all figures of speech describing the fellowship of the Kingdom.

He Had a Concept of the Church

There are some who say that Jesus had no concept of the Church. It is pointed out that the word for church, *ekklesia* (Heb. *qahal*) occurs only twice in the Synoptics: once in Matthew 16:18 where Jesus says to Peter, "You are Peter, and on this rock I will build my church;" and again in Matthew 18:17 where he is talking about church discipline, "If he refuses to listen to them, tell it to the church." Since these passages are both peculiar to Matthew, there is a real question as to whether or not Jesus used this term at all. Others point to his expectation of an immediate end of the world. If he believed that, then there would have been no necessity for talking about a church that would survive in the years to come.

I confess that I have great trouble with this logic. For one thing, I do not find Jesus predicting that the end of the world would come soon (cf. Chapter XV). But even if he did, one is reminded that some of those who wrote most voluminously about the church, like the apostle Paul, or the author of the book of Revelation, probably thought the end was near. Mainly I object to this approach to the question. What one must do to discover Jesus' concept of the church is not engage in prejudgment, or look for any particular word like *ekklesia*, but let the text speak for Jesus on his own terms. Throughout this book, I have shown that in this supremely creative mind we have someone who liked to use his own terminology, and who thought so individualistically that people often had difficulty understanding him. This, I think, is a case in point. If we will let Jesus talk in his own way, we will see a clear concept of the church emerging from these Gospels.

The Church in the Parables of the Kingdom

Although there was a perfectly good Hebrew word available for church or congregation, *qahal*, Jesus seems to have been reluctant to use it. Instead, he spoke in parables portraying the Kingdom experience as a corporate fellowship: a field of growing grain, a vineyard with many laborers, a net full of fish, or a household with many servants. So typical is this of his teaching, that I find it axiomatic that whenever a person is described entering the Kingdom, he finds himself in a close spiritual relation to others of like experience. There is something inevitably social about the experience of the Kingdom of God in Jesus' teachings. In the parable of the laborers, for example, the householder calls the idle workers out of the marketplace of their uncommitted existence into a working relationship with others who have also responded (Matt. 20:1-16). This is exactly the picture Paul gives of the church: a spiritual fellowship of those bound together by a new relationship of closeness and obedience to God (I Cor. 12:12-31). In Jesus' parable, these laborers have entered into a corporate experience of the sovereignty of God, and this is precisely what later Christian theologians called the church. It suggests that for a Christian to deny membership in and responsibility for the church is to deny the very nature of his existence as a servant of the Kingdom.

The Church in Certain Typical Words and Phrases

Jesus' concept of the church is further seen in a galaxy of special terms which he used to identify those who had entered the Kingdom. They are the "blessed" ones (*makarioi*), the sons of the Kingdom, the sons of Light, the brethren (*adelphoi*), who do the will of God (Matt. 12:50). These form a coherent group with a special relationship to Jesus and the Kingdom.

His favorite description seems to have been that of servant (*doulos*), and there are some fascinating patterns of consistency in his use of this term, especially if one correlates the way the servant appears in the parable with the audience to which it is given. In ten different parables, he identifies one of the central figures as a *doulos*. In each case, the way in which the servant functions in the parable depends on whether Jesus is addressing an audience of disciples or of opponents (ACHJ-99). Seven of these are addressed to disciple audiences, and there the *doulos* is always in the center of the parable, as an unforgiving servant, or an unfaithful servant (Matt. 18:23-35; Luke 12:41 ff.) who is judged for failing to respond in some way to the demands of the Kingdom. One can always identify the servant in the parable with the disciples in the audience to which it is given. But in those parables where the central figure is someone other than a servant, with the *douloi* running errands in the background, the audience is always an opponent one, made up usually of scribes and pharisees, and these must be identified as the wicked husbandmen or the reluctant guest of the parable (Mark 12:1-12; Matt. 22:2-14; Luke 14:17-24).

Such patterns of continuity point to a conception within Jesus' mind of a specially called out people with a unique relationship to the Kingdom of God. This had nothing to do with the use of a particular term, like *ekklesia*. Rather it permeated his entire thinking as a kind of basic premise, and in that way provided the theological raw material for the later concept of the church. Whether or not the church remained true to Jesus in its later self conception is perhaps another matter, and is one of the burdens of this chapter.

The Twelve Disciples: Primitive Clergy

Within this metaphorically identified company there were two distinct groups, both of which constituted the early developing church, and both of which were called "disciples" (*mathetes*). The first of these was the band of twelve. There are many different terms used by the evangelists to designate them, principally that of "disciple" (*mathetes*) or simply "the twelve" (*dodeka*) (ACHJ-34). The evangelists seem especially concerned to distinguish them from the larger group of disciples surrounding Jesus. This theme, clearly developed by all the Gospel writers, comes to sharpest focus in the Lucan version of the call: "And when it was day, he called his disciples, and chose from them twelve, whom he named apostles" (Luke 6:13; cf. Mark 3:13-14; Matt. 10:1; ACHJ-33).

Jesus also was concerned to distinguish this group, and there are nineteen words or phrases which he reserves exclusively for them (ACHJ-122). The three which predominate and show audience patterns are disciple (*matthetes*), servant (*doulos*) and little one (*mikros*). The word *matthetes* occurs five times on the lips of Jesus, each time to a disciple audience. In Matthew and Mark it always identifies the twelve as those who are not above their teacher (Matt. 10:24), who are compared to prophets and righteous men (Matt. 10:41-42). Luke records a wider usage where the disciple is one who comes to Jesus renouncing himself and his loved ones (Luke 14:26); and these are the salt of the earth.

A particularly interesting word is *mikros* (little one), which is a term of endearment occurring in five sayings, all directed to the twelve. The little ones are those who believe in Jesus (Mark 9:42), whose angels God always beholds (Matt. 18:10). They are those whom God does not will to perish (Matt. 18:14), those members of Jesus' "little flock," to whom God wills to give the Kingdom (Luke 12:32).

We have already pointed to Jesus' use of servant (*doulos*) to designate the disciples in his parables. This word seems closely restricted to the twelve, and is particularly prominent in Jesus' vocabulary. There is an interesting parallel in Matthew between this term and the other three, showing their interchangeability in Jesus' mind: "A *disciple* is not above his teacher, nor a *servant* above his master...Whoever gives to one of these *little ones* even a cup of cold water because he is a *disciple*...you are all *brethren*...He who is greatest among you shall be your *servant*" (Matt. 10:24, 42; 23:8, 11). This was a group which occupied a place of special importance in the thinking of Jesus, and would seem to justify the emergence at a primitive time of the office of the clergy, not just out of the exigencies of early Christian history, but rather out of the substructure of the Holy Word itself. It would seem that Jesus anticipated the office of the clergy. Whether or not the church remained true to his original conception is again a matter for much discussion.

If one does an audience analysis of the Synoptics, separating out all of Jesus' teaching directed to the twelve disciples, the special character of this group clusters around three headings. 1) They are first of all those to whom he gave *special instruction*. Forty-three percent of all the words of Jesus are directed to the twelve. They are therefore the principal focus of his teaching. Furthermore, it was primarily to the twelve and the few other disciples often with them that he is recorded explaining his parables: as he said in Mark 4:10-12, "To you (disciples) has been given the secret of the Kingdom of God, but for those outside everything is in parables" (ACHJ-103). This is a generalization in Mark that proves to be the rule throughout the Synoptics where Jesus seems particularly concerned to take the twelve aside from time to time and explain his parables more exactly (Matt. 13:10-23; Mark 4:10-20; 7:15-23; cf. ACHJ-103-109).

Audience analysis also points to another fascinating pattern supporting this point. There are many subjects Jesus deals with having what one might call two "poles" to their meaning. For example, there is the love and the wrath of God, or the present and the eschatological Kingdom, or the kingly and the suffering Messiah. The interesting thing is that he varies his teaching about these and other subjects consistently according to the audience (ACHJ-110-135). When addressing the opponents, he tends to defer to them and their needs or preconceptions by stressing only one part of what he seems to have believed about any particular subject. When speaking to them of God, he talked almost exclusively about his wrath. When referring to the Kingdom, it was almost always in its present sense. Eschatology was reserved for the disciples, as Mark makes clear in Chapter 13, a long sermon on this subject, given to the disciples in a private place. As one moves away from the twelve to the larger group of disciples, and then to the opponent groups, so do certain principles of selectivity go into increasingly sharp operation. It was, for example, to the opponents that he referred to heaven, Satan and other such cosmological terms in a more common first century fashion.

But when he was talking to the twelve, he gave a much more complete expression of his views. It was to them that he gave a fully balanced picture of the justice of God as both present and eschatological, both love and wrath. It was to them that he presented the Kingdom as God's sovereign presence at work both within history and at the end of time. It was to the twelve that he spoke of himself as the Son of man, both in the present and at the end, both as a kingly and a suffering figure. It was to them that he taught cosmology in his most characteristic fashion as both "horizontal" and "vertical" (cf. Chapter VI). It was to these disciples that he gave a concept of Satan far beyond the first century in its sophistication (ACHJ-125). The scene at Caesarea Philippi, where Jesus took the twelve to a lonely place for special instruction, would seem to be a Markan generalization of what Jesus was accustomed to do. He was preparing them by such special instruction for leadership in what later came to be called the church.

2)Beyond such special instruction, this group of primitive clergy is further distinguished by being given a *special function*, that of preaching. All of the major sources of the Synoptics agree that Jesus "appointed twelve...to be sent out to preach...saying, 'The kingdom of heaven is at hand'" (Mark 3:14; Matt. 10:7, 27; 24:24; Luke 9:2). The Gospel writers seem reluctant to use the term "preaching" (*kerussein*) for anyone except the twelve. Both they and the larger disciple group are told to bring the message that the Kingdom has come near (Matt. 10:5-8; Luke 10:9), but the twelve are told to "preach" (*kerussein*), and this word is used several times for what they are to do, whereas the larger group is told only to "say" (*legein*) that the Kingdom has come near (Luke 10:9). Never is the verb "preach" directed to them. This distinction between preaching and saying is a subtle one, and by itself would probably not be worth noting. But when coupled with the abundant use of *kerussein* to describe the preaching of both Jesus and the twelve, along with his special instructions to them, the distinction is more impressive. It would seem that the evangelists are concerned to set Jesus and the twelve in a separate category with regard to this special function. The laymen did present the Gospel of the Kingdom, but there appears to have been a subtle distinction in the minds of the evangelists between what the larger group of disciples did, and the preaching of the twelve.

3) This group of disciples was also given *special authority*, and here we come to a particularly thorny issue. There are twelve teaching units directed to this inner circle concerning church matters. The most dominant theme has to do with the question of authority, suggesting that this was a problem at a very early period. Ten sayings deal with this, and they reveal an interesting tension between giving authority to the disciples and denying it: "It is like a man going on a journey, when he leaves home and puts his servants in charge...;" "You know that...their great men exercise authority over them. But it shall not be so among you." "You are not to be called rabbi...father...master" (Mark 13:33, 41-45; Matt. 23:8-10). The key passage is of course Matthew 16:17-20: "And I tell you, you are Peter, and on this rock I will build my church...I will give

you the keys of the kingdom of heaven, and whatever you bind on earth shall be bound in heaven." Historically, the discussion over this passage has tended to divide along confessional lines. The Roman Catholic church has insisted that Peter *the man* is the "rock," and to him and his successors in the papacy the "keys" of Christian authority have been given. Protestants, on the other hand, have usually interpreted the "rock" to be Peter's *confession of faith*, "You are the Christ;" and the authority is understood to have been given not just to Peter, but to the entire group of disciples. There obviously is not space here to go into a lengthy discussion of this passage. With my Protestant bias, I note that Peter tends to be a representative figure in the Synoptics, and that Matthew 18:18 shows Jesus giving the authority to bind and loose in exactly the same words to the entire group of twelve. It would seem that one should go more deeply into the meaning of the rock and see it as a symbol of certain things about Peter that constitute his "rockhood." If one does that, then the rock would appear to symbolize the status of soul and the spiritual insight that made Peter a "blessed" one, to whom the Lord had revealed Jesus' messiahship (Matt. 16:17). This, then, would correspond with what has been said so far throughout this chapter, that the church is built on the foundation, not of a man, like some organization, but rather on the spiritual experience of the presence of God in Jesus Christ as Kingdom and power. The fact, then, that in Acts and the Epistles of Paul, Peter fades into the background, with James becoming the head of the Jerusalem church, and Paul its chief missionary, would tend to take Peter the man out of the center of authority and further support this interpretation. However one understands this passage, the pattern would seem to be clear that Jesus gave authority to the twelve. What he did was to warn them against "authoritarianism," which he perhaps saw emerging already in the claim of James and John to sit on his right and left hand (Matt. 20:21). So did one of the chronic problems of the clergy emerge at the very beginning.

The Larger Group of Disciples: Primitive Laity

There was a second group which Jesus and the Evangelists called disciples, and which constituted the early developing church. Sometimes the word "crowd" (*ochlos*) is used to describe them (Luke 7:11; 6:17); and a few times the Greek term *laos* occurs, which also means "crowd" and from which we get our word "laity" (Luke 6:17, 20; 7:29; 20:9, 19). Mostly they are described as "disciples" (*mathetai*) who were other than the twelve (Matt. 8:21; Mark 4:34; 8:34; Luke 10:1; 24:33 etc. cf. ACHJ-37-42). They were a large group of sympathetic listeners who seemed to depend on Jesus for healing, instruction and leadership, who called him "teacher" and "master," and from whom were recruited not only the twelve, but also the seventy, as well as others who served him in various capacities (Luke 6:13; 10:1 ff.). The Gospel writers go out of their way to identify these and distinguish them from the twelve, describing many different types of persons within this category. Here were the laity of the church, ranging all the way from ecstatic acceptance to active criticism, but all with one thing in common: a basic receptivity to Jesus. They were men and women of faith, and he called them "blessed" ones who heard and kept the word (Matt. 8:7, 10; 9:22; Luke 11:27-28, etc. ACHJ-26). Often they were those rejected by society; and Mark gives us a picture of Jesus at a meal surrounded by "many who followed him," some of whom were tax collectors and sinners (Mark 2:15).

Luke is especially interested in the female members of this group, identifying some of Jesus' disciples as "the women who followed him" (Luke 23:49; 24:22; 23:28; 10:38-42; 11:27 etc.) and ministered to him out of their means (Mark 15:40-41). There were those like Zacchaeus or Bartimaeus whose lives were liberated by Jesus; and certain ones who *almost* followed him wherever he went (Luke 9:57). There must have been many like this, for example the rich young ruler who was hindered by his wealth (Matt. 19:22). Some of this large company, at one point listed as five thousand (Matt. 14:21), were friends of the sick or demented and were credited with faith, like the centurian (Luke 7:1-10), Jairus (Mark 5:21-43), the man with the epileptic son (Mark 9;14-29) or the Syrophoenician woman (Mark 7:24-30). As Jesus said of some of these, "Truly...not even in Israel have I found such faith" (Matt. 8:10). There is often a record of faith connected with healing, as in the case of the woman with the flow of blood (Matt. 9:20-22) or the Samaritan leper (Luke 7:11-19), and one must assume that these would have been called "disciples."

The record of Jesus' approval of John the Baptist, whom he called "more than a prophet" (Luke 7:24-35), and the continuing contact between Jesus and some of John's disciples after his death (Matt. 14:12), suggests that we can list some of these as Jesus' disciples. This is exactly what the Gospel of John does (John 1:35 ff.). Finally, there was a large company of godly individuals with education, wealth and power, who can be called Jesus' disciples in this larger sense. One of these was a Roman Centurian whom Luke identified as a "worthy" man (Luke 7:4). Jairus was a ruler of the Synagogue, and Jesus called him a "man of faith" (Mark 5:21-43). Joseph of Arimathea was a "respected member of the council" (Mark 15:43), and apparently wealthy. Several scribes responded to his message and were called "not far from the kingdom" (Luke 20:39; Mark 12:34; Matt. 13:52; Mark 9:14). There were rulers of the Jews (Luke 7:3), and a number of pharisees, like Simon who invited him to dinner, or those who warned him of Herod's plot against his life (Luke 7:36; 13:31). This was the primitive laity, and they were distinguished by their religious faith and their high regard for Jesus.

These laymen did not seem to have any specialized function in Jesus' mind. Most of what he said to the twelve by way of mission instruction, he is recorded directing also to the larger group, especially in Luke (Luke 10:1-12). He called them to follow him, and to renounce all to serve the Kingdom (Matt. 8:22; Luke 9:61-62; 14:28-33; Mark 10:17-22). He instructed them to live as "blessed" ones, and serve the poor and needy (Mark 14:3-9; Matt. 5:1). He urged them in their mission activity not to be "anxious" about personal needs, just as he did the twelve. The evidence is less certain, but nevertheless there, that he expected them to "say that the kingdom of God has come near" (Luke 10:9), to heal the sick and cast out demons (Luke 10:9-12); and on one occasion he even noted with approval that one of these lay disciples had done a "mighty work" in his name (Mark 9:39). The disciples objected to this man because "he was not following us," but Jesus in a characteristic phrase told them his circle of followers was larger than they were prepared to admit. "He that is not against us is for us" (Mark 9:40). It would seem that the mission of these laymen was very comparable to that of the twelve, with the exception of their leadership role, and their particular calling to preach, based on his special instruction.

This was a powerful company, and the Synoptics are unanimous in their praise. They were humble, worthy, lovers of Israel, God-fearing, repentent men and women who did the will of God, whose names were written in heaven; and one can't help noticing the contrast with the twelve, who are called men "of little faith" (Matt. 14:31). The sinners, the demonic, the sick, the corrupt, the Samaritans, the Greeks, the soldiers, and even certain Jewish officials were often more receptive to Jesus' healing mission than were the twelve. The seventy disciples seem to have been more successful in their ministry to the sick than the twelve (Luke 10:17-20; Mark 9:18), and their assessment of his identity seems to have been much more theologically sophisticated. The twelve called Jesus "teacher" and "prophet"; but the larger group of disciples referred to him as the "one who is to come," the "Holy One of God," the "Son of God," the "Christ," "God visiting his people." Some of course did not continue their interest in him (Luke 9:59); but as far as the Gospel editors are concerned, these were men and women of profound religious conviction, who possessed ability, wealth and power, who responded to him with surprising insight, and followed him to the cross and the tomb, far beyond the dedication of that primitive group of clergy. If the Synoptics are any indication, the Kingdom power of the church resided first in Jesus, and then in that tremendous group of laymen.

The Organizing Church

Jesus had no special term for what was later called the "visible church." He did, however, seem to have a simple structure in mind. The disciples were a loosely organized group, wherein the twelve functioned in the special capacities described above, with Peter, James and John forming an inner circle, and Peter described most often as spokesman. Judas was the treasurer, and certain wealthy patrons, like Joseph of Arimathea or Mary Magdalene, supported them out of their substance. There were homes open to them, like that of Peter's mother-in-law in Capernaum where Jesus made his headquarters, or the upper room in Jerusalem where he served the last supper. During Jesus' lifetime there was a simple program of action, and on two occasions the Gospels show him organizing teams to go through the regions of Galilee to teach and heal. On one occasion Luke reports that he sent messengers ahead to a village in order to "make ready" for him (Luke 9:52), and one gets perhaps an insight here into the way Jesus insured that there would be a crowd to hear his teaching. Beyond this simple plan, however, a very loose structure seems to have prevailed at the earliest period.

But there was structure; there was a plan; there was a clear conception of a called-out community; and there were two unmistakable strata of disciples who fitted exactly into the theological concept of the Sons of the Kingdom as described in his teaching. It would seem clear that Jesus intended to found something similar to what later came to be called the church.

He Placed the Church under Judgment

But now we must face the question as to whether or not what developed before and after his death and resurrection was compatible with what he had in mind. The fellowship of the Kingdom begins in Jesus' teaching with an initial calling-out of the laborers from the market place into the vineyard, the fish from the sea into the net, the servants into the king's household, the grain into the growing experience of the field. But this is just the beginning, for the Kingdom society is a continuing process of judgment. There is no possible place in Jesus' conception for self-righteousness, for resting at ease in Zion. He constantly places the sons and daughters of the Kingdom under judgment, and some of his most highly critical statements are directed to his disciples.

Some of You are Masquerading as Servants

There are eleven such parables aimed directly at the disciples, which contain warnings of false discipleship. The visible Kingdom community was a mixed company, and these so-called servants stood under the judgment of God. One of the most interesting examples is Matthew 5:13, where Jesus calls his disciples "the salt of the earth," but then warns them that if this salt has lost its taste, if it is salt in name only, then it is good for nothing "except to be thrown out and trodden under foot by men." For the Hebrew, salt had special religious significance. Its preserving qualities led to its being regarded as an essential element in the making of an enduring covenant. As a symbol of incorruptness, salt was regularly offered with the sacrifices, and came to symbolize a covenant relationship with God. As I have already indicated, when Jesus said, "You are the salt of the earth," or "Have salt within yourselves," the suggestion is very strong that he is saying, Have the Kingdom, the covenant with God, within yourselves. Salt without saltness then would be a servant of the Kingdom who is a servant (*doulos*) in appearance only — but within would be a "wicked servant," a contradiction in terms, and destined to be cast out of the Kingdom fellowship.

Here is a warning against unconverted Christians, who, as Paul described them, were "holding the form of religion but denying the power of it" (II Tim. 3:5). This theme continues throughout Jesus' teaching in the image of the weed that only looks like wheat, the goat that only looks like a sheep, the bad fish that is only distinguished from the good in the practiced eye of the fisherman, the wicked servant who shows his incompatability with the King's household by

161

his lack of forgiveness, the five virgins who are only revealed as "foolish" when the time comes to light their lamps. The constant sifting process of God's judgment permeates Jesus' teaching from start to finish, and constitutes his indictment of the church. Some of you are masquerading as servants! And the day will come when your presence in the visible fellowship will not be enough. Jesus warned against over-zealous servants separating the weeds from the wheat (Matt. 13:27); and churches should be extremely cautious about trimming their roles, lest, as Jesus said, they root out some wheat with the weeds. The time will come when God will do that himself, and the harvest will be a sifting, sorting judgment upon the church.

The Judgment of Slow Growth

The process of judgment continues also with those who are in truth sons and daughters of the Kingdom, and it does so in terms of growth. Once the seed of the word of God comes alive in the soil of the soul (Mark 4:13), its first task is to grow. Jesus dramatized this in a series of parables about growing things. In one parable, the Kingdom of God is like a mustard seed sown upon the earth. It is the smallest of seeds (a bit of hyperbole), "yet when sown it grows up and becomes the greatest of all shrubs, and puts forth large branches, so that the birds of the air can make nests in its shade" (Mark 4:30-32). The Kingdom life begins with the new bursting life of the presence of God within; but it takes growth before that life is ready to lodge the birds of the heavens, to render the service for which it is intended. This is the task of every servant of the Kingdom, to grow up in his or her spiritual life that he or she may bear the "fruits" of the Kingdom (Matt. 7:20), what the apostle Paul called becoming mature in Christ (Eph. 4:13).

But spiritual growth can be very slow, and Jesus pointed to this in his parable of the seed growing secretly (Mark 4:26-29). "The Kingdom of God is as if a man should scatter seed upon the ground, and should sleep and rise night and day, and the seed should sprout and grow, he knows not how...first the blade, then the ear, then the full grain in the ear." Sons and daughters of the Kingdom do not immediately produce its fruits. When the seed of the Kingdom enters one's life, all our problems are not immediately solved. We are new persons, with a new source of power and some new orientations and commitments; but in many ways we are still the same individuals; with the same minds, the same misconceptions, the same habit patterns, and these slow down our growth in the spirit. We will grow,

162

and I see no evidence in Jesus' teaching that eternal life, once begun, ever ceases; but sometimes this growth can be painfully slow. The plant of the Kingdom life can be stunted, warped and twisted by the things in our lives that are hard to cope with. The children of the Kingdom are not always the nicest people, and Jesus recognized this when he distinguished between the "greatest and the least" within the Kingdom of God (Matt. 5:19). In this case, the "least" are those who break the commandments of Moses, and we see the importance of moral purity for growing up within the Kingdom. The sons of the Kingdom are constantly under the judgment of the moral process of growth to maturity, and it is by our "fruits" that we are judged to be five talent or ten talent persons; it is by the products of our love and joy and peace, our patience, kindness, goodness, faithfulness, gentleness, self control (Gal. 5:1-11), that the beauty, vitality and effectiveness of our Kingdom lives are judged. And this judgment is going on all the time within the church.

How Long am I to Bear with You?

Jesus' judgment on the church comes to peculiar focus in his indictment of the twelve disciples. Although he often expresses his approval of them as a "dear little flock," "good men," "blessed ones," "sons of the Kingdom," "sons of light," and "sons of God," the predominant picture of the twelve given in the Synoptics is a negative one. Jesus is constantly critical at three major points: 1) they lack understanding, 2) they persistently disbelieve, 3) they oppose him in his own understanding of mission. He calls them men of little faith, foolish and slow of heart to believe (Luke 12:28; Matt. 14:31, etc.). They consistently fail to understand his message, his person and his purpose until he cries out to Peter that he is not on the side of God but of men (Matt. 16:21-23; Mark 8:33). They are vain, exclusive, legalistic, unforgiving, complaining, inclined to be pompous, striving for preferment, anxious to lord it over others (Mark 9:35). His continuing disappointment over them takes the form of a running series of parables where some are described as unfaithful servants, as men not waiting for their master to return; weak, timorous sheep who will betray him and be scattered by the rigorous demands of discipleship (Matt. 24:45-51; Luke 12:47-48; 16:1-8; ACHJ-123). Mark records him crying out with frustration: "O faithless generation...how long am I to bear with you?" (Mark 9:19). This is an indictment of the primitive clergy, and is a warning to all sons and daughters of the Kingdom that Jesus Christ was a "severe" man (*austeros*, Luke 19:21), and the life of servanthood in the Kingdom is a cross (Mark 8:34), a narrow door (Matt. 7:14), wherein we all stand under the demanding judgment of God.

Judgment on the Modern Church

Jesus' three indictments of his disciples are still a valid critique of the church. Our *lack of understanding* is still reflected in the shifting moods in theology described in Chapter IX. We still need to understand what the Jesus of history meant by the Kingdom of God. That basic problem has not changed one iota; it has only changed its vocabulary. Our *disbelief* is still revealed in our reliance on programs and budgets, on political and economic power, instead of on the power of God whose Kingdom presence has come "near" in Jesus Christ (Luke 21:31). Our *opposition* to him still lies in wanting him to be our kind of Messiah. Some of us want him to be a teacher and prophet, but reject his role as radical social critic, sufferer, healer and miracle worker. Others of us reverse this and want him to be a radical critic, concentrating on the physical and social needs of men, but reject him as prophetic teacher, preacher, Messiah, Son of man. Nothing has changed, and Jesus is still putting his church under judgment, demanding that we take the "whole garment" of the Gospel, that we follow him completely in all our ways, and allow him to be our guide as to the nature and mission of the church.

One particular problem seems to stem from a misunderstanding of the nature of the church. A common indictment against denominations is that the conception of the church as a collective body has so dominated the minds of church leaders that great violence has been done to persons. It is often charged that the proclamation of the Gospel to individuals has been replaced by church programs, that evangelism has been redefined in terms of reorganization, or the church's ministry to collective social problems, ignoring or even vigorously rejecting what is sometimes called a "pietistic" fixation upon individuals.

There is, I think, substantial truth in this critique, especially in America. One very visible evidence is the widespread search for personal identity, personal salvation, personal meaning and liberation by so many within the Christian churches. The ranks of the drug sub-culture, the various Indian mystic cults, pop-salvation programs and the whole consciousness-raising movement, are drawn heavily from Christian churches which have failed to provide for the personal needs of their members. The church as a social entity has smothered individuals in some of the more "sober" denominations.

Another symptom of this has been the rejection of the church by those who are weary of the depersonalizing effects of church bureaucracy. Some have simply dropped out. Others have become intensely critical, especially college students I have known through the years. Others have gone into the so-called "underground church" movement. Some have created new support groups within denominations, while still others have become iconoclasts, smashing the old patterns of worship, structure, creed, anything that represents the image of the "Big Church." Mostly, I suspect, Christians in such churches just sit and suffer, and wonder why no one seems to care about them; and they ask what has happened to the glory and the excitement and the fire of the Gospel.

Certainly Jesus saw the church, or his primitive understanding of it, in a collective sense. As we have seen, he talked of households, and flocks, and fields of growing grain, and brethren and sons of the Kingdom; so there is within his teaching a justification for conceiving of the church as a corporate entity. Paul's concept of the "body of Christ" was, I think, an accurate development of this conception. But once one has said this, it must immediately be remembered that however social may have been Jesus' understanding of the Kingdom and the church, ultimately his emphasis was on the individual. The *douloi* are individually "servants" before they are members of the king's household. The *adelphoi* are individually "brethren" before thay are members of the family of God. The sheep are individually sons and daughters of the Kingdom before they are his "dear little flock" (*Mikroi*). In this heyday of the social sciences, with our concentration on people within groups, it is imperative to remember that when Jesus talked of the sons of the Kingdom, he did so as *individuals within fellowship*. They were precious as individuals before they counted as members of the corporate body. This suggests that to reflect accurately the theology of Jesus, any church polity or program should represent a total concern for both the individual and the collective group, but the stress should always be upon the individual.

Chapter XII

Jesus' Mission for the Church:
A Theology of Christian Education

Now let us take a closer look at the mission of the church as Jesus described it and see how it can be translated into a program for the church today. My thesis is a deceptively simple one: The mission of the church has always been to follow Jesus Christ. From those days beside the lake when he challenged them to follow him and become fishers of men, to these more complex times when the call is not so clear or so simple, and where the lake seems much broader and his words harder to implement, the basic call is still the same — to follow him in all that he is and all that he intends for mankind.

A Social Mission

Periodically the church seems to need to rediscover the social mission of Jesus; and in our age this has happened with peculiar force. The larger group of disciples discovered this immediately, and Jesus was besieged with requests for a ministry to human poverty and illness. The narrative material in the Gospels gives us a consistent picture of him responding to this need, but also resisting being swallowed up by it. At times he is pictured fleeing the crowds in a boat across the lake, only to have them meet him at the other side, clutching at him, even tearing off a portion of a roof to lower a paralytic before him (Mark 2:4). A common observation is that he healed them out of compassion; but his chief concern was to proclaim the Gospel of the Kingdom of God, so he did not want to get completely absorbed in a healing ministry. I think this is true. Nevertheless, he was concerned, and the parable of the sheep and the goats is still the charter of

Jesus' compassion: "I was hungry and you gave me food, I was thirsty and you gave me drink,...as you did it to one of the least of these my brethren, you did it to me" (Matt. 25:31-46). This much of Jesus' mission has been commonly accepted and widely practiced by Christians in every age.

But Jesus was also concerned about structures; and this is less well recognized, and even less consistently implemented. He vigorously challenged the status quo, which was certainly one reason for the official opposition to his ministry. "The scribes and the Pharisees sit on Moses' seat; so practice and observe whatever they tell you, but not what they do; for they preach, but do not practice...they bind heavy burdens...but...will not move them with their finger...They do all their deeds to be seen by men...they love the place of honor at the feasts" (Matt. 23:2-12). What a searing indictment this was of the official Judaism of his day, which he then portrayed with a bit of biting sarcasm in the parable of the good Samaritan: "A priest...a Levite...a Samaritan...Which of these three, do you think, proved neighbor to the man who fell among the robbers?" (Luke 10:29-37). "Woe unto you scribes and Pharisees, hypocrites!" Not the kind of critique calculated to make him and his religious following popular with the local power structure. Then when he went on to set himself above Moses, the temple and even the institution of the Sabbath, he was challenging the very fabric of first century society (Matt. 5:21; 12:6, 8). Jesus was an arch heretic, and in that theocratic environment, his critique of religious institutions was actually a challenge to the political situation of his day. There is a sense in which one could say that if the church is ever too comfortably allied with any government or any culture, it is in danger of losing the critical witness so apparent in the teaching of Jesus.

He was also concerned for issues of social justice. "Woe to you, scribes and Pharisees...for you tithe mint and dill and cummin, and have neglected the weightier matters of the law, justice and mercy and faith; these you ought to have done, without neglecting the others" (Matt. 23:23). Jesus did not see himself primarily as a social reformer, but the implications of his message for social justice are immense. This suggests that any church not actively engaged in a significant social critique and mission is not following Jesus at that point, and I would add, is missing a significant part of the power of the Gospel. One of the great heresies which the modern social Gospel is trying to correct, is the privitism and social passivity of many Christian churches.

167

A *Mission to Persons: A Theology of Christian Education*

But if we would follow Jesus in the mission of the Kingdom, we must direct our concern primarily toward persons and their needs. The church must remember that an effective social program has always been the result of the spiritual health and vitality of the individual members of the church. Any social mission that can be called Christian in these Gospel terms is a product, not an end in itself. It is not a cause in its own right so much as a symptom of an entire set of deeper motivations and commitments. This directs us to the major two-fold thrust of Jesus' mission to persons: teaching and preaching. The one aims primarily at the instruction of the intellect, the other at the commitment of the will. The two activities go so closely together, however, that Jesus is pictured shifting easily from one to the other, and more often than not blending them both.

Since he seems to have put his primary emphasis on teaching, directed most particularly to the disciples (cf. pp. 153 f), we are again reminded that *extensive* evangelism begins with *intensive* evangelism. Before the church can minister with power to society and its structures, it must first minister to itself; it must discover the power that will make it a "light set upon a hill." It is this total preaching-teaching task of the church which I am calling "Christian Education." Such is not the usual connotation of this term, but I think it is true to the Gospels. The artificial separation between the Sunday School and the Pulpit is one of the great sources of "anesthesia" within the modern church, and is not, I think, in accordance with a Gospel model.

Within the Synoptic Gospels there are many metaphors used to describe this mission to persons which is Christian Education. There is one, however, which Jesus seems to have favored and is particularly appropriate. In the parable of the soils, he describes his mission to persons in terms of the sowing of the seed of the Kingdom into the soil of the souls of men (Mark 4:1 ff.). There are four basic tasks required in the growing of a plant, which represent the four major activities of Christian Education. One can separate them for analysis, and there is a certain theological and practical progression, but they all tend to go on simultaneously.

Prepare the Soil

The first task in this Kingdom mission to persons is the preparation of the soil; for it is the condition of the soil that determines the ability of the seed to grow. "A sower went out to sow...some seed fell along the path, and the birds came and devoured it. Other seed fell on rocky ground...not much soil...it was scorched...Other seed fell among thorns...and choked it...And other seeds fell into good soil and brought forth grain" (Mark 4:3-8). This parable is describing the things that block the growth of the seed of the word within the human heart: "Satan...tribulation or persecution...cares of the world...the delight in riches,...the desire for other things" (Mark 4:14-20).

The first task of Christian Education is to prepare the mind and heart for the coming of the seed of God's word. This is a cleansing, enriching, often remedial operation that must be adapted to the individual; for the needs of the path are different from those of the rocky or the weedy soil. This is a vast subject, and there is only space here to discuss some of the major obstacles in our present situation that hinder the generating of the seed of the Kingdom. The first is pre-conditioning. One can begin very early to prepare an attitude of love and respect for God, for Christ and the church, that will predispose a child to accept the word of the Kingdom. The idealistic notion that children should be raised apart from the church so that they can make their own decision at a responsible age, unprejudiced by such conditioning, has one serious flaw. This very isolation is itself a negative conditioning, often filling the soil of the mind with all kinds of false and misleading ideas about the church which are a serious hindrance to the growth of the seed. The fallacy is that there is no such thing as a vacuum where the Kingdom is concerned. There is no neutrality possible in one's response to Jesus. As he said, "He who is not with me is against me" (Matt. 12:30). The empty soul is like an empty house, an open invitation to a flock of demonic intruders (Matt. 12:44).

One of the classic illustrations of the way this idealism of neutrality does just the opposite of what is intended, is the impossibly awkward stance of the American school system in its treatment of religious studies. Begun with the laudable concern to separate the church and the state, this policy was perverted by the mistaken notion that the Supreme Court forbade the teaching *about* religion in public schools. The result has been that an otherwise adequate and intellectually free public education has been unable to be either adequate or free. How can one teach the history of mankind and its institutions without teaching about religion? How can one teach human ideas without dealing with those of religion and ethics? How can one teach the great literature of human history without dealing

169

with the Bible or the Koran or the Bhagavad Gita? The abysmal ig-norance of students along these lines when they reach our college classes requires enormous remedial work, and makes it very difficult for them to get a truly adequate liberal education. Fortunately, this message has been getting through to American educators in recent years, and one state after another has undertaken a program of teaching *about* religion in the public schools. As a result, most public universities are beginning to catch up with private institu-tions in establishing strong departments of religion.

But the church should be more concerned than it is, not only on purely educational, but also on religious grounds. The problem has been that the radical divorcement of religion and public education has produced an enormous number of false and misleading attitudes that make it difficult for the word of the Kingdom to come alive within the minds and hearts of our children. The fallacious idea that science and religion are intrinsically incompatible has long created unnecessary obstacles to understanding and accepting Christian theology. The attitude that the concerns of religion and ethics are not legitimate parts of a high school education has unwittingly con-tributed to the degeneration of the lives of many students into a veritable moral wilderness, and then normalized this as the accepted pattern of life after leaving school. The panic of some of our educators tells me that they see all too clearly how this negative con-ditioning is providing the moral and religious vacuum into which all kinds of demonic problems are moving. The Christian church has a tremendous stake in the new move to introduce religious and value-oriented study into the public schools. Whether in public school or church school, we need to teach our children enough about the problems and options of morality that the soil of their souls does not become filled with the debris of attitudes and habit patterns that will choke the growth of the Kingdom life. Within the churches, the Christian ethic needs to be more clearly defined and more adequate-ly defended if our young people are to have a fighting chance of coming to know the sovereign God of absolute purity.

The soil also needs to be deepened and enriched so that the word can be received beyond the shallow and momentary enthusiasm that often so embarrasses people that it is a real hindrance to any genuine in-depth experience of the Kingdom life. This is the problem with those who were "burned" by some flaming evangelist, before their minds were ready for such potent exposure. It means that we must teach the facts of the Christian Gospel, the vocabulary of Christian theology, the language of Christian ethics soon enough, and with enough sophistication, that when the Kingdom "comes near" in some seeding, generating moment, there will be enough depth of soil, enough maturity of preparation, to sustain a genuinely life-changing experience. How many hyper-critics of the church there are whose only exposure to the Christian faith was that of a powerful word cast into a very immature and shallow understanding, and what resulted was unable to sustain the vital plant of the Christian life. And ever after, their entire attitude toward the church has been conditioned by this searing experience which stands in embarrassing contrast to their more mature experience in other areas of knowledge.

But there is deeper soil than that of the conscious, rational mind. The Christian educator needs to pay close attention to the cultivation of the subconscious levels of the personality, the areas of feeling and willing, if the seed of the word is to find sufficient depth to grow. We need to know the language of emotion, and have experience in expressing those feelings of love and awe, of wonder, fear and reverence, which are so important in the Kingdom life. This is done through prayer and worship, through art, music, poetry and drama, through all such forms of emotional expression that are effective for the opening up of the total person to a life-transforming encounter with the Kingdom. We need to help people develop an attitude of expectancy for the new life of the spirit, which goes beyond the intellect into the deeper soil of the heart, where love and surrender and commitment are born.

Finally, in preparing the soil, the Christian educator needs to help people understand themselves well enough to know what might be hindering their Christian commitment. This is most appropriate for more mature persons, but I suspect we can begin much earlier than we normally do. Each kind of soil has its own problems, and Christian Education must be intensely personal if it is to be effective. The inclusion of a program of personal counselling and group therapy is exactly to the point. So the soil must be prepared by being ploughed and cleansed and enriched, if the seed of the word is to take root within the lives of persons.

Sow the Seed

But then the seed must be sown. This is that for which the soil has been prepared. The word of the Kingdom must be presented so that the very presence of God is brought near. This is not simply telling *about* the Kingdom; it is casting the Kingdom itself, the word which is God himself, into the prepared soil of the human personality. And in the mystery of soil and seed, the inert human psyche — spiritually dead and dark, but pure potential — receives the seed of the word as spirit and power, and new life begins. Something wonderful takes place within the secret "innerness" of the soul, and this is the whole purpose of preparing the "good soil."

Many of the more educationally oriented denominations are very skillful at preparing the soil. They are well trained in educational methodology; but then they fail in the sowing of the seed, even as many of the more evangelistic churches fail in the preparation of the soil. There is a sense in which Plato, Aristotle and John Dewey have prevailed over Jesus in the Christian education programs of some churches. We are often more concerned to educate than to commit, to instruct than to redeem, under the mistaken notion that one can be educated into the Kingdom of God. Plato's model of the ideal educational system as he develops it in *The Republic* is fine for a liberal arts college; but its primary appeal to the intellect does not go far enough for the Christian faith. God is not just a subject to be studied, but a sovereign presence to be accepted. Jesus is not simply a biography to be learned, but a master to be acknowledged. The acceptance of the Kingdom into one's life involves the total personality in ways that go far beyond the discipline of the intellect and are peculiar to the religious experience; for we know God's love by *loving* Him. We know his sovereignty by *obeying* Him.

Every year I used to survey my Introductory students to discover where they were in their understanding of the New Testament. One set of answers recurred with significant monotony. "Have you attended Sunday School?" "Yes." "Are you a church member?" "Yes." "Does your religious faith have any meaning to you?" "No." It would seem that for many of these young people, graduation into the communicants' class had been perfunctory and spiritually meaningless. Somehow the seed had not begun to germinate. They were educated, but not committed. Although there were many subtle gradations within the Kingdom life, these gave the impression of being salt without savor, weeds instead of wheat, servants of the Kingdom in name only. The inevitable suggestion that comes to mind is that our churches need to aim their Christian education not only at the instruction, but even more at the redemption of individuals. Instruction can prepare for the Kingdom life, can discipline and guide it; but it cannot create it or be a substitute for it. This requires a deeper level of acceptance involving the will, the emotions and the living presence of God. It is the mystery of the sowing and generation of the seed.

It is in preaching and teaching that the seed is principally sown. In Jesus' parable, the seed is the word of God, and its sowing is the proclamation of the Kingdom. One of the most notable things about this word is its power. It presents us with a God who cannot be ignored, whose eternal power and justice command us with royal authority and will not be denied. God always brings men and women to the crisis of decision, for him or against him. And so he comes to us as a fire, and a sword, a net and an invitation, all analogies for the challenging, demanding, sifting action of his judgment. One of the great problems of the Christian family has always been that of unconverted Christians; of those who are holding to the form of religion but denying its power. Like so many Jews in Jesus' audience, or so many church attenders in ours, the word has never been sown and received with life-giving power. For the seed to be truly received, it must be truly sown. This means that at some moment, the sovereign God must confront the human soul in all his awesome power. This can be a time we are aware of, like a man finding a treasure in a field (Matt. 13:44), or it can be some quiet unobtrusive occasion that cannot be dated, like the germination of a seed beneath the soil (Mark 4:1 ff.); but there will be a moment when death becomes life, when darkness becomes light, when the poverty of our souls is redeemed by the treasure of the Kingdom. The preparation of the soil has no meaning if it is not the preparation for the new life of the Kingdom plant.

There are no doubt many reasons why the seed is not sown effectively, and the literature of recent years is replete with critical analyses. I shall make only three suggestions which come out of this Gospel study. The first is that the God we present may be too small, as J. B. Phillips expressed it some years ago. The God we proclaim must be able to drive men and women to their knees in fear and repentance, and raise them up into newness of life. If our God can be ignored, then he will be; and this is often a great weakness in the church's mission to persons.

A second reason may be that our Christ is too small. This was Peter's problem, until with God's help he came alive one day to the identity of him who was speaking to him: "You are the Christ, the Son of the living God" (Matt. 16:16). It was in those moments when Peter, and others with him, caught a vision of the presence of God in

Jesus Christ, that they became the rock on which Jesus could build his church. It is important who it is who is casting the seed upon the soil. We have seen this in Jesus' own teaching, as well as in the faith of the early church. It is in and through this Jesus Christ that the Kingdom has become especially available; and if the belief in Jesus as Son of God be significantly dimmed, the availability of the Kingdom will be significantly diminished. This is why the current Christological discussion is so important to the health and power of the church.

A third possible reason for our failure to sow the seed effectively has to do with our reluctance to confront people with the claims of the Kingdom, and this for a host of reasons. The image of the offensively aggressive evangelist haunts so many of us "proper" Christians, that one hesitates to use the word evangelism in sophisticated company. But a careful, critical analysis of the Gospel material reveals that although Jesus probably never used the term, it is quite adequate as a description of his chief concern, which was to sow the seed of God's word. Rightly understood, evangelism always has been and still is the heart of the church's mission to persons.

I suspect that some of us are victims of religious snobbery. In a recent student seminar, this matter was being discussed, and several began "putting down" the dogmatic evangelistic "sects" that preach on street corners. This aroused an interesting discussion, and the more we examined our attitudes, the more we realized that *we* were the dogmatic ones. Calling them "sects" automatically gave us a feeling of superiority. Our insistence that preaching be done only in a proper sanctuary by those regularly trained and ordained, and to those who accepted our right to preach, was pure snobbery. We began to see, to our chagrin, that we were victims of the acculturated captivity of the "proper" churches. And we were reminded that Jesus was a street evangelist, whose first priority was presenting the Gospel to persons, while doing what he could to heal the body and criticize the social structures. He spoke most often to those who were sympathetic, but also to opponents, wherever he could find them. And it became painfully apparent to us that one of the greatest difficulties for the religious establishment is to proclaim the message of the Kingdom to its opponents.

We "sober" Christians are so afraid of emotion that some of us have been avoiding one of the most important activities of Christian Education — the sowing of the seed. To compensate, we have concentrated on preparing the soil, but for what purpose? If carefully

174

done, an appeal to emotion can be as normal and dignified as any expression of our deepest selves. Surely modern psychology has shown us that the human personality is mostly subconscious. If the seed of God's word is to take root and claim our lives with life-giving totality, its impact will inevitably be mostly emotional. But if the seed never gets past the rational intellect to the sub-rational life of feeling and willing, nothing life-changing is going to happen. This means that Christian Education which attempts to follow this Gospel model, must prepare for, point toward and provide opportunity for a life-creating encounter with the Kingdom, which is partly rational, but mostly emotional. I cannot avoid the inevitable logic, that every teacher, every preacher, everyone involved in the total process of Christian Education, must in one way or another, consistent with good taste and with his or her abilities, be an evangelist, bringing the word of God's Kingdom presence near to the souls of persons.

Nurture the New Plant

With the coming of new life, with the spiritual awakening to the new dimensions of the Kingdom, the seed begins to grow, and the Christian educator is faced with the delicate task of nurturing the new plant. The challenge now is to grow up. The experience of new life does not immediately result in a mature son or daughter of the Kingdom, but rather in a tiny cotyledon of faith, emerging slowly within the soul, no matter how dramatic the experience. Here is new life, new power, new motivation, which needs strengthening, development, direction, refinement, application. The task of the new Christian, as Paul put it, is to grow up into the fullness of the measure of the stature of Christ, to mature manhood (Eph. 4:13).

One cannot expect mature fruit from immature plants, and it is pointless to criticize the immature sons and daughters of the Kingdom for their failure to act "like Christians." There is a strange intolerance at this point that besets both those within and ouside the church. One is often reminded by those outside, as they attempt to justify their own "outsideness," that those within the church are hypocrites. What they observe is no doubt correct. Christians are often not very nice people. But what the critics don't realize is that they are measuring immature Christians against some kind of absolute standard of perfection, not willing to allow them to be less than perfect. I do not know any perfectly mature Christians; but I do know many who are in varying stages of growth toward maturi-

175

ty, and some whose maturity is so slight that one could hardly tell that they had ever entered the Kingdom, except for a few telltale signs — a slight quickening of spiritual concern, which is often so subtle it takes a practiced eye to detect.

Pastors and church leaders, in their zeal, are often just as callous, expecting their people to bear mature fruits of love and service, of faithfulness and purity, when they are not yet mature enough to do so. The nurturing of new plants takes much patience, and one must allow the plant to be itself, or he will surely do it violence. How often I have gone from a church service with the feeling that I am surrounded by the bleeding souls of immature Christians who have been flayed, criticized and shamed by the preacher for not being or doing what they are not yet mature enough to accomplish! Ecclesiastical impatience is one of the greatest sins of the clergy. Love, or just plain common sense, demands sympathetic patience with immature growing things — and people.

Jesus' definition of maturity was to love God with all our heart and soul and mind and strength and our neighbor as ourselves (Mark 12:30). This is a total process that begins with the generation of the seed, and continues throughout one's life. It involves first of all the heart and the soul, the subconscious emotional life; and the Christian educator must provide means for the exercise of the willing, feeling, trusting experience of the deeply felt encounter with God. Worship and prayer, song and praise, exercises in trust and obedience: what an opportunity there is here for the expression of creative imagination! My first assignment as a theological student was as a Junior Assistant Pastor of a large city church whose sanctuary resembled a gymnasium, with the balcony looking for all the world like an indoor track. The more I thought about that, the more appropriate it seemed to me; for what we were doing in worship was going through spiritual calisthenics, helping "flabby" Christians to get in shape, helping immature ones develop their capacities to feel the presence of God, and to "will to do his will" (John 7:17). We need to be helped to express the love and the joy that is stirring deeply within; and we should be less concerned with whether or not this is done "decently and in order," and more concerned that it be done in ways that are meaningful to the individuals involved.

This process of growth also involves the mind, and it is at this point that the intellectual growth in the Kingdom is particularly meaningful; for it is only within an experience of the Kingdom that its theology is convincing, or makes much sense. This means that theology is especially important for the growing Christian. Even as Jesus concentrated primarily on teaching the disciples in what was a "school" situation, so the Christian church is not only a gymnasium, but a school. Theology is the process of understanding what has happened to persons in their new life within the Kingdom. It is the attempt to understand what Jesus is saying about God and our relationship with him. It is the concern to relate this new understanding to the areas of our lives outside the Kingdom, to science and literature, to history and philosophy, to economics and politics. It is the discipline of organizing our thoughts about the Kingdom so that we can relate our experience to others in an understandable way. The task of lay education must not stop with confirmation, but needs to continue indefinitely, lest the maturity of our intellectual growth in the Kingdom remain forever at an adolescent level. There is power in disciplined minds; and never before in the history of the church has there been as great a need for lay men and women to be highly educated in their understanding of the Kingdom. There is no other way for the church to confront a sophisticated secular world with redeeming power.

Christian nurture also involves the active life of the sons of the Kingdom, loving God with all our strength. This means that the subject of ethics is important as the application to one's ethos of his maturing spiritual power and understanding. We need instruction in the meaning of love and purity. We need research into the art of peacemaking. We need training in the skill of being persecuted for righteousness' sake. We need to learn how to be tolerant of people, yet intolerant of evil, how to respect ourselves, yet despise our own sin, how to be gentle and forgiving and turn the other cheek, and still command respect for ourselves and the cause we serve. There is a debilitating weakness in the church at this point. We are not practiced in the art of making difficult ethical decisions, and when forced to do so, the agony of the effort can often be heard across the land. We will deal more with this important subject in the next chapter. The point here is that the development of heart, mind and strength are all vital elements in the nurture of the new Kingdom plant.

Harvest the Fruit

This leads us to the final task of Christian Education, that of harvesting the fruit. The healthy and mature plant will bear fruit, and that is the purpose toward which the entire process of preparation, sowing and nurture is directed. Jesus applied this metaphor regularly to his discussion of the Kingdom. "Are grapes gathered from thorns, or figs from thistles? So, every sound tree bears good fruit...Thus you will know them by their fruits" (Matt. 7:16-20; cf. 12:33; Luke 13:6 ff.). The purpose of the Kingdom plant is to bear a certain kind of fruit. The servant of the Kingdom vineyard is to live a certain kind of life; and if it is not expressed, then we must face the possibility that the "wicked servant," the "salt without savor," is destined to be cast out of the visible company because he has never yet come alive to the sovereignty of God. In Chapter XIII we shall discuss in detail what Jesus had to say about the kind of fruit he expected — the meaning of Kingdom maturity toward which we are directed.

But sometimes in our churches "ripe" sons and daughters of the Kingdom are not being harvested. There are many mature Christians with talent, concern and training, who are not being put to work in the service of the Kingdom in ways that do justice to their maturity. They are like fruit that has been left to rot on the vine: frustrated, complaining, critical and often a source of obstruction to the clergyman or small power clique that sometimes controls the church. Their problem is usually their need to be harvested, by being given significant outlet for their energies and concern. Fruit is made to be eaten, and Kingdom motivation and commitment is made to be expended. It is my impression that the pews are filled with over-ripe Kingdom fruit that desperately need to be harvested. The church is wasting vast resources of power, over-ripe and under-expended.

A Theology for Lay Ministry

This chapter comes finally to focus on the laymen, for they are the substance of the church. Jesus was most complimentary in his appraisal of them. He was also dependent upon them for many things, from physical sustenance to the success of the disciples' preaching-teaching mission, and for faithfulness even unto death. As I have suggested, there were two major differences he seems to have made between this group and the twelve. The first was the authority to "bind and loose," and this seems to have been a difference in kind. The second was more a difference in degree. Although it would appear that he expected these laymen to teach and preach, the twelve were singled out for special instruction and were expected, therefore, to carry the burden of the preaching ministry. Nevertheless, I think it is clear that the laymen among Jesus' disciples were included in all his mission instructions. He gave them the same directions he gave the twelve, to proclaim the Kingdom by teaching, healing and preaching, by letting their lights shine through deeds of mercy and service. They, too, would be persecuted for righteousness' sake, and must trust God for strength and deliverance.

But why, then, have the laymen lost their place to the clergy in the teaching-preaching ministry of the Word? An adequate answer to this would be very complex. We see this distinction between the ministry of the Word and that of more mundane service beginning in the first few days after the resurrection over the issue of who was to wait tables in that early communal experiment. "And the twelve summoned the body of the disciples and said, 'It is not right that we should give up preaching the word of God to serve tables. Therefore, brethren, pick out from among you seven men of good repute...whom we may appoint to this duty. But we will devote ourselves to prayer and to the ministry of the word'" (Acts 6:2-4). That distinction may have had some practical justification at the time, and in those particular circumstances, but I believe it cannot be justified as a general principle in terms of Jesus' conception of the church. The ministry of the Word was given to both the clergy and the laity.

Through the years, however, this great reservoir of power, these Kingdom laymen, have too often been relegated to secondary duties, under-trained and ill used in ways that have frustrated committed and intelligent individuals. Because they are "faithful and good men," as Jesus called them, and I suspect because of centuries of being unduly impressed by the hyper-education of the clergy, they have remained in the background, with some gloriously notable exceptions. My experience with the laymen of the church in years of conducting the very kinds of laymen's Academies of Religion out of which this book arose, has been one of intense respect for the intelligence, good sense and dedication of the Catholic and Protestant laymen who represent an enormous, but largely undeveloped and untapped reserve of power for the church.

PART SEVEN

ETHICS, THE LIFE STYLE OF THE KINGDOM

Chapter XIII

An Ethic of Relationships

The Kingdom of God is infinitely practical. It is concerned with living real lives in the real world. Implicit within the experience of the Kingdom is a manner of living that stems from the nature of the Kingdom itself; and that very style of life is both an expression and a source of power. So before the power of the church can be fully realized, individually or collectively, the Kingdom life needs to be understood, disciplined and applied in intensely practical ways consistent with its nature. What does a son or daughter of the Kingdom look like? How does he or she behave, and how is the power of the Kingdom applied to the problems of daily living?

The term "ethics" is a neutral one, simply meaning how we act in our "ethos," our culture. It comes from the Greek, and means exactly the same as the word "morals," which comes from the Latin. The problem is that this empty term must receive some content. And one way or another it always does; for we inevitably act according to some set of ethical standards, whether consciously thought out, or unconsciously derived from our environment — usually the latter. Christians are no different from others in this respect, often acting unconsciously according to standards inherited from their surroundings, without thinking through the ethical implications of their experience as sons and daughters of the Kingdom. There is an urgent need these days to instruct, discipline and direct the power of the church in ways that are consistent with the Kingdom of God. The children of the Kingdom are called-out ones, different from the rest of mankind by virtue of their new life in the Kingdom. To deny this is to reject the new being; and to ignore it is to remain at a level of spiritual immaturity that fails to experience fully the power of the Kingdom life.

But how are the called-out ones different, and how can they relate this difference to their lives in the practical world? Without trying to give an exhaustive picture, I shall sketch some of the main outlines of what Jesus had to say on this subject, attempting to bring what I have already said about the Kingdom to specific focus on the practical matter of the life style of the Kingdom person. This is therefore a specialized ethic, and will have most meaning to those who have already entered the life of the Kingdom. To those who have not, it may help to explain some of the strange behavior of Christians.

The Radical Demands of Jesus' Ethic

The first thing one must be prepared for is the radical nature of Jesus' ethic. We must anticipate some dramatic new approaches to ethical problems that are not calculated to bring peace to the status quo, but rather to "cast fire upon the earth." And as one sharpens his understanding of the ethic of Jesus, he begins to see how far he went beyond the ethical demands of his own day.

One way to see this is to compare Jesus' teaching with that of John the Baptist. The first discovery is that in many ways their teaching was similar. This is perhaps not surprising since they were related, and must have had considerable knowledge of each other's ideas. Luke records a sermon of John in which the Baptist sounds strangely like Jesus: "You brood of vipers! Who warned you to flee from the wrath to come?" (Luke 3:7). Jesus also used these terms: "You brood of vipers, how are you to escape being sentenced to hell?" (Matt. 23:33; cf. 12:34). "Bear fruits that befit repentance," said John (Luke 3:8), and we are reminded of the many ways in which Jesus warned his audiences to bear the fruit that indicates what kind of tree or plant they are (Matt. 7:16). Speaking to the Jews who assumed they were included in God's Kingdom, John warned them not to presume too much, for "God is able from these stones to raise up children to Abraham" (Luke 3:8). Jesus also constantly taught that membership in the Kingdom of God was a matter of repentance and commitment, rather than racial inheritance (Luke 4:25-27; Mark 12:1-12, etc.). Finally, John warned his audiences of the imminent wrath of God: "Even now the axe is laid to the root of the trees," and this is the same message attributed to Jesus: "Every tree that does not bear good fruit is cut down and thrown into the fire" (Matt. 7:19; cf. 4:17; Luke 6:43; 19:44).

With these many similarities, it is especially interesting to note the differences between Jesus and John, particularly in their approach to ethics. John was a social conservative, but Jesus was clearly a radical. The multitudes came to John and asked him, "What then shall we do?" — an ethical question. John answered them, "He who has two coats, let him share with him who has none" (Luke 3:10-11). Jesus also had something to say about coats, but instead of sharing one's *extra* garment, he said to his disciples that "if any one would sue you and take your coat, let him have your cloak as well" (Matt. 5:40). Give him your overcoat also, a radical extension of John's rather conservative statement. The tax collectors also came to be baptized, and John said to them, "Collect no more than is appointed you," a sensible and highly moral bit of advice. But one is reminded of a man named Zacchaeus with whom Jesus spent a weekend, after which this tax collector pledged to give half his goods to the poor and to restore fourfold whatever he had exacted unjustly (Luke 19:8). The soldiers came to John and asked him, "What shall we do?" and John's reply was consistent with the rabbinic morality of his day: "Rob no one by violence or by false accusation, and be content with your wages" (Luke 3:14). Jesus also had some words about soldiers who were constantly pressing civilians into service: "If any one forces you to go one mile, go with him two miles" (Matt. 5:41). "If any man would come after me, let him...take up his cross and follow me. For whoever would save his life will lose it, and whoever loses his life for my sake will find it" (Matt. 16:24; Mark 8:35), "Sell what you possess and give to the poor" (Matt 19:21). John was a social conservative, but Jesus' ethic was breath-taking in its novelty and radicality; and if we would follow him in it, we too must be prepared for some solutions to ethical problems that are dramatically different from the ploddingly humdrum ethic of the "secular city."

A Kingdom Ethic

Any ethical system is a description of one's priorities — the distinctions we make between those things we put first in our lives and those which take lesser precedence. So Jesus' theology of the Kingdom demands that before our anxiety for food and drink, for clothing or length of days, or for physical life itself, we are to seek first the Kingdom of God, which is his righteousness (Matt. 6:25-34). "Man shall not live by bread alone, but by every word that proceeds from the mouth of God" (Matt. 4:4). "He who loves father or mother more than me is not worthy of me" (Matt. 10:37). "Do not lay up for yourselves treasures on earth...but lay up for yourselves treasure in heaven" (Matt. 6:19-20). What he is doing here is reversing the normal line of priorities which place the self and its physical needs first; and so again we are reminded of the radical nature of the Kingdom ethical economy. This comes to particularly sharp focus in one place where a scribe asks him about priorities; "Which commandment is the first of all?" Jesus' reply was in effect his summary of the theology of the entire Old Testament: "You shall love the Lord your God with all your heart, and with all your soul, and with all your mind, and with all your strength..." and "your neighbor as yourself" (Mark 12:28-31). Notice the order of importance here: God first, neighbor second, and last of all yourself. These are the priorities of the Kingdom.

An Ethic of Justice

What this means is that the Kingdom ethic is the acceptance of the imperative of God as Lord of our ethical lives; it is the affirmation that we do have freedom to make responsible decisions, and within God's justice, we must make them, and by them do we judge ourselves. "He has showed you, O man, what is good; and what does the Lord require of you but to do justice, and to love kindness, and to walk humbly with your God?" (Micah 6:8). We must act justly, not only because it is a good thing, but because God himself is justice. We must be merciful, not only because this, too, is a good thing, but because God is a loving God, and his imperative is that we express his nature in our lives. As Jesus put it, "Seek first his Kingdom *and his righteousness*" (Matt. 6:33). Righteousness is a synonym for justice, and is a description of the nature of the Lord of the Kingdom. That is why it is so very important ethically to understand the nature of God; for he is the basis of the Kingdom ethic.

A Relational Ethic

There are several major ways one can approach ethical questions: in terms of a set of rules, in terms of the interplay of institutional power, or in terms of relationships. The Kingdom ethic is clearly a relational ethic rather than a code spelled out like the provisions in a book of law. It is an ethic that develops out of the relationship between God and the sons and daughters of the Kingdom; it is the redemptive power of the love of God working within individuals and then through them in the life of the Kingdom community, and from that into the world. This is also why Jesus' ethic only makes real sense to those within the Kingdom, whose relationship with the

Lord of the Kingdom has led them to a new set of commitments which make the strange reverse logic of the Kingdom ethic completely reasonable: "The last shall be first...lose your life to find it...put yourself last...take up your cross...don't worry about what you shall eat.

An Inner Ethic

It is therefore an intensely personal ethic. It is an ethic of attitude before it is one of action, for it begins with the quickening of the sovereignty of God within the human heart.

In the Sermon on the Mount, Jesus says, "You have heard that it was said to the men of old, 'You shall not kill;'...But I say to you that every one who is angry with his brother shall be liable to the judgment...For out of the heart come...murder" (Matt 5:21; 15:19). This is actually an extension of an old Hebrew principle that it is not the taking of life (*harag*) that is to be condemned, but it is killing out of hatred and evil motive that is murder (*ratsach*, Ex. 20:13; Deut. 4:42; 5:17 etc.). Jesus was merely taking this principle one step further by saying that even without the act of killing, hatred itself was a form of murder, for it was the ultimate rejection of persons. And so with the other commandments of the decalogue. Whoever looks at a woman lustfully has committed adultry in his heart. I don't think Jesus was saying that the Kingdom life is one of lust-less perfection, but rather that adultery begins in the heart, and the Kingdom ethic goes beyond the external act into the innermost recesses of the human personality. "If your eye is sound, your whole body will be full of light" (Matt. 6:22). It is out of the abundance of the heart that the mouth speaks (Matt. 12:34). In all these ways, Jesus is going beyond Moses by plumbing more deeply into human personality and the essence of the Kingdom of God. He called it "fulfilling" the law (Matt. 5:17).

A Resultant Ethic

For any act to be Christian in this Kingdom sense, it must not be an end in itself, but a product of the Kingdom life. "You will know them by their fruits." That is, the fruit tells us something about the inner life because it is a product of the inner life of the plant. "The good man out of his good treasure brings forth good" (Matt. 12:25). So within this context, an ethical act is not an end in itself, nor is it a means to an end by which we might gain some personal benefit, but it is the result of the presence of God acting within that life. It is the power of the sovereign God producing the fruits of the spirit. It is the natural overflow of one's inner treasure of the heart. As one student put it in an examination paper: "It is the in-breaking Kingdom of God breaking out." This suggests strongly that outside of the Kingdom life, it is impossible to live or act according to the Kingdom ethic.

Jesus was constantly fighting the externalized legalism into which the noble pharisaism of his day had sunk, where, as he said, "you cleanse the outside of the cup...but inside...are full of extortion and rapacity" (Matt. 23:25). For the Judaism of his day, ethics was a matter of obeying the religious law, which was spelled out in such great detail that there were over fifteen hundred rules in the Mishnah for the honoring of the Sabbath day. In its highest conception, this life of minute obedience to law was a joy and an expression of deep love for God. But the problem with the way of the Torah has always been that the doing of the act becomes an end in itself, until men literally forget why it is that they do it, and attitudes degenerate into perfunctory ritualism, or baptized self-interest, where the act is done in order to gain favor with God. Jesus saw that this was the state of the religious life in his day, and he condemned the pharisees for paying attention to the externalities of the law, and ignoring the matters of the human heart.

But Christian people have great difficulty in separating themselves from a Jewish ethic of law, and more disastrously from that first century pharisaic ethic of religious self interest condemned in the Gospels. Each time I teach New Testament I realize this problem, for it is common for Christians to interpret the beatitudes in this fashion: *If* you are poor in spirit, *then* the Kingdom will be yours; *if* you mourn, *then* you will be comforted; *if* you are meek, *then* you will inherit the earth. These qualities are seen as ways of getting into the Kingdom of God, of being comforted and especially of inheriting the earth. What this interpretation is doing is just rehearsing the old self-serving legalism that Jesus tried so hard to overcome. The problem with such a bargaining approach to the Kingdom is that it doesn't go deeply enough into the meaning of that which brings the Kingdom rewards in the first place. Mourning and poverty of spirit and meekness and the rest are all descriptions of an attitude that puts God first and self last, and by their very nature exclude the kind of self interest that says, I am going to be meek *in order* that I may inherit the earth.

Jesus was realistic about the rewards of the Kingdom; and there is some evidence that he described the blessings of the Kingdom in physical terms. In Mark 10:29-30, the "hundredfold," which all those who have turned their backs on home and family are to receive, is apparently some reference to physical reward. The presence of the Holy Spirit automatically signals the expulsion of the demons that cause physical disorders (Luke 10:1-17). In the parable of the empty house (Luke 11:24-26), the "unclean spirit" driven from the house describes metaphorically the dumbness that Jesus has just healed by the "finger" or Kingdom of God. But the point is that these more mundane benefits are only the result or by-product of the deeper commitment to his righteousness. One notes, furthermore, that the rewards of the Kingdom described in the beatitudes are mostly spiritual, that is, rewards that can only flow from a genuine Kingdom experience that puts God interest before self interest. Jesus constantly warned against the hypocrisy of such pseudo-God interest which he called "the leaven of the Pharisees and Sadducees" (Matt. 16:6). He admitted that physical blessings come from living life God's way, but warned against putting them first. The problem is that if we make the benefit an end in itself, it tends to vanish, for it is a by-product of the inner life of the Kingdom.

A Social Ethic

This ethic is also intensely social. It requires God, ourselves, and our brothers and sisters to be complete. In the sermon on the mount Jesus says, "Do not resist one who is evil...turn your other cheek...give him your cloak also...if he asks you to go one mile, go two." Why? Not, I think, to avoid a fight, although this would accomplish it. The point is that this is the way to redeem our brother; more concerned to redeem him than to save ourselves. That is why we are to take up our cross, and lose our lives and deny ourselves. This ethic of the Kingdom drives us outward into the arms of our brother. This is the essential activity of the light on the hill: shining out into the darkness, expending ourselves that men may see our good works and glorify, not ourselves like the self-righteous pharisee (Luke 18:11), but our Father in heaven (Matt. 5:16). So this ethic of the Kingdom begins with an upward look, by putting first the Kingdom of God; it then involves an inward look, an ethic of the heart, whose fruits are the result of a Kingdom relationship; and this inevitably makes it an outward look to the hurts and injustices of the world. God, others, self, these are the dimensions of a total Kingdom ethic, and any decision which attempts to operate within a

Kingdom context must involve all three areas of concern, and in that order of priority.

It Bears a Particular Kind of Fruit

As an ethic of relationships, Jesus' teaching did not contain a code of behavior. There is no Christian Mishnah, that ancient Jewish book with its thousands of ethical rules. The closest to it is perhaps the sermon on the mount (Matt. 5-7), where someone within the early Christian community gathered together Jesus' ethical teaching into one long sermon. This is the way he taught on the hillsides of that natural amphitheatre in Galilee, and this is the kind of thing he was accustomed to say about ethics. But no one had a tape recorder, and a quick look at the parallels to these Matthew sayings in Luke shows Luke locating many of them elsewhere in Jesus' ministry. Here in this sermon is an editorial distillation of his ethical instruction, which reveals five major characteristics. 1) He clearly supported the law of Moses, which in this case meant the ten commandments: "I am not come to destroy the law...You have heard that it was said to men of old, 'You shall not kill...not commit adultery.'" Jesus was no antinomian, and one can begin by assuming the decalogue as basic to his thinking. 2) Jesus went beyond Moses, to a deeper level of ethical instruction, what he called the "fulfilling" of the law; and I shall say more about this later. 3) In contrast to the rabbis, he taught mostly in terms of general principles rather than specific cases, although on occasion he did cite particular instances (e.g., Matt. 5:25). 4) With some exceptions (Matt. 5:34), he taught positively, rather than in terms of a series of negative prohibitions, preferring to hold up examples of ideal behavior. 5) In characteristic fashion, he taught ethics both directly and metaphorically, often setting up a vivid contrast in a parable as a way of dramatizing the ideal ethical person.

Jesus did, therefore, have a clear conception of what the son and daughter of the Kingdom looked like ethically: "You will know them by their fruits" (Matt. 7:20); and this sermon on the mount is a collective picture of the ideal servant of the Kingdom. The mature fruit of the Kingdom is distinctive, and following Jesus' practice, I want here to gather together from the sermon, as well as the entire Synoptic material, an idealized portrait of the child of the Kingdom — what Jesus called the "blessed" one.

The Kingdom son or daughter is first of all a humble person: "Blessed are the poor in spirit." He is not one who exalts himself, or abuses others by his pride; but his humility is a sign of his reverence for God and his respect for others. Jesus warned against "practicing" one's piety before men (Matt. 6:1-16), and one can see something of the despised publican in Jesus' ideal servant of the Kingdom. Two men went up into the temple to pray, one a pharisee and the other a publican (Luke 18:10-14). The pharisee thanked God that he was not as other men, for instance the tax collector; for did he not fast twice a week and give tithes of all that he possessed? He was an officer in the most prestigious church in town, attended worship services twice a week and was a regular giver to the benevolence budget. But the tax collector, beat his breast, saying, "God, be merciful to me a sinner!" "I tell you, this man went down to his house justified rather than the other; for every one who exalts himself will be humbled, but he who humbles himself will be exalted." The sons and daughters of the Kingdom show that they have entered the Kingdom by their humility. No "proper" people, these blessed ones — just those who are aware of their need for God; and humility is an inescapable sign of such awareness.

The child of the Kingdom is secondly a concerned man or woman: "Blessed are those who mourn." I think Jesus is talking here about one who mourns for his own sins and for the troubles of others. He is a sympathetic person, which literally means "suffering with" other people. This is one of the ways of understanding Jesus' command to take up the cross and follow him; to look at life as he did, to weep over Jerusalem as he did, to take upon ourselves the agony of the world as he did. But this is not the mourning of despair. Jesus was not an existentialist in this modern sense. For if we take our place beside him on that cross, we make a wonderful discovery. Jesus was not alone, and we are not alone; and in that transfiguring fellowship, our mourning becomes a song of joy in the discovery that "all things are possible with God" (Mark 10:27).

This ideal servant of the Kingdom is, furthermore, a gentle person: "Blessed are the meek," not the cowardly, but the powerful meek, blessed with the power of God which shall ultimately inherit the earth. Gentleness is, I think, a sign of power rather than weakness, for it takes great confidence and great self-control to be gentle. The apostle Paul called it a sign of Christian maturity (Gal. 5:23).

The son of the Kingdom is one who hungers and thirsts after righteousness. This is not the sanctimonious reticence to soil one's life that is sometimes associated with this term. To hunger for righteousness is to yearn for God; it is to desire above all else to express his justice in our lives, to reflect his love, to do his will. Not because of some pious self interest, but because this is a natural and inevitable response to our relationship with the God of righteousness and justice. And the fascinating thing which is implied here is that unlike the hunger for food, this is a hunger which is never satisfied. In the economy of the Kingdom, the more one partakes of God's righteousness, what Jesus called in John, "the bread of life," the more one wants. And this divine hunger itself is the mark of the blessed one. The true atheist is the person in whom there is none of this hunger, no sense whatever of the presence of God; and this, as I have suggested, is the inescapable symptom of spiritual death.

Who is this child of the Kingdom? He is one who is "pure in heart," (Matt. 5:8), "full of light, having no part dark" (Luke 11:36). He is the "good soil" who is able to cradle the new life of the Kingdom (Mark 4:1 ff.), the "sound eye" who receives the light of God's presence (Matt. 6:22), the "sound tree" who bears the good fruit (Matt. 7:17). And this ideal servant of the Kingdom is one whose life is clean enough to reflect the light of the God of infinite purity without undue distortion. Piety is a lost word today, but I suspect God is not mocked. Whatever we sow, we do indeed reap (Gal. 6:7), and one of the great reasons for lack of power within the church today is the impurity within the personal lives of some of the sons and daughters of the Kingdom. We have taken our freedom in Christ too literally, and have felt that somehow this exonerates us from the judgment of God. But the impurities in the soil still hinder the mature growth of the plant. The unsoundness of the tree still prevents the production of fruit.

This blessed one is then a "peacemaker." Not just one who avoids conflict, but who agonizes over the making of peace. Of all the conditions of men that require intense effort, enormous maturity, prodigious love, that of making peace is, I believe, the most difficult. What a world this would be if we spent just half the time and money making peace that we spend making or preparing for war! We have a department of defense; but its efforts are spent almost exclusively in preparing for war. When will we learn this simple, yet profoundly difficult, Gospel lesson, that the greatest defense lies in preparing for, and spending great amounts of defense budget money for, peace? And even as we say this, we must remind ourselves of the deeper message in this simple beatitude. The peace that Jesus was talking about was not just the absence of war, or peace between neighbors. These are symptoms of something deeper. For him, peace was a description of the Kingdom of God. In Hebrew, the word peace, *shalom*, ultimately refers to God's salvation. And so again Jesus points not to symptoms, but to causes, and this is where the church must put its emphasis. John was on target when he reports Jesus describing this peace: "My peace I give to you; not as the world gives do I give to you" (John 14:27). In more Synoptic terms, outside of the justice of God's Kingdom, there is no peace.

This Kingdom person is, moreover, a faithful man or woman; faithful to the trust of being left in charge of the vineyard. He is a light shining in the world like a faithful lighthouse. He is a good witness, proclaiming abroad the word he has heard. He is "persecuted for righteousness' sake," because he has dared to stand for God's righteousness. And if no one ever opposes us; if we are never criticized for the stand we have taken, individually or collectively; if no one ever persecutes us because he doesn't agree with what we believe, then we have cause to wonder if we have really been faithful to our trust as servants of the Kingdom of God.

But this is a joyous life. The Kingdom is a wedding feast; and the ideal servant is described as a radiant person, "full of light...not like the hypocrites" with their dismal, disfigured countenances (Matt. 6:16). Again John has accurately described the Synoptic mood when Jesus says, "These things I have spoken to you, that my joy may be in you, and that your joy may be full" (John 15:11).

He is also a person of understanding. In his special instruction to the twelve, Jesus said, "To you has been given the secret of the Kingdom of God" (Mark 4:10). The seed sown in the soil of the soul is described as the word of God, which is at one and the same time a source of power and a source of understanding. The light that illuminates the mind comes from God who is the light; and the very experience of loving God is an experience of the mind (Mark 12:30). As it is made more explicit in John, "If any man's will is to do his will, he shall know..." (John 1:17). Paul further elaborated this idea by saying that spiritual things are "spiritually discerned" (I Cor. 2:14). With the Kingdom experience comes a new depth of understanding into the person and nature of God that represents the word of God growing within the soil of the Kingdom life.

The blessed one is a disciplined person. His thoughts are disciplined. Jesus said, "Every one who is angry with his brother shall be liable to judgment" (Matt. 5:21). His speech is disciplined: "Men will render account for every careless word they utter; for by your

191

words you will be justified, and by your words you will be condemned" (Matt. 12:36-37). Love itself is a discipline, and the forgiveness
which is its symptom is a necessary product of the life of Kingdom
servanthood (Matt. 18:23-35). The imperative of God's justice is
particularly strong in Jesus' message of the Kingdom, and so in his
teaching he called himself a "severe" (*austeros*) man, reaping where
he had not sown (Luke 19:22).

Who is the servant of the Kingdom? He is a committed person,
seeking the Kingdom first, before money, or job, or food, or even
family. The order of priorities is clear: God first, others second and
self last. He is an integrated person, and the core of his integration is
the living presence of God within. There is nothing more powerful
than the presence of God to unite the personality, to focalize one's
energies, to centralize his thinking, and so to bring the health that is
the product of the wholeness of body, mind and spiritual potential.

An Ethic of Maturity in Love

Finally, the ideal son of the Kingdom is a loving person: "Blessed are
the merciful." The sermon on the mount is filled with this theme:
"Love your enemies and pray for those who persecute you," "By this
shall all men know that you are my disciples, if you love one
another." And then he sums it all up in a phrase that is often
misunderstood: "You, therefore, must be perfect, as your heavenly
Father is perfect." And at that point we lay down the Bible with a
sigh and say to ourselves, this ethic is too demanding! Who can be
perfect? The answer is, obviously, no one. As Jesus said, "One there
is who is good," and that is God alone (Matt. 19:17). This entire sermon presents an awesome picture, and places us all under judgment; and it can be discouraging unless we keep two things in mind.
The first is Jesus' central metaphor. He is describing *mature* fruit;
the Christian ethic is a *process* of growth toward maturity. We are
not sons of the Kingdom by moral attainment, but by spiritual
generation; and our growth in the Kingdom life is a slow process of
maturation where, like the metaphor of the growing tree, the
various fruits of the Kingdom mature at various rates. It is interesting to note that the description I have been giving of the
mature child of the Kingdom, the "blessed" one, is almost exactly
the same as the one Paul gives us of the fruits of the spiritual life:
"love, joy, peace, patience, kindness, goodness, faithfulness,
gentleness, self control." This is Paul's portrait of "those who belong
to Christ" (Gal. 5:22-24), and is actually a collective picture of Jesus

192

himself, who epitomizes and transfigures all those human characteristics, and who calls us to grow up into him, into what Paul later called "mature manhood...the measure of the stature of the fulness of Christ" (Eph. 4:13). We are not expected to duplicate the character of Christ, but we are called to grow up into him, and in this sermon, the "perfect" experience of the Kingdom comes to most mature expression in the life of love.

The second antidote to moral discouragement is a deeper understanding of what Jesus meant by being perfect. What we need to realize is that the word translated "perfect" (*teleios*) is often, and perhaps most accurately, translated "mature," which takes away the image of moral spotlessness as the Kingdom ideal, and supports the Christian ethic as a process of growth toward varying degrees of spiritual maturity. But even further, this word *teleios* is ultimately a description of the love of God: "As your heavenly Father is perfect." Jesus is here summing up his many sayings about loving others in terms of the fulfillment of the law, which is nothing less than the reflection of the love of God in our lives. Paul got the point when he called such love "that which is perfect" (*teleios*), or "mature" (I Cor. 13:10). The Kingdom ethic is a life lived within an experience of the love of God; not a set of rules to be obeyed, but a divine communion to be experienced; not an ideal of spotless perfection, but a set of loving relationships that reflect the maturity of God himself.

There is no greater ethical power on earth. Mankind groans with longing, our institutions cry out with desperation for mature sons and daughters of the Kingdom of God.

PART EIGHT

THE ESCHATON, THE FINAL CONSUMMATION OF THE KINGDOM

Chapter XIV

There Will Be an End

The power of the Kingdom stems finally from its awareness of the manner in which the ongoing stream of history stands in relation to the eschaton, which is the end of time. The size and adequacy of one's understanding of the theology of Jesus depends on many things; and ultimately on the sense of movement and direction in the activities of men and nations of stars and galaxies; on the knowledge that there is meaning and purpose behind it all; on the awareness that this physical life is but a prelude to a greater life beyond; on the realization that in the end, all mankind will stand before the final judgment of God. These are the ponderous, inexorable, awesome elements within the Gospel which chasten our pride and drive us to our knees in reverence before the ultimate mystery. A theology that has no eschatology has no real depth of perspective, for it has not thought life through to the end.

Some Definitions

First we must define one term and make an important distinction between two others occurring regularly in what is to follow. They are prophet, eschatology and apocalypticism. It is common to identify a prophet as one who predicts the future; and certainly there was a predictive element in the message of the Old Testament prophets. A more comprehensive understanding of prophecy, however, reveals that prediction is actually a minor part of a much larger phenomenon. As John Bowman pointed out years ago in his book *The Religion of Maturity*, a prophet is most basically a person with an intense awareness of God: Moses confronted by God in a burning bush, Isaiah driven to his knees in a temple that seemed to

195

be filled with the smoke of God's holiness. Out of this confrontation comes a sense of a word to proclaim; and Jeremiah cries out with the burden of the word of God which is like a burning fire within him: "Thus says the Lord." This is regularly a word of warning and of promise, filled with the judgment of God. Its prediction of doom or salvation is always conditional upon the choices of men and women. This is then a word of justice, and contains a characteristically strong concern for society: "What does the Lord require of you, but to do justice and love mercy and walk humbly with your God" (Micah 6:8). The ancient prophets were not sooth-sayers, nor clair-voyants; they were men and women whose lives were specially in tune with the presence, the word, the justice of God. Whatever the prophet had to say about the end was then said within a much stronger concern for his present time, and all within a consuming orientation to the justice of God. Eschatology comes from the Greek word *eschatos*. It is a large concept, and refers to a general treat-ment of the entire subject of the end of time. Any one saying something about the end is dealing with eschatology; and this is an important concern of both Old and New Testament. Most prophetic figures were eschatologists, in that their vision of God's plan tended to leap forward to the ultimate consummation of his judgment.

Apocalypticism, on the other hand, is a more limited term, describing a particular kind of eschatology. It arose within the Hebrew culture at the end of the period that produced the Old Testament (about 300 B.C.), and was particularly strong in a large body of Jewish literature emerging at that time. As a result, it was especially active during the time of Jesus and the half century out of which the written New Testament emerged (65-100 A.D.). This type of eschatology is evident in the books of Daniel and Ezekiel in the Old Testament, and Revelation, II Thessalonians 2:1-12 and Mark 13 in the New Testament. There are three ways in which apocalyp-ticism may be characterized: 1) It is a *point of view* that is non-prophetic; that is, it has little awareness of the immediate presence of God, and little concern for applying his justice to the personal and social sins of men. It tends to be pessimistic about man's ability to accomplish justice within history, and looks primarily, if not ex-clusively to the end time for the manifestation of the justice of God. 2) It is also a *method* of presenting religious thought that has a more self-consciously literary style than the prophetic material. The characteristic motif is that of the vision; and the common formula is, "I looked and lo I beheld." This gives the appearance of being more a literary device than a reference to an actual spiritual experience. The religious thought is regularly presented in the guise of strange symbolic figures, secret numbers, and intermediaries who act as God's messengers. 3) Apocalypticism is also characterized as an *emphasis* upon God in his complete transcendence, and a veritable fixation upon the *eschaton* as immediately near, coming in cataclysmic ways with strange signs and portents and typically strident in its concern to predict the time. There is always a "horizontal," temporal urgency about apocalyptic material that contrasts with what I have called the more "vertical," spiritual urgency of the prophetic (Chapter VI).

Normative Old Testament eschatology is prophetic, and contrasts sharply with the apocalyptic, which the Hebrew has admitted into canonical literature in Daniel and Ezekiel as descriptive dress for what is otherwise thoroughly prophetic. Whether or not Jesus allied himself with the apocalyptists is one of the critical questions of this chapter, and failure to make this careful distinction between eschatology and apocalypticism is one of the major sources of confusion in discussions of biblical eschatology.

The Basic Themes of Jesus' Eschatology

The most powerful argument for giving eschatology an important place in Christian theology is that Jesus seems to have done so in his teaching about the Kingdom of God. The Passover he ate was to be fulfilled in the eschatological Kingdom (Luke 22:16). The judgments men pass on others, and so on themselves, were placed under the surveillance of the end time (Matt. 7:2). The cities where most of his mighty works were done were brought under the condemnation of the "day of judgment" (Matt. 11:24). As we have already noted, Jesus had a very real concern for time in a horizontal sense, bounded by creation and eschaton. This linear history would continue only "till heaven and earth pass away" (Matt. 5:18; 24:3 ff.). There is actually a mass of data to document his interest in this subject, within which there are three basic themes constantly appearing. These are the same eschatological themes found in the Hebrew Old Testament and inter-testamental literature, but contain modifications characteristic of Jesus' Kingdom theology.

The Day of Judgment

The first of these great themes is the "day of the Lord." In the Old

Testament, this concept has many meanings, beginning on a rather low level, and reaching toward the kind of spiritual heights with which Jesus identified. On its lowest level, it merely refers to any punishment or calamity which befalls men and nations (Joel 1:15; Jer. 46:10). On its highest level, it represents an eschatological judgment intimately linked with the Kingdom of God and the messianic age (Is. 24-27). It is a physical judgment on all men and women, a short, climactic day occurring at the end of history, and yet somehow within the stream of ongoing time. It centers in and around the city of Jerusalem, which becomes the scene of the judgment of God. At these high points of Old Testament prophecy, the three dimensional categories of time — past, present and future — are strained with what John Marsh called the trans-historical tensions of eternity; but they never quite get beyond time as horizontal extension.

Jesus seems to have borrowed this concept from his Hebrew environment, and then put his characteristic stamp upon it. There are two terms he is recorded using regularly in this connection. The first is "day" (*hemera*), which occurs in five different but inter-changeable phrases throughout all the underlying Gospel sources: "on that day...the day of judgment...that day...in his day...the day of the Son of man" (Matt. 7:22; 11:22; Mark 13:32; Luke 17:22, 24, 30 etc.). These formulas are primarily seen in warnings against final judgment, and contain several patterns typical of Jesus' eschatology: finality, suddenness, preparedness, the Kingdom of God and the reward and punishment of judgment. There is a similarity and wide usage that argues strongly for their authenticity as words of Jesus. One thing clearly suggested here is that the eschaton will not be a gradually unfolding, indefinite period of time, but rather a short, limited experience, like a day or an hour (Matt. 25:13; Mark 13:35). We will know that it has come, and it will have a clear beginning and ending.

The Age of the Coming Messiah

A second eschatological theme Jesus borrowed from his Old Testament sources is the age of the coming messiah who is to be God's special emissary to redeem Israel at the end of time. It is in this material that the main reference to the Kingdom of God in the Old Testament is centered. This age is typified by the direct sovereignty of Jehovah in Jerusalem: "The Lord of hosts will reign on Mount Zion and in Jerusalem" (Is. 24:23). It is an age that will come only in the "latter days" (Micah 4:1). It will be an extended period, a "year of the Lord's favor" (Is. 61:2). It will be characterized by peace (Micah 4:3), by the exaltation of Zion over all the earth (Obad. 21; Micah 4:1-8), by the rule of righteousness (Is. 32:1), by salvation and the revelation of Jehovah's love to his people (Is. Chs. 65-66). This messianic age is often linked with the pictures of Israel restored to Jerusalem from captivity (Zeph. Ch. 3; Is. 52:7), but then again there are hints of a truly universal Kingdom (Zech. 14:9). In all this Old Testament material, the messianic age is identified mainly with an eschatological Kingdom to be localized in the physical city of Jerusalem, a real theocracy at the end of, yet within, history. The important thing to remember is that for the Hebrew, then as today, the messiah comes only at the end of time, and so Hebrew messianism is always eschatological.

The Christian Gospel, on the other hand, is the proclamation that the messiah has already come in Jesus Christ, and this is still the crux of the difference between Judaism and Christianity. We have already seen that Jesus viewed himself as the fulfillment of Hebrew messianic prophecy. This means that when he talked of an eschatological messiah, he did so in terms of the *return*, or the *second* coming of this figure.

There are two forms in which Jesus identifies with, and then goes beyond, this Old Testament theme. The first is his series of parabolic descriptions of the returning messiah, which contain all the characteristic themes of his eschatology, and portray the reward and punishment of God's judgment with special vividness. This is a time when the master (Luke 12:42-44), the householder (Matt. 20:1-16), the nobleman (Luke 19:11-27) and the man on a journey (Mark 13:33-37), return and reward their servants for their faithfulness. It is a time When the bridegroom returns and takes the wise virgins with him into the feast (Matt. 25:1-13), when the owner of the field comes with his harvesters and brings the field into judgment (Matt. 13:24-30). In all these parables, there is a finality about his coming that brooks no further trifling, no extended time, no second chance. The issue has been decided. Now there is only blessedness, or terrible rejection. In every parable the judgment is based on the issue of moral-spiritual preparedness, faithfulness, the response to the call, fruitfulness, the possession of oil, the status as wheat, all typical Synoptic symbols of souls prepared for the *eschaton*.

The other form Jesus uses in this connection is that of the eschatological Son of man. This, too, has been a subject of considerable debate in recent years. Some, like Dodd, Glasson, Jeremias, and J. A. T. Robinson have insisted that the so-called *parousia*, the second coming of the Son of man, was a creation of the early church. Others like Beasley-Murray, Fison, Cullmann, Kummel, Fuller and Ladd, insist that this is not only a valid doctrine, but one of the focal points of Jesus' thought and of the faith and hope of the early church. The battle is not over, but I sense that in recent years it has waned considerably, and that few scholars today would attempt, with T. F. Glasson, to rid the Synoptics of all eschatology. What we have perhaps learned from this debate is to be more aware of our presuppositions, not make sweeping generalizations, and allow each passage to stand or fall on its own merits. As I see it, the evidence of the Synoptic teachings of Jesus suggests a genuine eschatology and future *parousia*, adorned and complicated by the fairly obvious enthusiasm of some around him for apocalyptic and eschatological concerns.

One of the most explicit examples of this theme occurs in Luke's description of "the day of the Son of man" in terms of five graphic similes: it is like lightning; it is like the days of Noah; it is like the days of Lot; it is like two in a bed, like two grinding corn, the one will be taken and the other left (Luke 17:22-37). Jesus is warning the disciples that the day of the Son of man will be delayed, and is urging them not to let their impatience cause them to follow those who will be ready to point out the signs of the end and to set the date for its arrival.

All five similes converge at four points, which are typical of Jesus' eschatological teaching elsewhere. 1) This will be a day when God will judge the souls of men and women. He will separate the righteous from the unrighteous as Noah was separated from those whom the flood destroyed, as Lot was separated from those in the wicked city, as one woman or one man is separated from another in the midst of their daily tasks. This is strongly reminiscent of Jesus' parabolic teaching elsewhere about the *eschaton*, where the sheep are separated from the goats (Matt. 25:31-46), the good fish from the bad (Matt. 13:48-49), the wheat from the tares (Matt. 13:30). 2) This day will be as sudden as a bolt of lightning, as unexpected as the flood that caught Noah's contemporaries unprepared, as unattended by warning signs as the fire and brimstone that rained on Sodom and Gomorrah, or the selection that catches men in bed and women grinding grain. 3) This day will be as definite and unmistakable as the lightning, as the flood, as the fire and brimstone, as the wrenching apart of friends and loved ones. There will be no need to say, "Lo, here!" or "Lo, there!" for all will know that the day has come. 4) This will be a universal judgment, occurring wherever there are bodies over which the vultures may gather (Luke 17:37; cf. Rev. 19:17-18), a judgment that cannot be localized with a "here" or "there." It would seem that all four of these meanings are implicit in each one of the five similes of this passage, and it would be only arbitrary speculation for us to attempt to say which one receives the strongest emphasis in the mind of Jesus.

The basic point being made by all this language about the age of the coming messiah, is that it will be an experience of the presence of Jesus Christ who has gone away in humiliation and returned in glory, gone away as a crucified man and returned as the focal center of the ultimate judgment of God.

The Glorified Kingdom of God

The third and most characteristic eschatological theme which Jesus borrowed from his Hebrew environment and then "fulfilled" in his Holy Word is that of the glorified Kingdom of God. The Old Testament uses the word Kingdom (*malkuth*) in three main ways. 1) The Kingdom of God is first of all identified with the Kingdom of Israel. This is usually spoken of as an everlasting Kingdom. It is a real political theocracy within the present age (I Chron. 28:5; Ex. 19:6; II Sam. 7:13). 2) The Kingdom is God's sovereignty in the heavens. It is an everlasting sovereignty over all mankind, and in this sense breaks out of the first more parochial usage (Ps. 22:28; 103:19; Dan. 4:3; I Chron. 29:11). 3) The Kingdom of God refers to the future, final reign of God, instituted at the Final Judgment, and localized in Jerusalem. It is, nevertheless, a real, physical theocracy, existing on earth within time (II Sam. 7:13; Is. 9:7; 65; Dan. 2:44; Obad. 21). This is the glorified Kingdom associated with the coming of the messiah, which the religious Jews are still awaiting.

Through the centuries, Christians have taken this prophecy seriously, often more so than the Jews. The author of the book of Revelation portrays the climax of the great eschatological drama to be "the new Jerusalem, coming down out of heaven from God, prepared as a bride adorned for her husband" (Rev. 21:2). He goes on to describe the *eschaton* in terms of Jerusalem whose walls will be of jasper and adorned with jewels; the gates will be made of pearls and the city of pure gold, "clear as glass." The glory of God will be its illumination, and the river of the water of life, flowing from the very throne of God, will run through the city and water the tree of life. Highly idealized, highly metaphorical and located in Jerusalem.

Several years ago I spent eight weeks in a hotel atop the Mount of Olives. Just outside my window was the tiny chapel of the ascension, where for centuries Christians and Moslems have located the site of the messiah's return. At almost any hour of the day one could look out and see Christian groups worshipping in the circular compound surrounding the small domed structure, many of them no doubt anticipating the glorification of Jerusalem at any moment.

The interesting thing is that Jesus, in the Synoptic Gospels, made no such prediction. He promised to return again, and he did speak of the end in terms of some elements of the Old Testament glorified Kingdom, but coming specifically to Jerusalem was not part of the promise. This is pure Old Testament, and runs quite counter to the teaching of Jesus. What he did was to take this horizontal, local and highly parochial vision of the *eschaton*, and turn it on end. He universalized and spiritualized the Old Testament concept of the glorified Kingdom, as he did every other idea borrowed from his environment. Ultimately for Jesus, God's time is vertical; time and space come together in the eternal presence of God. This means that the horizontal point of time called *eschaton* must ultimately be understood not in terms of cities and the tiny country of Israel, but in terms of the eternally present time of God, for whom such symbols as return and wedding feasts and judgment thrones are analogies for ultimate reunion with God, within or outside of Jerusalem. Jesus did have a lot to say about the glorified Kingdom, but much that passes for Christian eschatology, especially in its twentieth century Jerusalem orientation, is pure Judaism, and not part of his Holy Word.

The Little Apocalypse (Mark 13)

One section of the Gospels seems to contradict what I have just said — Mark 13 and its parallels (Matt. 24:1-36; Luke 21:8-36). Here it would seem that Jesus is predicting the end of the world and the destruction of Jerusalem as part of the same impending experience: "But when you see the desolating sacrilege set up where it ought not to be...then let those who are in Judea flee to the mountains...for in those days there will be such tribulation as has not been from the beginning of creation." This passage has been the subject of extensive discussion in recent years. Vincent Taylor, in his commentary on Mark, has clearly stated the conclusions of a host of New Testament scholars before him and since with regard to this passage. I agree with this and will document my agreement more extensively in the next chapter.

"It is now widely agreed that 1) the chapter is composite and that with reasonable certainty the last Markan modifications can be determined; 2) that doctrinal and catechetical interests have affected the material which Mark used; and 3) that genuine sayings of Jesus are embodied in it and adapted to later conditions."

The confusion seems to be this: Mark 13 is introduced with two questions, not one. 1) The first question deals with the destruction of Jerusalem. "When will this be?" that is, "not one stone left upon another" (v. 2); 2) the second question is about the *eschaton*. "What will be the sign when all these things are to be accomplished?" (Matthew says, "the sign of your coming and the close of the age," 24:3). With this clue, we see that this passage contains two strands of tradition, one dealing with the first question and the other with the second, but woven together in such a fashion as to give the impression that the two events would occur simultaneously. The following outline is suggestive of the order in which the two strands have been interwoven.

Mark 13:1-4 The substance of the two questions
　　　5-13 Concerning the Second Coming and the end of the world
　　　14-23 Concerning the destruction of Jerusalem
　　　24-27 Concerning the Second Coming and the end of the world
　　　28-30 Concerning the destruction of Jerusalem
　　　31-37 Concerning the Second Coming and the end of the world

If this is a correct analysis, then the rather artificial alternation between the two themes strongly suggests that although much of this material doubtless represents authentic teaching, the final form is a literary work carefully composed by some editor to give the impression, found nowhere else in the Gospels, that Jesus taught that the end of the age would center upon the city of Jerusalem. This is what I call an "anti-pattern," and would seem to be a later Christian adaptation of Jesus' thought in the direction of Old Testament, Jerusalem centered prophecy.

The Nature of the Final Judgment: Eschatological Reward

Jesus' description of the end involved all three of these basic eschatological themes, the day of judgment, the age of the coming messiah, the glorified Kingdom of God, interwoven in the kinds of simile and metaphor typical of the rest of his teaching. He did not try to talk explicitly and factually about the *eschaton* — when, where and how — for he knew that in describing that which transcends our three dimensional world he must of necessity use pictures, symbols, parables, metaphors. He is therefore speaking analogically, and these analogies of proportion (cf. pp.47 f) are only valid within limits and when understood as analogies. The problem comes when we try to take them as factual descriptions, or push the analogies too far so they become distorted and begin to contradict other more widely established ideas of Jesus' teaching. The interpretation of any eschatological symbol must be compatible with the generality of patterns in the Holy Word, otherwise we must say either that it is not an authentic saying of Jesus, or our interpretation is inaccurate.

My general impression of this material is of its lack of extravagance, and its continuity with all else that Jesus said about God and his Kingdom. As men and women respond to the claims of the sovereign God, so are they judged. This judgment begins during each person's lifetime, and comes to its climax in the *eschaton*, the universal termination of history, beyond which physical life as we know it has no meaning, and in which our souls are dealt with on the basis of the judgment they have already elected. From the judgment of this *eschaton* there is no appeal, no opportunity for reconsideration, but only the reward and punishment that is the dynamic fulfillment of the crisis going on within history.

The *eschaton* resolves itself into two great poles, which are the final expression of the love and the wrath of God. It is the person and nature of God who gives meaning and character to the *eschaton*, as to every other aspect of the Kingdom. Jesus was a painter of word pictures; and although we cannot push them too far, there are several clear ideas that emerge as patterns from this eschatological exhibit. Let us begin by looking at the positive side of God's judgment, which is the ultimate fulfillment of his plans and purposes for men and women, for horizontal history, for time and the universe.

The Fulfillment of the Promise of Eternal Life

The *eschaton* is first of all the inheriting of a promised Kingdom, of eternal life fully realized, which the righteous already possess in ways that are limited by human considerations. The parable of the laborers in the vineyard is a good illustration (Matt. 20:1-16). It is a drama in two acts that answers precisely Peter's question: "Lo, we have left everything and followed you. What then shall we have?" (Matt. 19:27). Each act represents one phase of the historical-eschatological process. In the first act, the owner of the vineyard, God, or the messiah figure, invites persons to come and work in the vineyard, which is the symbol of the Kingdom of God. They are called early and late in the day — an indication of the passage of horizontal time. Each is promised the same reward; and so while they are working, they possess the reward, but as a promise for the future.

Then comes the second act of this drama, which is introduced by the crucial phrase, "And when evening came, the owner of the vineyard said to his steward, 'Call the laborers and pay them their wages'" (Matt. 20:8). There is now a decided shift in emphasis and plane of reference. The day when the householder continues to call men to the Kingdom vineyard is over. No longer is there opportunity for entrance. Now there is only reward for those who have already answered the call.

And so the promise if fulfilled, and Luke underscores the theme of reward as promise and fulfillment by placing the parable at the end of a long discussion about Kingdom benefits. There are several factors that give us a clue to the nature of the wages. Since this is a parable of the Kingdom, then the eschatological reward should be consistent with its spiritual nature. This is also an absolute reward. Each man, no matter how long he has worked, receives the same *denarius*, a Hebrew coin worth a day's wages for a farm worker. It would seem to be the automatic result of merely being in the Kingdom vineyard. This implies that there is no reward that could more fully compensate the laborers for being in the vineyard. In Luke's context, Jesus has just paralleled the phrase, "enter the kingdom of God" (Mark 10:23-25) with "receive...eternal life" (Mark 10:30). There would seem to be justification for identifying the *denarius* as that crucial reward which is the result of a life lived in the vineyard of God's presence — eternal life, possessed as a promise and a certain quality of life in this historical age, and inherited in all its fullness at the *eschaton*.

Inclusion in a Consummated Kingdom Fellowship

The most characteristic picture of the reward of God's final judgment is one of inclusion in the consummated Kingdom fellowship, a glorified communion with God. The parable of the waiting servants is a graphic illustration which deals mainly with the positive side of the final crisis. "Let your loins be girded and your lamps burning, and be like men who are waiting for their master to come home from the marriage feast, so that they may open to him at once when he comes and knocks. Blessed are those servants whom the master finds awake when he comes; truly, I say to you, he will gird himself and have them sit at table, and he will come and serve them" (Luke 12:35-37). The first half of the parable speaks of the kind of moral-spiritual preparation that God demands within human lives, couched in terms of girded loins and burning lamps. The second half carries this theme to its eschatological fulfillment with the figurative description of the rewards of blessedness. The repeated emphasis on the word "come" confirms this as a description of the second coming of the messiah. The identification of the disciple audience with the servants of the parable follows Jesus' consistent pattern, and shows this to be one of those parables where he describes the disciple band as a mixed company. Only those who have obeyed the master's command to stay awake, whose loins are girded, whose lamps are lit, who are therefore spiritually alive, are worthy of being called servants, and of receiving the reward that is compatible with their present spiritual condition.

The description of the eschatological reward as a messianic feast is common to both Jesus and his Jewish contemporaries. The creative mark of Jesus' mind is seen in another of those bizarre elements running counter to the customs of the physical world, and also to Rabbinic and Old Testament descriptions of the *eschaton*, but which he loved to use as pegs upon which to hang his major emphases. The master comes and serves his servants (cf. Luke 22:27; John 13:4-5). Here is a beautiful description of the incomprehensible love of God, forever coming near to persons, and at the *eschaton* coming near in a very special way.

So often does this picture occur that we seem to have here the heart of Jesus' concept of eschatological reward. It is the beginning of a new fellowship with the Lord that is the natural and "theological" culmination of a relationship already possessed. The wise virgins already know the bridegroom, but then they are with him in the wedding feast (Matt. 25:1-13). The invited ones are already guests by their acceptance of the promise, but then they actually experience the joys of the banquet where God is host (Matt. 22:1-10). The stalks of wheat already know the generating activity and care of the householder, but then they have reached that which symbolizes the epitome of the owner's value and protection: they are in the barn (Matt. 13:24-30). The good fish already know the enfolding limits of the fisherman's net, but then they know the more intimate confines of the fisherman's jar (Matt. 13:37-50). The sheep are already part of the shepherd's flock, but then they are with him in the fold (Matt. 25:31-46; Luke 15:3-7). All of these symbols describe the consummation of the judgment that has already taken place. In spiritual, human terms, the servant, the sheep, the wheat, the fish, the wise virgins, all describe the soul that has begun to live in the dimension of the spirit, although imperfectly, because as he said in other figures, the soil is never quite free of rocks and weeds (Mark 4:1 ff.), or the house of demons (Luke 11:25). When the *eschaton* comes and the Son of man returns, then these sons of the Kingdom will enjoy in all its radiant fullness that which they have already experienced in part, and that is the spiritual sovereignty of God. The continuity between the present and eschatological reward of God's judgment is nothing less than the continuity of the love and the presence of God.

The Nature of Heaven

Jesus seems to have had little to say in explicit terms about the exact nature of the resurrection life. He is recorded using the technical terms for resurrection, *anastasis* and *egeiro*, on only three occasions (Mark 12:18-27; Luke 11:31; 14:14), and typical of his practice, he talked about the "stuff" of heaven almost exclusively in simile and metaphor. As we have seen before, when one talks about reality that transcends the three-dimensional world, then he is driven by the very nature of words and the human mind to talk in analogies. So Jesus said it was like a wedding feast, like a master returning, like a harvest time, like the evening when the door is shut and the master rewards his servants. Whatever else one says about the *eschaton*, it would seem to be mostly characterized by Jesus in terms of the Kingdom and glory and eternality of God. At this point, all categories of time and space become what we have called "vertical" in the consummate presence of God. The "stuff" of eschatological heaven is God in his love as presence and power.

There are two further words that characterize this experience. The first is "identity." In the recurring sense of continuity between

God's judgment as promise and fulfillment, Jesus clearly implies an identity between the historical and the eschatological person. Here is no disappearance of the personality in some timeless sea, but rather the judgment of souls on the basis of their historic decisions and spiritual conditions. It is the same wheat that is gathered into the barn; the same fish stored in the jar; the same ten and five talent men rewarded when the nobleman returns. It is the same servant who receives the evening *denarius* who has been working throughout the heat of the day.

The idea of reunion with loved ones in heaven is not a Synoptic one; but the teachings of Jesus would seem to be compatible with it. The one passage that touches on this question, however, suggests that such things as marriage relationships as we know them will be quite different from their expression in this life. There was a woman who had been married to seven brothers successively. The sadducees asked Jesus whose wife she would be in the resurrection. He answered, "When they rise from the dead, they neither marry nor are given in marriage, but are like angels in heaven" (Mark 12:25). Since the common pattern of Jesus' teaching suggests a clear continuity between individuals before and after their resurrection, this singular statement to the sadducees must either be an anti-pattern, or we must understand it in some way that is compatible with the eschatological retention of our identity. This is just the sort of brilliant reply that would be remembered, and fits very well with Jesus' general view of cosmology (See Chapt. V); so we must probably understand it as some subtle point about three-dimensional priorities where the question as to which husband came first would be resolved by the fact that in the resurrection life, in the vertical dimension of the spirit, such things no longer would be a problem.

The other word is "responsible." This impression of distinct and separate existence is strengthened when we see Jesus hinting that eschatological reward involves a certain responsible activity. In the parable of the faithful and unfaithful servants (Luke 12:42-48), the present blessedness of the servant (v. 43) is given its final fulfillment in these words: "Truly I tell you, he will set him over all his possessions." In like manner in the parable of the pounds (Luke 19:11-27), the final reward is described in responsible terms: "You shall have authority over ten cities." If the nature of God is imperative, and man's earthly experience of him is one of command and responsible activity, then it would seem that the glorification of this relationship would also involve a glorified life of obedience. If man's obligation as a child of the Kingdom is to reflect the nature of God, his justice, his love and righteousness, then one might hazard the suggestion that the eschatological imperative involves the amplification of this historical responsibility: to reflect in perfect measure the nature of God.

The Nature of the Final Judgment: Eschatological Punishment

But now let us examine the eschatological negative. This is the most difficult aspect of eschatology; to sort out, because it is so complicated, and to discuss, because it is so painful. We must do so, however, for Jesus had a great deal to say about this subject, and unless we have come to grips with the ultimate wrath of God, we have not really finished our understanding of his theology of the Kingdom. In general, the final act in the drama of judgment against unrepentant souls involves the consummation of the crisis going on in the present; the making final and complete of that which is conditional and incomplete as long as human life is capable of making responsible decisions. In the teaching of Jesus there are two basic pictures of final retribution, and these represent the theological extension of his concept of the wrath of God.

Exclusion from the Kingdom of God

Jesus describes present punishment as man's self-exclusion from the Kingdom of God. In keeping with this the final consummation is portrayed as an abysmal rejection that plumbs the dark night of God's wrath. Exclusion from the Kingdom of God is the primary way in which Jesus expressed the awful eschatological negative. The parable of the closed door is a case in point. "When once the householder has risen up and shut the door, you will begin to stand outside and knock at the door, saying, 'Lord, open to us...we ate and drank in your presence, and you taught in our streets.' But he will say, 'I tell you, I do not know where you come from; depart from me, all you workers of iniquity'...there you will weep and gnash your teeth" (Luke 13:25-30). There are two characters in the parable. The one, described simply as "you," identifies the audience before him. The other, the householder, probably pictures Jesus himself. The audience is made up of Jews who assume they are sons of the Kingdom, but Jesus is reminding them that in reality they are not. They are those casual listeners whose only real claim to Kingdom entrance, aside from birth, would be their passing acquaintance with him who closed the door, who ate and drank in their presence. The phrases "when once" and "risen up" locate this as the eschatological judgment, that clearly defined time when the closing of the door will terminate any further possibility of gaining access to the Kingdom, when the Jesus of the streets will be the eschatological judge (cf. Matt. 25:31-46).

Although the Lord has eaten and drunk in their presence, at that day he will not know them, for this is a spiritual judgment, and this must be a spiritual recognition. They have not yet accepted the Kingdom, and the closed door is the symbol of the great eschatological rejection. These persons are excluded from the joy and fellowship of the eschatological Kingdom feast, and the nether side of that Kingdom, outside the door, is a terrible place for cast-out things, before which there can only be gnashing of teeth. It is the tragedy of darkness, whose agony is the remorse of rejection. Here is the eternal night of wrath, the absence of God, the consummation of man's earthly blasphemy against the spirit.

This theme of final exclusion occurs in many different guises. In the parable of the faithful and unfaithful servant (Luke 12:42-48), Jesus warns the disciples that the master of the unfaithful servant "will come on a day when he does not expect him...and will punish him, and put him with the unfaithful." In the Lukan apocalypse (17:34-37), some will be "taken" and others simply "left," ignored, abandoned on the physical plane where the vultures gather together. The salt that has "lost its taste" will be thrown away (Luke 14:35). The plant that the Heavenly Father has not planted will be "rooted up" (Matt. 15:13). The unprepared guest will be cast "into outer darkness" (Matt. 22:11-14); the foolish virgins shut out in the night (Matt. 25:1-13); the bad fish "thrown away" (Matt. 13:48); the weeds thrown out and "burned" (Matt. 25:30); the goats told to "depart" into eternal fire (Matt. 25:31-46).

The emphasis throughout is that men and women will be excluded from the Kingdom presence of God. The eschatological stress is not so much on a place *into which* unrepentant souls will be cast, but rather on that *from which* they will be excluded, the glorified Kingdom communion. The darkness of that outer realm receives its meaning from the fact that it is the opposite of that experienced by the sons of light. It is the radiance of the Kingdom feast that gives the realm outside its awful darkness. In reality it is a "nothing realm," a kind of terrible negative. This is the expression of God's ultimate wrath, where the divine self-control, the divine imperative-condition, resolves itself in a cosmic negation. The darkness is not a place, for when the light goes out it doesn't go anywhere. It simply ceases to be. It is that which is obliterated by the light. Man is cast out into nothingness. The emptiness within his soul, that human pinprick of the "black hole" of God's wrath, has become cosmic as man's negation of God is confirmed by God's negation of him.

Hades, Gehenna, Fire: The Descent Into Hell

The most sensitive and most sharply debated material in Jesus' eschatological teaching centers around the interrelated concepts of *hades*, *gehenna* and fire, what is commonly called hell. Before descending into this abyss of conflicting interpretations, it would be well for us to re-affirm certain observations emerging from our study of the Jesus material. 1) The first is that there is nothing uniquely Christian about these symbols. Any rabbi in Jesus' day might have used them. 2) Secondly, we have noted throughout, that Jesus regularly changed the meaning and use of the concepts and phrases he borrowed from his Jewish environment. This opens at least the possibility that much of the Jewish apocalyptic geography of hell was actually foreign to his creative and independent mind. 3) We should also be aware that the Synoptics record Jesus using *gehenna* and *hades* on only four and three occasions respectively. This suggests that although it is safe to attribute the use of these terms to Jesus, they do not form a major part of his message. 4) Finally, we are reminded that the overwhelming abundance of his teaching about the eschatological negative is done in terms of exclusion from the Kingdom. This clearly demands that whatever we say about these three controversial concepts must be said in light of this over-riding stress on exclusion. The problem with so much of the discussion of this subject is that many have taken the concepts of hell and fire, which are really peripheral, and certainly metaphorical, and brought them into the central place in Jesus' teaching in a highly literalized fashion. This is bound to give a distorted picture of the Holy Word of Jesus.

But these terms have had an enormous influence on Christian eschatology through the centuries, so we must deal with them in some detail. In summary of the evidence which I have presented at length elsewhere (JGTJ-218-227), there is a pattern of development in the use of *hades*, *gehenna* and fire which is visible throughout the literature. 1) In the Old Testament, the Hebrew equivalents, *sheol*,

211

maweth and *esh*, refer almost exclusively to the fact or place of physical death or destruction, either as a natural phenomenon or as the judgment of God, and all in a completely historical, non-eschatological sense. The word *hades* was appropriated from the classical literature of Greek religion to translate *sheol*, which regularly refers to the fact or place of physical death. It appears in a few places in the Greek Old Testament to translate *dumah* (silence) and *maweth* (death or the place of the dead). In its six occurrences in the New Testament outside the Synoptics, *hades* is used entirely in this Old Testament sense as a synonym for physical death (Rev. 6:8), or the place of dead bodies (Acts 2:27, 31; Rev. 1:18; 20:13). The Greek word *gehenna*, transliterates the Hebrew *ge hinnom*, which occurs thirteen times in the Old Testament to identify the Valley of Hinnom south and west of Jerusalem, the site of fire worship from the time of Ahaz (II Chron. 28:3; Jer. 7:31), which became the dumping place for the offal of the city; that is, a place for dead things. The symbol of fire (*esh*) takes on a more consistent reference to the judgment of God; but in each of its twenty-four Old Testament occurrences, it, too, describes the utter physical annihilation of sinful men on the stage of history. Whether just a reference to death, or to the judgment of God, the pattern is clear: these terms in the Old Testament describe the physical death of persons within the ongoing stream of history.

2) In the Jewish inter-testamental literature produced after 300 B.C., we see the introduction of the eschatological dimension, with some accompanying adaptations. These three terms continue to refer primarily to the complete physical extinction of the body and soul, but now in a thoroughly eschatological and even apocalyptic framework. Among interpreters of this literature, *hades* is usually considered to be a more general concept, describing death or the abode of dead bodies, both righteous and sinners, whereas *gehenna* depicts the torment or destruction of the wicked only, although there is no general agreement. The metaphor of fire becomes part of the symbolism of the final abode of the wicked, the result of the vengeance of the Lord on the Day of Judgment (Judith 16:17). It is part of the "abyss" (I Enoch 10:13; 18:11). It is eternal (I Enoch 67:13), and is described as a furnace (I Enoch 98:3). In general, it describes the final, total destruction of the bodies and souls of the wicked (I Enoch 10:13; Sir. 7:17). But now in this literature there is a further adaptation. At times, both *gehenna* and fire describe not the death, but the contradictory idea of the eternal torment of

unrepentant souls (II Bar. 59:10-11; IV Ezra 7:36; Judith 16:17; II Enoch 10:1-6). The pattern here is that in the inter-testamental literature we find these three symbols becoming thoroughly eschatological, and for the first time, the idea of unending torment is introduced, although the major emphasis is still upon final extinction.

3) With Jesus in the Synoptics, this developing pattern receives its final adaptation in a combination of Old Testament and inter-testamental ideas along with his own creative additions. Of its three Synoptic occurrences, *hades* finds its most vivid and ornate use in the parable of the rich man and Lazarus (Luke 16:19-31). This parable teaches explicitly that *hades* is the awful abode of the unrighteous dead to which men and women go immediately at death. It is separated from the realm of the blessed by a great chasm, over which none may pass. If we could take this at face value as Jesus' conception of eschatological judgment, then we might follow Ethelbert Stauffer and search no farther than first century Judaism for Jesus' thinking on the subject. The fact is, however, that there is a fairly large body of evidence suggesting either that Jesus did not give this parable at all, or he did not give it as an expression of his own views on the subject of *hades*. The parable is so untypical of Jesus' teaching as to represent an "anti-pattern." It uses artificial symbolism, whereas Jesus regularly used what has been called "natural symbolism." He never uses a personal name, like Lazarus, elsewhere for a character in a story. Perhaps the most striking evidence is the complete absence of any of those creatively new ideas so typical of the Holy Word, the familiar Kingdom language and symbolism which made Jesus' parables stand out as new wine. The language and teaching is Jewish in character and content. The central figure is not God but Abraham. The one explicitly stated reason for the rich man's punishment is not his rejection of the Kingdom, but the fact that he did not "hear Moses and the prophets" (v. 31); and the only remedy suggested is that they listen to them (v. 29). This shows a mind predominantly Jewish and quite different from Jesus.

This impression that the parable is not representative of the mind of Jesus is strengthened when we see that it has striking similarities with several portions of inter-testamental Jewish literature: with I Enoch 103:5-9, with Wisdom 4:20, and most especially with the story of the wealthy man in the underworld which Gressmann discovered in a Jewish papyrus of the first century. Jesus was not in the habit of using popular material without adding certain characteristic touches, such as the lessening of the apocalyptic, the heightening of the spiritual and the adding of the messianic. If he gave this parable at all, it was certainly not given in characteristic fashion; and we would do well not to place much emphasis on it as an indication of Jesus' view of *hades*. A more characteristic usage occurs in Matt. 16:18 where Jesus turns to Simon and says, "on this rock I will build my church and the powers of death (gates of *hades*) shall not prevail against it."

The term "fire" is the most graphic, and by far the most characteristic symbol of these two eschatological themes of rejection and destruction. In the Synoptics, the image of fire occurs twenty-two times. Representative of the material is Matthew 7:13-27, in which the condition and destiny of the Kingdom man is compared with that of the "evil" man. In verses 13-14, the few that find the narrow gate leading to life are compared with the many who enter the wide gate leading to *destruction*. In verses 21-23, he who does the will of the Father, and so is destined to enter the Kingdom of Heaven, is compared with the "evil doers" who are told to "depart." In verses 24-27, the wise man whose house will not fall in the eschatological testing, is compared with the foolish man whose house on the sands is destined to be *destroyed*.

Within this context, Matthew 7:16-20 would seem to follow exactly the same pattern: the good tree that is not cut down is compared with the bad tree destined to be cut down and cast into the fire. The casting into the fire is then parallel to, and an extension of, being "cut down." If one carries out the logical imagery here, the fire would seem to refer to the destruction of a tree already dead. It is also noteworthy that the agent of the cutting and the casting into the fire is the same, presumably God. This is similar to the saying in Luke 12:5: "Fear him who, after he has killed, has power to cast into hell." It would seem that in this symbol of fire, here as elsewhere we have a combination of both themes emerging from this study: rejection and destruction (Matt. 13:47-50; 5:21-22).

In summary, what Jesus seems to have done with these three Jewish terms for hell is this: 1) Like so much other popular Jewish terminology, Jesus made sparing use of the common language of hell; but he did so in his own ways, which are quite compatible with his more characteristic parabolic description of eschatological punishment in terms of ultimate exclusion from the Kingdom of God. 2) In the Synoptics, all three retain a strong reference to the physical destruction of body and soul. 3) All retain their character as descriptions of the judgment of God's wrath. 4) They all have a distinct eschatological reference, although at times Jesus uses them to refer to God's judgment in the present — for example, where he calls the pharisees "children of hell" (Matt. 23:15; cf. Luke 12:49). 5) With the exception of the parable of Dives and Lazarus, which is anti-typical, Jesus avoids the highly descriptive and apocalyptic language of Jewish literature which gives *hades*, *gehenna* and fire a geographical location. The geography of hell is the language of Jewish apocalypticism, and is not in keeping with the Holy Word of Jesus. 6) He spiritualizes hell and eschatological fire by placing them in direct opposition to the Kingdom of God. They do not describe a place, but a condition of non-being, the inevitable result of failing to be in the Kingdom; for hell is a negative; it is where God is not.

The Nature and Extent of Final Punishment

And so we have descended into the pit of hell. The deep night of God's wrath presses in upon us, and we must explore more fully this which is one of the most important of all theological problems. Seldom is it discussed outside of highly conservative circles, and so there is a particular need to examine it in terms of critical scholarship. The crux of the problem is the question of the natural immortality of the soul. In the history of theology, three classic alternatives have suggested themselves, and most positions can be related in some way to them.

Eternal Torment

The first is eternal torment, often identified as the "orthodox" one by more conservative theologians. This position views hell as an experience of unending torture for unrepentant souls. It assumes that the human soul is indestructible, and takes very seriously the wrath of God. It is this doctrine which lies behind the awesome pictures of Dante and Milton, of sinners forever burning in a fiery pit, with vultures tearing eternally at their entrails. There is some evidence in the Synoptics that seems to support this view; but upon critical analysis does just the opposite. The parable of Dives and Lazarus is often presented as evidence, but because this is untypical of Jesus' teaching, we cannot build anything upon it with confidence.

The most impressive evidence is the phrase, "weeping and gnashing of teeth," which recurs like a formula on seven separate occasions in Jesus' teaching to describe the eschatological negative

(Matt. 8:12; 13:42, 50; 22:13; 24:51; 25:30; Luke 13:28). This is assumed to portray the never ending agony of damned souls in hell. On close examination, however, this phrase demands a surprisingly different interpretation. The problem is that interpreters have not understood this as the thoroughly semitic idiom that it is. The figure of weeping is a common symbol among Hebrews of Old Testament, inter-testamental and New Testament times for extreme grief, fear, or misery, often because of the judgment of God upon sinners (Joel 1:5; II Macc. 13:12; Is. 22:12; Baruch 4:11; I Esdras 5:63). One of the most common uses of weeping is for grief because of the death or destruction of others (Is. 16:9; Jer. 48:32; Rev. 18:9). In two particularly important parallels, weeping is the sign of the mourning of the living for the dead (Sir. 38:17), the sorrow of those who know of the perdition of others (IV Ezra 7:131). Some such reference to the Hebrew funeral feast and the injunction of the living to weep for the dead would seem to be the closest parallel we can find to Jesus' use of this figure: "Weep for the dead, for he lacks the light; and weep for a fool, for he lacks intelligence" (Sir. 22:11). In IV Ezra 7:81, the damned grieve in seven ways; the seventh and most terrible is their reaction to the sight of the glory of God before whom they are to be judged. Not physical torture, but *sorrow* over the reality of death and the judgment of God.

The phrase "gnashing of teeth" is particularly Hebrew in its idiomatic character. Although it occurs at least once in the Old Testament for the extreme grief of the wicked (Ps. 112:10), it most commonly describes the wrath of an enemy about to kill his victim (Job 16:9; Ps. 35:16; 37:12; Acts 7:54; Sir. 51:3 etc.). To gnash one's teeth against another is to show extreme anger. It would seem much more likely that Jesus used this phrase to picture the wrath of God, the occasion for this sorrow, rather than the torment of persons in hell. When seen against Jesus' regular association of "weeping and gnashing of teeth" with eschatological exclusion from the Kingdom of God, we see that he was not referring to unending torture, but to something quite different — much more idiomatically Hebrew, and much more in keeping with all we have been saying about his eschatological teaching. The "gnashing of teeth" seems to have been a strengthened reference to the wrath of God, the destructive force of eschatological exclusion, so vividly described by the terms *hades*, *gehenna*, and fire. The "weeping" was a reference to the extreme sorrow that would accompany the realization, either by rebellious souls themselves, by living friends, or by the hosts of heaven, of the terrible nature of the impending wrath of God.

The remaining evidence for a doctrine of eternal torment comes in the inter-testamental use of the terms *hades*, *gehenna*, and fire. I have suggested that these are symbols which Jesus borrowed from his Jewish environment, but used in their more Old Testament sense as reference to destruction and death, not eternal torment. Aside from the fact that there is little or no Synoptic evidence for it, there are further weaknesses in the doctrine of eternal torment. Its logic demands a never-ending human rebellion, which is a denial of the sovereignty of God. It necessitates the construction of a geography of hell which cannot be supported by any strong Synoptic evidence. It expresses a vindictiveness that offends against Jesus' teaching about the love of God. It is a Jewish, inter-testamental doctrine that has been perpetuated in Christian circles by a naive literalism that fails to understand the spiritual quality of these eschatological symbols in the teaching of Jesus.

Universal Salvation

Another view of eschatological punishment assuming the indestructibility of the human soul is that of universal salvation. All souls, including those who die in a state of rebellion against God, will eventually find salvation. The soul is capable of growth and decision after death, and the love of God alone is the final determining factor in eschatological matters. This doctrine, held as a "pious hope" by many scholars, has certain assets. It provides a positive stress on the love of God, offers an ultimate hope for those whose loved ones die in an obviously sinful condition, and lays a strong emphasis on the sovereignty of God. It is understandably a popular idea.

Despite its attractiveness, universalism has many inherent weaknesses that make its tenability as a Christian doctrine extremely dubious, and as the teaching of Jesus, impossible. First of all, it lays such stress on the love of God that it all but ignores his wrath. The inevitable result of universalism is a weak doctrine of sin. To assert the final salvation of every person is really to deny any ultimate risk in the moral life. To be sure, there is the risk of protracted misery, of the struggle to regain lost ground, but in the last analysis, this is not a risk but merely an inconvenience.

Along with a weak doctrine of sin, goes an easy concept of salvation. If man is naturally immortal, then salvation is not a matter of life and death, but of pleasure instead of pain, of sooner instead of later. Perhaps most important of all, this concept runs quite counter

217

to Jesus' teaching about the spiritual potential of the souls of men, and the condition which is inherent within the justice of God (cf. Chapter IV).

Conditional Salvation

The third alternative for the nature and extent of final punishment is that of conditional salvation. This view assumes that the human soul is not naturally immortal, which is a Greek, inter-testamental Jewish doctrine, rather than a Christian one. What Jesus taught was that the human psyche is only potentially capable of the eternal life (*zoe aionios*) that transcends death. The inevitable corollary to this is that at the time when men's souls receive their final disposition, those who have not already received the eternal life of the spirit will be destroyed along with their physical bodies.

All the evidence examined so far in the teachings of Jesus points in this direction. Aside from the passages we have looked at, there are several other specific references that bring the terrible risk, the awesome alternative, of the condition of God's justice into sharpest focus. In the parable of the sheep and goats (Matt. 25:31-46), for example, the Son of man tells the goats on his left hand to "depart...into the eternal fire," and this is later underscored as "eternal punishment." There are two keys to the eschatology of this passage. The first is the word "eternal" (*aionion*). The fire and the punishment partake of the nature of the eternal (*aion*). The "glory" attending the Son of man, and the parallel between "kingdom" (v. 34) and "eternal life" (v. 46) indicate that Jesus is using eternal (*aion, olam*) in what I have called its vertical, spiritual sense (cf. Chapter VI). This does not describe torture that is unending in a horizontal sense, but rather the punishment of the *aion*, which is the eternal absence of God.

The second key resides in the word "punishment" (*kolasis*). There are no Old Testament passages where this term (*mikshol*) refers to correction. Often it describes God bringing the judgment of death upon sinners (Jer. 6:21), and Jesus seems to quote one such passage (Ezek. 3:20) in Luke 11:50. Although the meaning "correction" is familiar in the later usage of the common Greek, the sense of being "cut short" seems to be the original meaning, and that most current in the first century. In the book of Wisdom, *kolasis* describes punishment (11:13) and torment in general (16:2), but the main reference is to the punishment of "pittiless wrath to the uttermost," which is death (19:4; 16:24). If Matthew is using this term in its almost universally current sense, it would seem that here Jesus is identifying the punishment of the *aion* as the fire of destruction and the consequent separation from God's love, precisely the two themes that recurred throughout his use of *hades, gehenna* and fire.

The same conclusion must be drawn from the parable of the two houses (Matt. 7:24-27) where the fate of the soul built on sand is described as a falling (*ptosis*), a word referring in the Old Testament to the divine judgment of destruction (Ex. 12:13; Is. 8:14), further strengthened by Luke's use of the term "ruin" (*hregma*, 6:49), which literally means to rend asunder. In the Lukan apocalypse (Luke 17:22-37), the punishments of the day of the Son of man are identified as the losing of one's soul, and this is compared to the destruction by flood in the days of Noah, by fire and brimstone in the days of Lot, and to an experience of the gathering of vultures. In Mark 8:35-38, Jesus warns those who reject the Kingdom presence of God that they will "lose" their souls; and the parable of the rich fool (Luke 12:13-21) closes with the warning that "this night your soul is required of you." In Luke 12:1-12, the denial of one's very existence "before the angels of God" is closely linked with the destruction of both body and soul in hell (Matt. 10:28). So abundant is the evidence, that one can say with a rare degree of certainty that Paul had the mind of Christ when, in describing eschatological punishment, he summarized these two recurrent themes: "They shall suffer the punishment of *eternal destruction* and *exclusion* from the presence of the Lord" (II Thess. 1:9; cf. Jude 5; Heb. 6:2, 8; 10:27 ff; 12:25-29).

The chief virtue of this interpretation of Jesus' theology is that it is one of the inescapable conclusions toward which the logic of the justice of God has been driving us. Conditional salvation is the inevitable resolution of the condition coming right out of the nature of God. This which provides for human freedom is an indispensible ingredient in Jesus' view of the cosmos, and lies at the very heart of his concept of man, where he confronts us with the terrible alternatives of light and darkness, life and death. As we respond to the imperative of God's justice, so do we choose for ourselves the love of his presence or the wrath of his absence, inclusion in the eternal life of the Kingdom, or exclusion in the eternal death of outer darkness. And so the symbol of exclusion, which is the hell of spiritual death apart from God, and the symbol of destruction so graphically identified by *hades, gehenna* and fire, are merely two ways of talking about the same eschatological negative; the one in terms of the more spiritual language of the Kingdom, the other in terms of the more physical language of men as found in Jewish apocalypticism.

The Problem of Hell

This is another of those lost doctrines in much of non-fundamentalist theology, whose absence has weakened the church. Even as much of American critical biblical theology has avoided the concepts of the wrath of God and the sin of man, so it has also ignored the doctrine of hell; for they go together as the under-side of the love of God. Sin describes God's wrath in terms of man; hell describes it in terms of cosmology and the end time. Much of the dismissal of hell is part of a general tendency in recent years to de-mythologize biblical eschatology, and re-interpret it as the qualitative experience of the ultimate within the present time.

From where I sit, I can see *gehenna*, the valley of Hinnam, running down the west and south sides of the old city of Jerusalem. I attended a concert there given by the Israeli Philharmonic orchestra, in a grassy, rock-bound outdoor amphitheater. The rest of the valley is filled with lovely old olive trees. This symbolizes to me what many have done to Jesus' concept of hell. We have turned it into a park, and in doing so, we have lost much of the agonizing concern which made Jesus weep over this city, and sent him out to proclaim a Gospel that must not be ignored. When you can ignore hell, then you have stripped the Gospel of an important element of its power, for you have done something to the justice of God.

The issues are awful and the stakes are ultimate; and the agony over loved ones who die without seeming to acknowledge God's sovereignty is the inevitable result of facing this issue squarely, as Jesus presents it in the Synoptics. There are no easy answers; for the fact of evil and injustice and the death of our hopes and dreams can never be anything but painful. But I think that the Gospel does give us some answers. One is that death, like birth, is part of life. And like the other "givens" of God's creation, it must be accepted as fact, and kept in proper perspective. An increasing amount of research is revealing that the bodies and minds of the dying are prepared to accept death in ways it is hard for the living to understand. I think a loving God has provided for the dying. He has also provided for the living by calling them to greater degrees of maturity, and by offering them the sustaining power of his presence in the Kingdom. He does not remove the offense of death, but he does help us to surmount it, and to be able to say with Paul, "O death, where is thy victory" O death, where is thy sting?"

The ultimate answer to this question called theodicy, which is really a challenge to the justice of God, is to be found within the nature of God himself. It is not God who needs to be justified; it is he who justifies us. If he is a just god, and this is the greatest affirmation of Old and New Testaments, of both Moses and Jesus, then whatever be his answer to the fate of our loved ones, it will be a *just* answer, far beyond any justice which we can imagine, more loving than any love we ourselves could express. If justice is the conclusion to the story of mankind, then the resolution of the problem of evil, the disposition of those who seem to flout God's justice with impunity, will be a *just* resolution. And if that is true, then Job can cease his complaint and we can rest content.

The Nature of the Eschaton

Jesus was reluctant to go into detail with regard to the nature of the *eschaton*. Although at times he spoke in the eschatological language of his day, mostly he taught in metaphor concerning that whose nature transcends the three-dimensional, and can only be described analogically. As Donald Baillie has said, "The beginning and ending of sacred story are outside historical time altogether, and can only be described 'mythically' because they belong to another world, another dimension." Perhaps the best we can do is to summarize what has been said so far about God, the cosmos and persons, and bring that to focus upon the end time.

In terms of God, the *eschaton* is the consummation of the sovereignty of God, the glorification of his presence, the resolution of the love, the wrath, the imperative, the condition of his justice. Ultimately, the *eschaton* is the experience of God, enthroned and perfectly revealed. Wrath has ceased to have meaning, for rebellious man has ceased to be. God's justice can now exist as perfect love.

In terms of the cosmos, the universe, the *eschaton* is the complete establishment of the spiritual realm of the Kingdom. The axioms of the physical dimension are replaced by those of the spiritual. The conditional tension between earth and heaven becomes resolved in the eternal oneness of the Kingdom of God. The horizontal history of creation, process and conclusion is replaced by the vertical history of God. Time is caught up in eternity. The eternally present *aion* of God's time is revealed as the time of the *eschaton*.

In terms of persons, their relation to God as conditional growth and development is concluded and made final. The historic involve-

221

ment in the dimension of the spirit becomes in the *eschaton* the ultimate fulfillment of our spiritual potential: our perfect reflection of the being and nature of God. The axioms of the physical dimension cease to have meaning in the transcendent freedom of perfect spiritual communion. On the other hand, the present loneliness of persons outside the Kingdom is climaxed in the terrible cosmic loneliness of final exclusion from the Kingdom of God's presence. The aching darkness within the souls of men and women is blotted out by the solar explosion of God's light. The spiritual non-life of our natural condition is confirmed in the cosmic nothingness of eternal death. The process of present, physical, non-spiritual deterioration is concluded in eschatological destruction. The opposition and rebellion of the satanic force of the physical is consumed in the cleansing fires of God's eternal justice. Indeed, Satan is cast into the lake of fire (Rev. 20:10, 14, 15).

In terms of Christ, the *eschaton* is the return of Christ "with power and great glory," which are symbols for the presence of God. Our fellowship with him is then complete, and this can only be described in metaphorical terms that are highly mystical and completely inadequate: as a bridegroom returned to take us with him into the wedding feast; as a shepherd come to separate the sheep from the goats; as the master of servants, returned to his own from the far country.

In all of these ways, however it be described, the *eschaton* is the ultimate experience, where God and man are in perfect communion, and where the children of the Kingdom, the whole cosmos and all of time and eternity sing together one perfect word, "God!"

Chapter XV

The Time of the End

There is one final question: when is it to come, this *eschaton* which Jesus so confidently predicted? We have touched on this at several points, but we must now confront it directly, for one's answer to this question has an enormous effect on his interpretation of Jesus' theology of the Kingdom. This has been one of the great biblical debates of our century, and has operated at both a popular and scholarly level. With a bewildering array of variatons, there are four main views to which all others are more or less related.

Apocalyptic Eschatology

The first operates on a more popular level. Characteristic is its concern to predict the coming of the end, and always within the immediate future of the person interpreting the biblical material. According to this interpretation, Jesus, and the authors of the books of Daniel and Revelation, were giving us the signs of the end so that we could identify them when they come. The main task of the interpreter then is to match up those signs with events occurring in history. Hal Lindsey caught this mood in his book *The Late Great Planet Earth* which has become an all time best seller. The key to it is the rebirth of Israel as a modern state in 1948. Within one generation, approximately forty years from that date, according to many scholars who have studied Bible prophecy from this point of view, the end "could take place" (p.54).

This Nervous Apocalyptic Age

Lindsey's book typifies the nervous curiosity of what has emerged as a highly apocalyptic age. Whenever any particularly catastrophic event occurs, or even threatens, it is interpreted as one of the woes which the books of Revelation and Daniel say will precede the end. In the fall of 1978, the International News Service in a highly slanted article reported a scare in Adelaide, Australia, when a man named Johan Nash, a house painter and a self-styled clairvoyant, announced that God would destroy Adelaide with a giant earthquake and tidal wave that would usher in the end of the world. He was so certain of this vision that he took out a fifty dollar advertisement in the Adelaide newspaper, warning people to flee for their lives. Literally hundreds did, and there was a period of frenzy in the city. There were also the debunkers. The article went on to say that about two thousand non-believers gathered on the beach nine miles from Adelaide for earthquake parties. These skeptics were wearing business suits, bow ties, snorkels and flippers, sipping champagne and eating meat pies, while waiting for the end to come. There were also bikini-clad girls with signs on their backs, "Sin now, tomorrow it will be too late." We have had our own share of that kind of thing in America. The prediction that California was going to slide off into the Pacific ocean, a not implausible thing given the nature of the San Andreas fault, was taken by some as a sign of the end.

The most sensitive spot of course is the Near East. As I look out of my window at the city of Jerusalem nestling beautifully within its enfolding hills, I am aware of many persons who have come to the holy city at this moment to await the end; for the Old Testament says that the focus of the great judgment day will take place on this exact spot.

Certainly this is an age when it is possible, as perhaps never before, to believe in the coming of the *eschaton* in our time. I was crossing the college campus some years ago with Arthur Compton, one of Wooster's distinguished alumni who was part ot the Manhattan Project which produced the first atomic bomb. As we walked along to a class on ethics where he was going to defend the dropping of the bomb on Hiroshima to a group containing many pacifists, I asked him if he thought it was possible for us to create our own apocalypse. His answer was clear and unequivocal: "Yes, there is enough hydrogen in the ocean, which, if exploded, would drive the earth into the sun." And it would seem that we have the potential capability of doing just that. The possibility of ecological disaster has convinced several generations of my students that mankind will not survive much longer the pollution of land and sea and air. Scientists for years have been reminding us of the second law of thermodynamics which states that according to the principle of entropy, the energy of our universe will eventually come to a zero state. This kind of knowledge, coupled with our media awareness of potential global suicide, has produced a particularly intense climate of receptivity to the Hebrew-Christian expectation of the end.

The Problem with Modern Apocalypticism
Within this welter of modern speculation, there is a clear and compelling need to maintain our perspective, and to understand these concerns in terms of the theology and mission of the Kingdom of God as found not only in Daniel and the book of Revelation, but more importantly in the teaching of Jesus. What I want to do here is to bring the thinking of Jesus about the Kingdom to bear upon this dark and fearsome subject, and to point out what I think are some very real problems in the apocalyptic eschatology contained in Hal Lindsey's book.

The first has to do with the kind of biblical interpretation he represents. There is not space here to argue this in detail, but only to record the fact that Lindsey's uncritical interpretation of the Bible fails to come to grips with a vast amount of data, amassed by professional scholars through the years, to the effect that Daniel, Revelation and Mark 13 are all talking about events which were assumed by the authors to take place not in our day, but in the immediate period in which the books were composed. This view may be inaccurate, but one cannot simply dismiss the evidence, especially when so much of practical importance hinges upon it. Modern apocalyptists need to pay more responsible attention to critical scholarship.

A second problem is that this nervous attention to the signs of the times is contrary to the spirit and teaching of Jesus. As we shall see later, not only did Jesus not give his disciples any clear predictions of the end, but he strongly resisted their anxious curiosity. The spirit of his rejection of such apocalypticism is perhaps best summarized in a statement that seems to have been made more than once: "An evil and adulterous generation seeks for a sign" (Matt. 12:39; 16:4; Mark 8:12). I think Jesus would say the same thing today.

Another problem with modern apocalypticism is that it fails to pay proper attention to Jesus' entire Gospel of the Kingdom. When one almost equates the Christian religion with speculation about the end time, it tends to crowd out the deeper areas of faith. This takes a valid concern for the consummation of the Kingdom and blows it up out of proportion with all the rest that Jesus had to say about God and his justice, about man and his need, about himself and his

225

uniqueness, about the church and ethics, and the practical business of daily living within the Kingdom society. What it produces is a distorted image of the Kingdom that has all kinds of adverse effects, both theological and practical.

For one thing, it tends to keep faith immature by its concern to "prove" the validity of the Gospel through its fulfillment in modern political history. In the Gospel of John, there is recognition of the importance of signs, like miracles, or the resurrection, to enable people to believe in Jesus (John 7:31; 10:38 etc.). But he is pictured constantly driving people like Nicodemus beyond this superficial belief to a deeper level of faith where they are confronted by the spirit of God (John 3:1ff.). Redemption within the Kingdom of God does not come from believing that Jesus performed miracles, or that he predicted what is to happen in the twentieth century. This apocalyptic disorientation hinders Kingdom entrance by concentrating on superficial concerns that divert our attention from the deeper matters of faith.

Another adverse effect has two closely related products. Such apocalyptic belief that the end is coming soon has always, since its inception in inter-testamental Judaism, promoted an historical pessimism that God's purposes of justice can in no way be fulfilled within history, but only at the last judgment. This attitude has led to a social quietism that is simply not interested in addressing the problems of sin, poverty and injustice within history, but concentrates its attention upon awaiting the end. It tends to create introverted persons and communities, who in extreme cases drop out of society and gather in a cave or on a mountain top — or in Jerusalem — to watch for the end.

It also tends to be divisive; and the disruptive shattering of community, caused by this which can become a genuine nervous disorder, is familiar to most Christians. It promotes a highly subjective type of pseudo-prophetism, where a vast number of imaginative, and no doubt highly dedicated, Christian leaders presume to interpret the signs of the times with utmost confidence. And rarely does one agree with another. As far as I can see, this interpretation is usually based upon some highly arbitrary assumption, and a completely uncritical study of the Bible, and is often done with a spirit of partisan polemic that shatters the peace of the Christian community.

What happens is that the Christian faith is turned into a kind of pagan sideshow. It makes the primary Christian concern that of getting a front seat on the grandstand of history, in order to be there when the great apocalyptic parade comes by. An Israeli friend tells a wonderful story to this effect. During the British Mandate, he was district officer for the British administration in the region of Megiddo, where Jewish tradition has said the eschatological battle of Armageddon will occur. He received a letter one day from a woman in America with the request that she be sent a ticket for a front row seat to the battle of Armageddon. His reply was that he didn't think this was the battle being fought at that particular time. Sideshow eschatology! This is a subtle but unmistakable form of self interest running completely counter to the central concerns of the Kingdom ethic which put God first, others second and ourselves last. It is actually paganism, and I believe has only a secondary relation to essential Judaism or to the Gospel of the Kingdom of God. The loss of eschatology on the part of so many of the more liberal denominations is perhaps understandable as a reaction to the excesses of those who exploit this nervous concern.

Consistent Eschatology

The second approach to this question is a more scholarly one, and is epitomized in Albert Schweitzer's book, *The Quest of the Historical Jesus.* For Schweitzer, whenever Jesus talked about the Kingdom of God, he was referring to the end of time. He confidently predicted that it was imminent, and when it failed to appear, he altered his plans and changed his attitude toward the multitude. From then on, the whole inner history of Christianity has been based on the non-occurrence of the second coming, and the necessity to remove this eschatological blunder. Christian theology has been put on the defensive, and many questions have been raised concerning Jesus' general fallibility. This position has had a surprising following through the years, for example, in Howard Kee's recent book *Jesus in History.* The main difficulty with this view has been its handling of those Synoptic passages where Jesus presents the Kingdom as an immediate, inner sovereignty and power, what I have called the "Anthropology of the Kingdom" (Chapter VII). If Jesus did teach that the Kingdom "comes" whenever an individual accepts God's presence, then we cannot limit his conception of its advent to the end time. Oscar Cullmann perhaps sounded the death knell for what he termed "the relentlessly applied prejudices" of consistent eschatology when he wrote "this oversimplified, unproblematical view of the early church's thought really should be abandoned" (*The*

Christology of the New Testament, p. 319).

Realized Eschatology

The opposite extreme is represented by the so-called school of "realized eschatology" which found its most consistent expression in C. H. Dodd's book, *The Parables of the Kingdom*. For him, Jesus viewed the Kingdom as "neither an evolutionary process nor yet a catastrophic event in the near future, but a present crisis" (p. 178). Dodd's emphasis on the present, eternal nature of the Kingdom was a welcome corrective to the exclusively horizontal and eschatological view of Schweitzer; but in this case, one extreme was hardly the answer to another. Dodd's concern to remove all eschatology from Jesus' teachings failed at many points of detailed exegesis where, as I think we have shown in the last chapter, genuine futurist eschatology must be accepted. Dodd's method failed principally in his rigorous application of Adolf Julicher's thesis that Jesus could only have told parables with a single point, in the style of the classical Greek parable. According to him, further teaching within the parable, and this would include large sections on eschatology, would be the later development of the parable within the early church. This is a good illustration of the problems of interpretation that come from the application of Julicher's method (cf. pp. 7 f).

Dodd's emphasis lives on in the influence of Rudolf Bultmann who thoroughly existentialized Jesus' eschatology. That is, he saw Jesus' eschatology in terms of the inner intellectual and emotional dynamics of human existence. Unlike Dodd, he accepted the eschatology of the Synoptics but interpreted it not as referring to the end of the world at some future date, but as a description of any moment in the present, when persons are called to make fundamental decisions that liberate them from the present and open them to the future. This, too, has had a large influence on a certain segment of modern theology, which talks a lot about eschatology, but usually does not refer to a future end in time. There is validity in Bultmann's awareness of what I have called the present nature of the Kingdom which is always "vertically" near (Chapters V, VI). But Bultmann's interpretation was plagued by two major problems: the one was philosophical, and involved his enamorment with European Existentialist philosophy which led him away from the historical realism of the Synoptic life and teachings of Jesus; the other problem lay in his form critical method, which enabled him to dismiss any futurist eschatology, and whose inadequacies we have dealt with at some length (Chapter I).

Comprehensive Eschatology

There has been emerging an increasing number of scholars in recent years who have been forced to recognize the validity of both the eschatological and realized aspects of the Kingdom in Jesus' teaching. There is no one scholar who would tie this loosely identified group together as a school of thought, but I would identify it as "comprehensive eschatology," and it is here that my own exegesis has directed me. The crucial question is, what is the Kingdom of God? If, as this book has extensively shown, the Kingdom is a vast concept with many facets, and is essentially a description of the spiritual presence of God, then the Kingdom crisis is not centered primarily on the eschaton as a point in horizontal time, but rather on the realm of God's eternal presence, which enters into linear time at two points: when the Kingdom enters an individual life; and when for all creation the Kingdom is finally consummated. This Kingdom, which is both realizable and eschatological, overarches and encompasses all of time in the person of the eternal God of justice. Amos Wilder, in his book *Eschatology and Ethics in the Teaching of Jesus* (1939), rejected what he called Schweitzer's "otherworldliness." He pleaded for a balance that recognizes a Kingdom having to do with last things, but also resting on first things; a Kingdom directed to the present moment and the actual scene in concrete history, but conveying "an intimation of the ineffable fruition of life." In this third group, a synthesis and accommodation is being worked out between the extremes of Schweitzer and Dodd, and study of the Kingdom since Wilder's book has shown that it is here that the future of this discussion will probably lie.

Apparent Predictions of an Immediate End

But the sharp point of this critical question still remains. Did Jesus predict that the end would come within his generation? Many who interpret the Kingdom "comprehensively" still think that he did. Two key passages clearly seem so to predict. The first is Mark 9:1, "there are some standing here who will not taste death before they see the kingdom of God come with power." Mark would seem to have understood this eschatologically by placing it at the conclusion of a saying about the eschatological Son of man; and Matthew and Luke follow suit (Matt. 16:28; Luke 9:27). Several factors, however, lead me to the conclusion that Mark has misunderstood Jesus at this point; and by locating the saying in this context, has given it a falsely apocalyptic sense. 1) There is a "seam" between the eschatological section in Mark 8:38 and the verse in question, which suggests that Mark 9:1 circulated independently within the early church, and its location in that context is due more to Mark than to Jesus. 2) If, as the argument of this whole book suggests, we can look for the Kingdom as a present, inner presence as well as an end-time event (cf. Chapter IV), then Mark 9:1 need not necessarily be eschatological. 3) While the Matthew parallel strengthens the eschatological flavor of Mark 9:1 by rendering this, "the Son of man coming in his Kingdom," Mark retains the less eschatological "see the kingdom of God come with power." Luke makes it even less so: "see the kingdom of God." 4) There is good evidence that Jesus was accustomed to using the metaphor of "seeing" with regard to the spiritual perception necessary for the understanding of his message. This was in effect an indication of the internal activity of the spirit, the first step to the full coming of the Kingdom within that life (Matt. 13:13; Mark 4:1-12; Luke 11:33).

I would suggest that Jesus' meaning was something like this: "There are some standing here who will not die before they have gained the spiritual perception to see the Kingdom coming in their own lives, in the lives of others, or in the church." This would place the emphasis not on the external, physical considerations of death, but rather on the internal, spiritual consideration of life; not on the linear, horizontal time of the end, but upon that which was the most central emphasis in Jesus' teaching about the Kingdom, the power of God *within* the lives of persons on the plane of history (cf. Chapter IV). If this is correct, then both Mark and Matthew have probably misunderstood Jesus; and his warning to those who overstress the apocalyptic and miss the spiritual quality of the Kingdom is in order: "The kingdom of God is not coming with signs to be observed...for behold, the kingdom of God is in the midst of (within) you" (Luke 17:21).

In establishing his thesis that Jesus predicted an immediate second coming, Schweitzer laid great stress on Matthew 10:23: "When they persecute you in one town, flee to the next; for truly, I say to you, you will not have gone through all the towns of Israel, before the Son of man comes." Superficial observation would seem to agree with Schweitzer but a more thorough analysis suggests that Matthew has again created an "anti-pattern" by interpreting a saying of

Jesus apocalyptically when it probably did not have that connotation originally. In this long discourse containing Jesus' instructions to the twelve (Matt. 10:1-42), Matthew has conflated in somewhat disjointed fashion several sections from Mark and those places where Matthew and Luke agree. None of these was originally apocalyptic, but they receive such an emphasis in Matthew (cf. JGTJ 44). For example, in Luke 9:2, Jesus instructs the disciples to "preach the kingdom," but Matthew 10:7 expands this to say, "The kingdom of heaven is *at hand.*" It would seem that the linking of the evangelistic mission and the imminence of the *eschaton* is more peculiar to Matthew's apocalyptic interests than to Jesus as reported elsewhere (cf. JGTJ-144-145). My assessment is that wherever any editor shows Jesus predicting the end to come immediately, we are probably justified in identifying an "anti-pattern" which is untypical of the general tenor of Jesus' teaching, and so some kind of intrusion or misunderstanding by the editors or the early church.

Warnings Against Expecting an Immediate End

Instead of being an apocalyptist, the evidence of the Synoptics points to Jesus as an "anti-apocalyptist," surrounded by those who obviously thought the end was coming soon. The chief problem with this apocalyptic interpretation is the refusal of both fundamentalists and radical liberals to distinguish between the teachings of the historical Jesus and the various sectarian concerns of those surrounding him, including his editors. Bultmann refused to do this, and such refusal continues as one of the most basic and deeply imbedded fallacies of his extreme historical skepticism. Probably the most important evidence of this phenomenon is the Markan Apocalypse (Mark 13), which seems to teach that both the destruction of Jerusalem and the end of the world are coming soon, with strange signs and portents: "the moon will not give its light, and the stars will be falling from heaven" (v. 25). There are, however, at least three lines of evidence that clearly suggest that in this chapter some early editor has gathered together many sayings of Jesus dealing with eschatology from various points in his ministry, and edited them in such a fashion as to make him sound like an apocalyptist. 1) The first I have already presented (p. 203). The chapter interleaves Jesus' words about the two questions asked, the destruction of Jerusalem and the end of the world, in such a way as to make it appear that they were coming simultaneously, and soon. The artificiality of this suggests editorial activity, and is in keeping with our emerging realization that some, at least, of these editors, like many in the early church, believed the end was upon them.

2) There are seven verses imbedded within Mark 13 which contain the highly apocalyptic language familiar to inter-testamental Judaism (7, 8, 14, 18, 20, 24, 25). Certain characteristics these have in common suggest that they come out of Jewish apocalyptic, and are uncharacteristic of the teaching of Jesus; that is, they represent an anti-pattern. a) None of them has a clearly attested parallel in any other part of the Synoptic words of Jesus, whereas every other portion of this chapter can be paralleled elsewhere in Jesus' teaching. b) As Bousset pointed out, they all contain expressions typical of the language of Jewish apocalyptic. c) Of all the material in Mark 13, this has by far the strongest reference to Old Testament and Jewish literature. d) One of the most striking facts about these seven verses is their complete lack of ethical and spiritual content, even though they contain such meaning in their Old Testament context. These seven verses would seem to be so completely untypical as to represent an intrusion into the text, and are more characteristic of the apocalyptic early church than of the teachings of Jesus.

3) Even though the over-all tenor of Mark 13 suggests an immediate *eschaton*, the editor has been careful enough with his material to include nine separate warnings against that very misunderstanding — "they will lead many astray...the end is not yet...this is but the beginning of the sufferings...the gospel must first be preached to all nations...do not believe it...False Christs...will...lead astray...of that day or that hour no one knows...you do not know when the time will come...you do not know when the master of the house will come" (Mark 13:5, 7, 8, 10, 21, 22, 32, 33, 35). It is this basic contradiction within Mark 13 that has caused many scholars to see the chapter as a classic example of editorial collation. It unites genuine sayings of Jesus with material from Jewish apocalyptic, giving the whole a sense that is untypical of his teaching, yet retaining material that contradicts this editorial picture. The authentic Jesus material is in conflict here with the apocalypticism of his generation, which misunderstood his eschatology. These constant warnings against such misunderstanding reveal Jesus as an anti-apocalyptist, who could get quite disturbed by such misconception: "An evil and adulterous generation seeks a sign, and none shall be given" (Matt. 12:39).

Misunderstanding Jesus

The theme of warning against expecting an immediate end continues in a series of sayings that stress the delay of the returning messiah. This is mostly in parables, and all in a context heavy with evidence for the widespread misunderstanding of Jesus on this subject. Luke makes this quite clear: "As they heard these things, he proceeded to tell a parable, because he was near to Jerusalem, and because they supposed that *the kingdom of God was to appear immediately*" (Luke 19:11). Both Matthew and Luke place the parable of the pounds, which follows this passage, in the context of that last week in or near Jerusalem. Jesus has led them to expect dramatic and climactic things (Mark 10:33-34; Luke 18:31; Matt. 20:18-19). There are several indications that this whole phase of Jesus' ministry was a mystery to the disciples. When the sons of Zebedee came with their mother asking to sit on Jesus' right and left hand in his Kingdom, he replied, "You do not know what you are asking" (Mark 10:38). Luke confirms this misunderstanding by adding, "But they understood none of these things; this saying was hid from them, and they did not grasp what was said" (Luke 18:34). John indicates such lack of comprehension with regard to his intentional fulfillment of the prophecy of Zechariah 9:9: "His disciples did not understand this at first." The manner in which the enthusiastic crowd and the disciples forsook him suddenly, the charges that he called himself, and others called him "Christ" and "king" (Mark 14:62; 15:2, 9, 12, 32), the derision of the soldiers (Mark 15:18), and the superscription on the cross(Mark 15:26), all indicate a general misunderstanding and bitter disillusionment as to the nature of Jesus' messiahship and his purpose in coming to Jerusalem. He spoke on his own terms, which were often quite different from those of his contemporaries. He came not as a political leader, nor as a herald of the apocalypse, but as the humble Suffering Servant and Son of God, to lay upon them the burden of God's justice, and to inaugurate God's spiritual reign within their souls. In this sense, in him and through him, the Kingdom of God was "at hand" (Mark 1:15), had "come near" (Luke 10:9), had "come upon" them (Luke 11:20); and they regularly misunderstood.

With these things in mind, let us now go back to the explicit statement in Luke 19:11, "They supposed that the kingdom of God was to appear immediately." If Luke is correct in assessing the situation, and if the parable of the pounds is rightly located, then to find it contradicting the idea of an immediate *eschaton* is exactly what one might expect. One of the emphases of this parable is on the delay of the eschatological reward, on the "far country," on the necessity that men must trade until he comes; and that would not occur until the nobleman, here representing Jesus, had "received the kingdom."

This same emphasis on delay continues elsewhere. In the parable of the talents, "after a long time" the master came and settled accounts with his servants (Matt. 25:19). In the parable of the wicked husbandmen, the man went into a far country (Mark 12:1) before returning. In that of the faithful and unfaithful servants, the wicked servant says to himself, "My master is delayed in coming" (Luke 12:42-46). There are at least four indications that Jesus expected the Gospel to be preached to the whole world before the end would come (Matt. 24:14; 28:19; Mark 13:10; Luke 24:47), and at least one place where he hinted that none of the disciples would see the day of the Son of man (Luke 17:22). In the face of all this, it would seem quite clear that Jesus not only did not teach an immediate *eschaton*, but went to considerable lengths to warn against this misunderstanding, which was causing so much trouble among his disciples then, and continues to plague the church today.

Understanding the Misunderstanding

But we must go even farther to get to the center of the issue. If we would understand Jesus on his own terms, we must take an entirely new approach to eschatology and view it from the vertical, spiritual dimension of God (cf. Chapter VI). The whole discussion must be turned on end, from the horizontal to the vertical. We must see eschatology in relation to God and the doctrine of the Holy Spirit. Jesus did speak of the nearness of judgment, of the Kingdom and the Son of man; but this must be understood in terms of the eternal immediacy of the dimension of the spirit, where time and space come together in the eternal presence of God. The nearness of the spiritual dimension is primarily what we have called a "spatial," dimensional nearness, and any sense of temporal immediacy derives from the eternally "present" nature of God.

Actually, when describing the eschatological advent, Jesus is seldom if ever recorded using whatever underlay the Greek word for second coming, *parousia*. More typical is the adverb "near" (*eggus*, *qarob*), or the verb "come near" (*eggizo*, *nagash*, *qarab*). Perhaps the most significant uses of these terms are the places where *eggizo* describes the coming near of the Kingdom of God in both a temporal and a spatial sense. It is near in the person of Jesus (Matt. 3:2), in his preaching (Mark 1:15), and in the healing and saving power at work in the disciples (Matt. 10:7). In Luke 10:9, Jesus instructs the disciples to announce that "the kingdom of God has come near to you," and this is a description of the coming near, through the ministry of the disciples, of "peace" (v. 5), which essentially means salvation, the "mighty works" of the spirit (*dunameis*, v. 13), the person of Christ and the God who sent him (v. 16). It is the dimension of God, focused in the person and work of Jesus and his disciples, that has "come near," and this is both a spiritually temporal and spatial nearness.

Now if the eschatological Kingdom, the final judgment, and the second coming of the Son of man are realities that partake of the spiritual nature of the *eschaton*, they must also partake of the eternally present nature of the God of the *eschaton*. This means that there is a temporal as well as a dimensional continuity between the incursion of the Kingdom and judgment of God on the plane of history, and that which is consummated at the end. If the time of the Kingdom that "came near" in the mission of the disciples, and the time of the final coming of that Kingdom at the *eschaton*, both are the time of the "*aional*" presence of God (cf. p. 82), then they are the *same time*; they are in the *eternal present*. This is why an inevitable awareness of the nearness of the end — what is sometimes called "the foreshortening of history" — goes along with an intense awareness of the spirit in the prophetic Old Testament and in the teachings of Jesus. What we have here is time and space viewed from the point of view of God, for whom the three-dimensional passage of moments between that Galilean mission and the end of history have no meaning, but are replaced by the eternal "nowness" of the Kingdom dimension. The tense eschatological expectancy that regularly accompanies the prophetic message is the inevitable result of the spirit of God pressing vertically upon the prophetic mind. God is always about to come, for he is eternally present. In him the eschaton is always near, spatially and temporally; the day of the Lord is always "near in the valley of decision" (Joel 3:14).

The whole problem has come from the distortion by the early church of Jesus' vertical point of view. This was because of its thorough preoccupation with Jewish apocalyptic conceptions of the Kingdom and eschatology. The first century apocalyptists had caught the urgency of the prophetic message, without having been caught up by its spirit. They suffered from a kind of spiritual myopia, where the vertical nearness of the Kingdom of God appeared as the horizontal nearness of the *eschaton*. When Jesus' divine, vertical point of view was translated into the terms of early Christian apocalypticism and seen from its traditionally non-prophetic standpoint, it came out de-spiritualized and horizontal. It was a prophetic, spiritual vacuum into which Jesus moved with his message of the Kingdom, and its spiritual content was often distorted by the lack of eyes to see and ears to hear; and this is still going on today.

The Time of the Eschaton

Jesus saw the time of the eschatological Kingdom and judgment of God from two planes of reference. In terms of the horizontal flow of time, it is a limited period, a day, an hour at the end of human history when God will make final the judgments which persons have already made upon themselves. It is a sudden and unexpected moment for which we are to be spiritually prepared. He described it in terms of indefinite delay, and warned against apocalyptic attempts to predict the signs of its advent.

Vertically speaking, however, the *eschaton* is eternally present; spatially, as the dimension of God impinging upon people's lives within history; temporally, as the eternal "now" of God's salvation, which is always "near." Horizontally speaking, the *eschaton* is both present and future. One begins living eschatologically now, in this life, as he begins to live in the eternal time of God; and this ultimate quality of existence which Jesus called "eternal life," is then fully consummated at some future moment when time and space become vertical in the consummate presence of God.

This clearly suggests two horizontal moments of final judgment: the death of any individual, and some future collective time when all will be judged together. The logic of Jesus' eschatology suggests them both, and, I think without contradiction. For if the time of the *eschaton* is the time of God's eternal presence, then when the physical drops away, and three-dimensional considerations cease to affect our souls, all time becomes eschatological, that is, eternally present, and the time of death and that of the future final *eschaton* are the *same time*.

The Power of the Eschaton

The final element of power in the Holy Word of the Kingdom is this message about the *eschaton*. It is God's ultimate word that the drama of salvation is supremely serious. In the threat of hell or the promise of heaven, in the radiant glory of the divine presence, or the awful darkness of his absence, one sees the culmination of his justice. In the conclusion to the direction of God's will, we know that life has meaning from beginning to end. In the assurance of divine judgment, we know that God is not mocked. There is an end to the frustration of injustice. Ultimately we all stand before the complete honesty of God's purity and are thereby judged; with no artificial advantages from power or money or treachery or special privilege. We are all on a par before God. The *eschaton* is the great leveler. Death is entirely democratic. And this is the conclusive vindication of God's justice that enables us to hang on, even though the forces of injustice seem for a moment to triumph. The *eschaton* is the decisive expression of the faith that the universe does work God's way. Petty kings and tyrants of all kinds may strut their tiny dance on the stage of history, but the last act is God's. And in that assurance we can take courage, and find hope and comfort; for it is the way the story comes out in the end that makes for joy and peace and redeeming power.

CEDS LIBRARY

32113984